I0762545

50 STATES

The Ultimate Travel List

50 STATES

The Ultimate Travel List

The Best Things to See and Do in Every State

CONTENTS

PREVIOUS Exploring the narrow passages of a slot canyon

INTRODUCTION

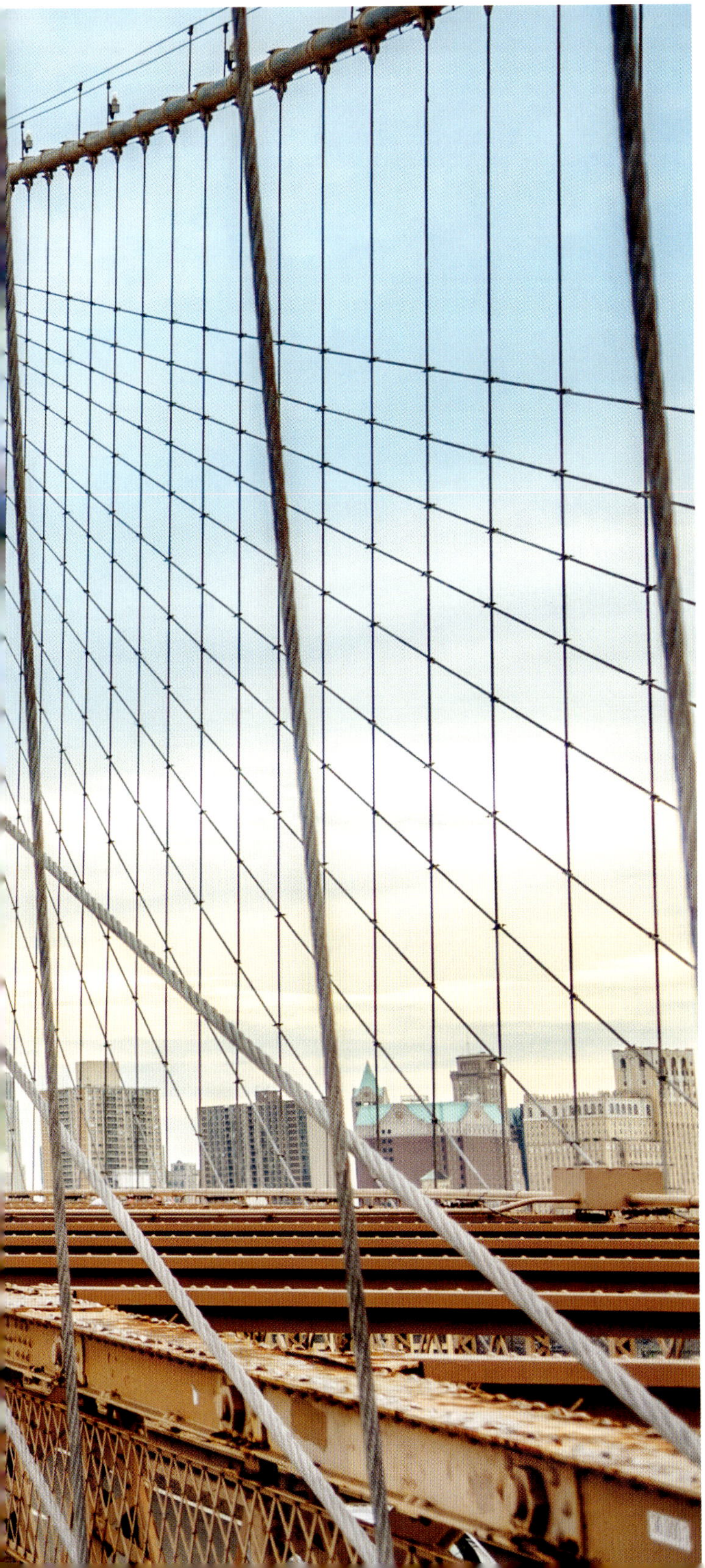

Welcome to the United States of America. Stretching from the Atlantic to the Pacific, from snow-capped mountains to scorching deserts, home to 50 states, 63 national parks, and countless cities and towns, this is a country whose nickname–the land of opportunity–couldn't be more apt. There are so many things to see and do here, even the longest of bucket lists would run out of space.

But, here's the reality. Vacation days are precious. Weekends vanish in the blink of an eye. And those dream "one day we should..." travel plans? They have a habit of staying just that: dreams. That's why this book gets straight to what matters most. From Alabama to Wyoming, our U.S. travel experts shine a light on the places and experiences that show America at its very best, state by state.

So, discover the moments that make every state unforgettable. Stand on Civil War battlefields in Virginia, trace the roots of the blues in Mississippi, soak up the art scene of New Mexico, and go honky-tonkin' in Texas. When nature calls, you're spoiled for choice. Will you go whale-watching off the coast of California, see bison roaming in South Dakota, or marvel at The Mighty 5 national parks of Utah? Hungry for more? Feast on lip-smackingly good barbecue in Missouri, buttery lobster rolls in Maine, and sweet, juicy peaches in Georgia.

Think of this book as a starting-point, the friendly nudge that gets you out the door. Whether you're making time for one state, or you're setting your sights on all 50, you're guaranteed to discover something special.

One country. Fifty states. Countless adventures waiting to happen.

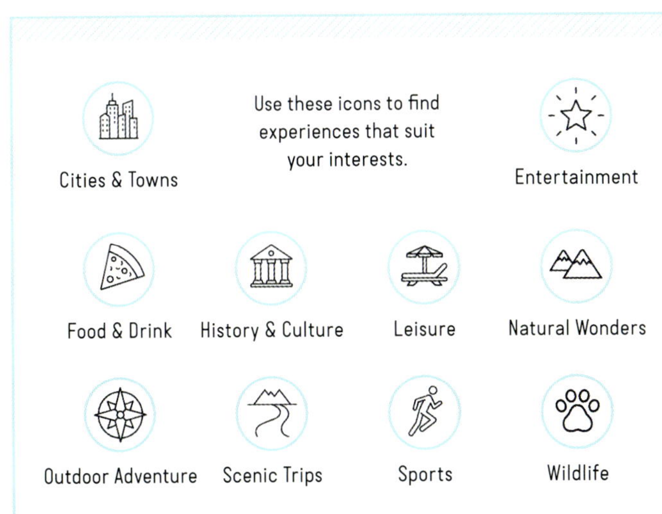

← New York City's iconic Brooklyn Bridge

ON THE MAP

WASHINGTON
232
MONTANA
128
NORTH DAKOTA
170
ALASKA
16
PACIFIC OCEAN
OREGON
182
IDAHO
66
SOUTH DAKOTA
200
WYOMING
246
NEBRASKA
134
NEVADA
138
UTAH
216
COLORADO
38
CALIFORNIA
32
ARIZONA
22
NEW MEXICO
154
PACIFIC OCEAN
PACIFIC OCEAN
HAWAII
60

MINNESOTA
116
WISCONSIN
242
MICHIGAN
110
IOWA
80
ILLINOIS
70
INDIANA
76
OHIO
174
KANSAS
84
MISSOURI
124
KENTUCKY
88
OKLAHOMA
178
ARKANSAS
28
TENNESSEE
204
MISSISSIPPI
120
ALABAMA
12
GEORGIA
56
TEXAS
210
LOUISIANA
92
FLORIDA
50
NEW HAMPSHIRE
146
VERMONT
222
MAINE
96
NEW YORK
160
MASSACHUSETTS
106
RHODE ISLAND
192
PENNSYLVANIA
186
NEW JERSEY
150
CONNECTICUT
42
DELAWARE
46
MARYLAND
100
WEST VIRGINIA
238
VIRGINIA
228
NORTH CAROLINA
166
SOUTH CAROLINA
196
ATLANTIC OCEAN
N

The winding route of Hawaii's scenic Road to Hāna

50 STATES

The Yellowhammer State

You might already know Alabama for the powerful place it holds in American Civil Rights history, but did you know it's also home to stunning white-sand beaches, a once world-changing music scene, and rockets that famously soared to the stars? From its bustling big cities to its small towns, there's a little magic (and some big ol' Southern cheer) to discover in every corner of the Yellowhammer State.

STATE MOTTO We Dare Defend Our Rights

STATE FLOWER Common camellia

STATE ANIMAL Black bear

STATE BIRD Yellowhammer

FUN FACT Ever lost a bag during a flight? It might have ended up in Scottsboro, Alabama, at the Unclaimed Baggage Center, the only store in the U.S. that buys and resells unclaimed airline luggage.

Spend a weekend in Birmingham

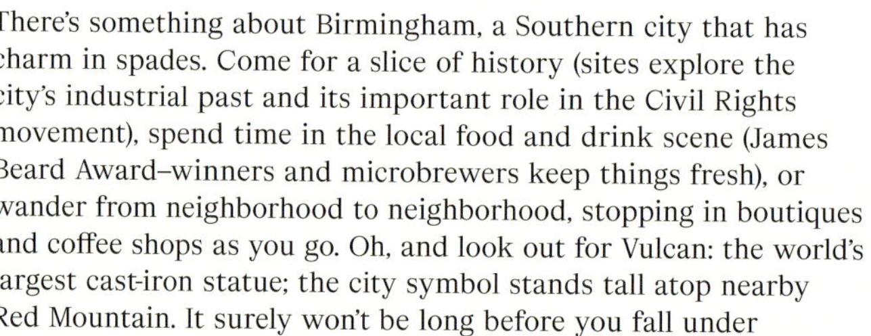

There's something about Birmingham, a Southern city that has charm in spades. Come for a slice of history (sites explore the city's industrial past and its important role in the Civil Rights movement), spend time in the local food and drink scene (James Beard Award–winners and microbrewers keep things fresh), or wander from neighborhood to neighborhood, stopping in boutiques and coffee shops as you go. Oh, and look out for Vulcan: the world's largest cast-iron statue; the city symbol stands tall atop nearby Red Mountain. It surely won't be long before you fall under Birmingham's spell—it is called the "Magic City," after all.

◉ Birmingham's highlights include the Civil Rights Institute (bcri.org), botanical gardens, and Alabama Sports Hall of Fame (ashof.org).

Chill out in Gulf Shores

Turquoise waters, soft white sand, relaxed vibes: no, this isn't the Caribbean, it's Gulf Shores, a tight-knit beach community on Alabama's southern coast. During the day, vacationers venture from their beachfront condos to lounge on the sand, paddleboard in the lagoon, or swim the Gulf's tranquil waters. At night, they don their breezy best and head to the local crab shacks and beach bars for fresh-caught seafood served Southern-style (read: fried). And after dinner? It's all elegant cocktails and sunset views. If that sounds like your idea of the perfect vacation, then come on down—the water's fine.

◉ Because of its warm climate, Gulf Shores (gulfshores.com) is popular year-round. The spring and fall offer a respite from the crowds while still being warm enough to get in the water.

When to visit

You can't beat college football season in Alabama; the state comes alive with game-day parties September through November. This is also a great time for an off-season beach vacation, with fewer crowds but warmer temperatures.

Party at Mardi Gras in Mobile

Though New Orleans gets the spotlight when it comes to Mardi Gras, the first celebration in what is now the U.S. was actually held in Mobile, 15 years before New Orleans was even founded. While many of the ingredients—lively parades, elaborate floats, brass bands, and colorful beads—are the same, Mobile has carved out its own traditions, like the locally run "People's Parade" and the act of throwing Moon Pies (a popular Southern snack) into the crowds. Can't make it for Fat Tuesday? The Mobile Carnival Museum displays elaborate costumes, carnival relics, and replica floats from past festivities. Let the good times roll all year long!

◉ The Mobile Carnival Museum is open Mon, Wed, Fri, and Sat, 9am–4pm; for more information, check out mobilecarnivalmuseum.com.

Visit the home of Helen Keller

Many people know of how Helen Keller, a deaf-blind child, learned to read and write with the help of her teacher Anne Sullivan. Fewer may know that she became a leading disability rights activist, visiting multiple countries, befriending U.S. presidents, and fighting for women's suffrage. Her story began in a cottage called Ivy Green, which has been immaculately preserved as a museum. Here you can view original 1800s furniture, her library of Braille books, and the water pump where Sullivan famously spelled letters onto the palms of Keller's hands, leading to a language breakthrough. It's a fascinating look into how Keller navigated disability, and a celebration of two remarkable women who proved that anything is possible.

◉ Located in Tuscumbia, Alabama, Ivy Green is open Mon–Sat (helenkellerbirthplace.org).

Step into music history at the studios of Muscle Shoals

They say there's something in the water in Muscle Shoals, a small city with an outsized musical legacy. It was here that two studios, FAME Studios and Muscle Shoals Sound, created some of the greatest records of the 1960s; Aretha Franklin, Otis Redding, and the Rolling Stones all came here to make music magic. The studios' success was thanks in large part to the Swampers, FAME's house band, known for its bluesy Southern style. Find out all about them—and plenty more besides—on a studio tour, and who knows, you might just hear the next big thing laying down a track while you're there.

◉ FAME (famestudios.com) and Muscle Shoals Sound (muscleshoalssoundstudio.org) offer tours.

Delve into Civil Rights history in Montgomery

For those interested in the Civil Rights movement, a stop in Montgomery is a must. During the 1950s and 60s, the Alabama capital saw Rosa Parks refuse to give up her seat on a city bus; Martin Luther King Jr. lead the congregation of the Dexter Avenue Baptist Church (later renamed in memory of King); and the arrival of thousands of activists who marched from nearby Selma to the state capitol. The city's churches and a number of museums mark these historic events (and many more), including Troy University's Rosa Parks Museum, the Legacy Museum, and the Freedom Rides Museum.

◉ The U.S. Civil Rights Trail traces sites across 15 states that played a key part in progressing the Civil Rights movement; find out more at civilrightstrail.com.

Expand your mind at Huntsville's U.S. Space & Rocket Center

It's not where you'd expect the largest spaceflight museum in the world, but Huntsville–a city of just over 230,000–is home to the U.S. Space & Rocket Center and a NASA project that put a man on the moon. The Apollo program used the Saturn V rockets originally developed here to propel astronauts beyond the earth's orbit to the first lunar landing. At the space center, peruse artifacts, see old rockets, and ride a simulator that mimics the g-force and weightlessness of a rocket launch. Though you won't go as far off the ground as the rockets, you'll return to earth with a greater sense of wonder–and perhaps a new appreciation for gravity.

⦿ Have some budding astronauts in the family? Look up the center's space camps for a one-of-a-kind experience (rocketcenter.com/SpaceCamp).

Tailgate in Tuscaloosa

In the South, football is serious business. On game days, fans make the pilgrimage to the University of Alabama for tailgating: outdoor parties that are the can't-miss social event of the season. Alumni sport the likes of houndstooth jackets and crimson dresses while serving tasty spreads under outdoor tents (think barbecue, mimosas, even fresh-cut flowers). Meanwhile, students sip beer in the back of pickup trucks before the pregame pep rally. Attending a tailgate solo? Just say "Roll Tide," and you'll be invited to a tent in no time.

⦿ College football season runs Sep–Nov, with games usually played on Saturdays.

Catch a race at Talladega

Travelers, start your engines! It's time to burn rubber. Alabama claims one of the most iconic speedways in the motorsports world: Talladega. Earning just about every plaudit at one time or another, this fan-favorite track sees stock race cars zoom around at speeds of up to 200 mph (320 km/h). Expect deafening noise (earplugs are recommended) and plenty of close calls. If that's not exciting enough, make a pit stop at the infield campground, where the party lasts all weekend long; tire tug-of-war, barbecue sauce wrestling–you'll wonder why you've never come before.

⦿ The NASCAR race season typically runs Feb–Nov, but you can tour the Talladega Superspeedway year-round (talladegasuperspeedway.com). Tour times vary based on the event calendar, so reserve ahead.

The Last Frontier

You don't even have to leave Anchorage airport, surrounded as it is by the fierce profile of the Chugach Mountains, to see why Alaska is known as the Last Frontier. It's full of wild beauty—and we do mean wild. Nowhere else in the U.S. can match the state for sheer miles of forest, tundra, alpine cliffs, and coastal rainforest, nor even sandy desert. If you're drawn to the raw and the remote, Alaska's untamed wilderness will happily oblige.

STATE MOTTO North to the Future

STATE FLOWER Forget-me-not

STATE ANIMAL Moose

STATE BIRD Willow ptarmigan

FUN FACT Alaskans like to fly high. There are six times more pilots per capita here than in any other state, in large part because only some 20 per cent of Alaska is accessible by road.

Take a day trip into the wilderness of Chugach State Park

Despite being Alaska's biggest, most populated city, Anchorage has wilderness and beauty right on its doorstep. Just a stone's throw away lies Chugach State Park, one of the largest state parks in the country, and an explorer's paradise of mountains, glaciers, and valleys, all accessible via a more than 280-mile (450-km) network of trails. Looking for a short but rewarding hike? A popular gateway to Chugach State Park, the Glen Alps Trailhead offers easy access to multiple routes of all lengths and ability levels, plus stellar views over Anchorage and—on a clear day—the top of Mount Denali.

◉ The park is easy to access from Anchorage, located just 7 miles (11 km) away; for maps and trails, visit dnr.alaska.gov/parks.

See bears in Katmai National Park

Positioned on a remote peninsula between the Gulf of Alaska and the Bering Sea, Katmai National Park is the epitome of untouched wilderness. Its isolation and lack of established trails make it a true haven for wildlife, especially the star attraction: brown bears. There are over 2,200 of these carnivores in the park, and they're massive, feeding on five species of Pacific salmon that famously "run" through the region each year. Visitors flock to well-known spots like Brook Falls to witness the bears scooping salmon from the rushing river, but for those who can't make the journey, the park's seasonal "bear cams" offer a front-row seat.

◉ Katmai National Park can only be accessed by seaplane or boat; check nps.gov/katm for information and resources.

When to visit

Here for the Northern Lights? You might witness them anytime from mid-August through early April, but February, March, September, and October are your best bets. As for exploring national parks, summer promises warm, dry weather.

Sail past fjords in Kenai Fjords National Park

A Tolkien-like land of deep fjords and huge glaciers, Kenai Fjords National Park promises scenery on the most epic scale, and there's no better way to see it than on a boat tour. Half-day tours are available, but push the (literal) boat out, and spend a day on the water. Aboard, keep your eyes fixed on the surroundings to catch sight of Steller sea lions, Dall's porpoises, and migratory whales. There's great bird-watching here, too: kittiwakes, oystercatchers, puffins, and the like. Hear a loud crack? Active glaciers here regularly calve, sending boulders of ice into the waters with an almighty noise.

◉ The closest town to the national park (nps.gov/kefj) is Seward, accessible via the Seward Highway.

Walk onto the Matanuska Glacier

For a truly magical experience, make for the fantastical Matanuska Glacier in summer. As a result of global warming, this 27-mile- (43-km-) long icefield is shrinking but it's still accessible to tour on foot. With crampons strapped to your boots, you'll pick your way across azure-blue ice ridges, listening to the trickle of freezingly cold water beneath your feet. After a day of trekking, there are a number of spots to camp or "glamp" nearby, where you can watch the midnight sun cast a golden glow over this icy landscape. It's an experience like no other.

◉ You must be on a tour to hike on the glacier; see alaska.org/detail/matanuska-glacier for details.

Cruise the Richardson Highway

There's no escaping it: overland travel in Alaska is usually an unhurried affair. But, thankfully, this means you can really slow down and soak in the state's truly dramatic scenery for which it's best known. And nowhere is this more true than the Richardson Highway, easily one of the nation's most scenic drives. Officially marked as Alaska Route 4, and then Route 2, this nearly 370-mile- (595-km-) long road runs south from Fairbanks to the coastal town of Valdez. Road-tripping along the highway, you'll pass white rushing rivers, stormy gray lakes, and the mighty Alaska Range, where towering, jagged peaks rise like dragon's teeth over fields of tundra.

◉ The Richardson Highway is a long road, but there are areas to stay or camp along the highway, such as Delta Junction, Glennallen, and Tonsina.

Learn about the Indigenous peoples of Alaska

The rich well of Alaska's Indigenous history is tapped into at Anchorage's Alaska Native Heritage Center (ANHC), a museum... well, is it a museum? Yes, and then some. Just as Indigenous peoples are more than their history, the Native Heritage Center is more than a catalog of things past. Rather, you may run into an exhibition opening one day or a celebration of contemporary Indigenous dance on another. It's a living institution for an organic people and a showcase for cultural expression and voices of the past.

◉ The Alaska Native Heritage Center (alaskanative.net) is open all year. A free shuttle connects it to Anchorage Jun–mid-Sep.

Get into the frontier spirit

Step back in time in McCarthy, a remote hamlet nestled deep within Wrangell–St. Elias National Park, a preserve that, at over 13 million acres (5 million ha), is bigger than Switzerland. Founded in the early 1900s, McCarthy was known as a "vice town" for the strict nearby mining community of Kennecott; things are less raucous these days, though it's no picnic reaching this outpost. Travel the challenging McCarthy Road, a 60-mile (97-km) gravel path that follows the route of a former railway, and you'll stumble upon a street of old frontier buildings surrounded by stunning wilderness. Looking to stay a while? Wrangell–St. Elias has ample opportunity for glacier hiking and river expeditions.

◉ Specialized wheels or a charter van are needed to get to McCarthy (alaska.org/destination/mccarthy).

Drive along the Dalton Highway

Even the north has a north, an edge to the edge. And usually in Alaska, you have to fly if you want to get to some of the northernmost towns in the Arctic Circle. But not if you're on the Dalton Highway. Also known as the Haul Road, this vein of concrete and gravel (and quite a lot of it is gravel) ribbons north from Livengood, near Fairbanks, all the way up to Deadhorse and the oil fields of Prudhoe Bay. As you drive along the highway, you'll pass through taiga and tundra typical of the area, spot herds of musk ox, and cross the mighty Yukon River, before finally reaching journey's end.

◉ It takes two days to safely drive the highway, and only some companies rent the 4WDs needed for the trip. Visit explorefairbanks.com for a good list.

Traverse Denali National Park

Denali is one of Alaska's most visited parks, with hundreds of thousands of people flocking here each year to witness life on the wild side. It's huge—more than 6 million acres (2 million ha)—and only one road runs in and out. Visitors can drive along it, but only up to mile marker 15; lucky road lottery winners, however, can drive the entire length. Beyond scenic drives, hiking, cycling, and flightseeing await, all great ways of seeing the park's natural wonders, not least its main character: Mount Denali itself. Whatever way you get around, one thing's for sure: the wild is never more than a breath away.

◉ The town of Denali Park is just outside the gates to the national park (nps.gov/dena).

Go north with a visit to Utqiagvik

The land is flat, the sky either steel gray or cornflower blue, and everywhere the wind howls. Welcome to Utqiagvik, the northernmost town in the country. While it may feel like this town is on the edge of everything, Utqiagvik (once known as Barrow) is in fact a central locus of the Iñupiat people, who have lived here for centuries. No visit to this town is complete without a stop at the Iñupiat Heritage Center, which has a variety of exhibits as well as in-house craft programs. After that? Wander to the whalebone arch by the waterfront and look out to sea—you might just see a beluga whale breaking the chilly waters.

◉ You'll need to fly to Utqiagvik and then rent a car or join a group tour; good planning is essential (alaska.org/destination/utqiagvik).

Marvel at the northern lights in Fairbanks

If you want to see the northern lights, come on over to Fairbanks. Around 200 miles (320 km) south of the Arctic Circle, it's perfectly positioned beneath the auroral oval (a ring-shaped zone above the earth's geomagnetic north pole, where auroral activity is at its most frequent and intense), and sees plenty of aurora nights every year. Base yourself in downtown, and you'll be in a prime spot for quick nighttime excursions, like to Aurora Pointe, a facility in private, scenic land. Aurora a no-show? The skies are so dark here, you'll no doubt see starry constellations, at the very least.

◉ Fairbanks has many tour operators, such as the Aurora Chasers (theaurorachasers.com), who visit several locations nearby, including remote areas.

The Grand Canyon State

At the heart of all things Arizonan lies its landscape, and it's anything but normal. In this sun-struck state, red rock buttes rise from desert floors, canyons cut deep into the planet's history, and wide skies seem to stretch on forever. Against all this, a cast of characters—cowboys, artists, road-trippers, and Indigenous groups among them—have added to the state's story, creating a chart-topper you'll surely want to enjoy for yourself.

STATE MOTTO God Enriches

STATE FLOWER Saguaro

STATE ANIMAL Ringtail

STATE BIRD Cactus wren

FUN FACT Arizona used to have a town called Nothing, which was given the name as a joke. Marked with a roadside stop in the 1970s, it's now a ghost town with, well, nothing there.

Tour Antelope Canyon with Diné (Navajo) guides

The Diné (Navajo) people have lived and hunted in northeast Arizona for hundreds of years and today, the vast Navajo Nation Reservation sprawls over this corner of the state, spilling into New Mexico and Utah, too. Mother Nature has had her way with this land: it unfolds in a riot of bear-toothed peaks, buttes, mesas, and plunging canyons. A highlight is Antelope Canyon, a masterpiece of rain and wind erosion. Guided tours are the only way to visit, offering not just access to the canyon's flame-colored walls, but also a deeper connection to the region's Indigenous culture.

⦿ Page is the nearest major town to Antelope Canyon and most visitors use it as a jumping-off point for tours.

Ride the Grand Canyon Railway

The Grand Canyon might just be Arizona's, nay, the United States' most impressive natural wonder. Carved out by the Colorado River over millions of years, its magnificent rock formations stretch as far as the eye can see. There are few more memorable ways to arrive at the canyon than aboard the Grand Canyon Railway, a historic train that's been operating since the 1900s. The scenic journey begins in the cute mountain town of Williams and covers 65 miles (105 km) to reach Grand Canyon Village, at the South Rim. Expect views of sweeping prairies and pine forests, and charmingly kitsch entertainment, including banjo-strumming musicians and even a train robbery reenactment.

◉ The train runs daily from Williams and takes just over two hours to reach the canyon. For schedules and tickets, visit thecanyon.com/grand-canyon-railway.

Photograph Horseshoe Bend

It's a competitive field, but Horseshoe Bend might just be one of the most recognizable views in all of the Southwest. A towering butte surrounded by the meandering Colorado River, it's a hit with photographers, who come to claim the perfect shot. Join them at the overlook, perched high above the river and reached via a sandy trail that winds down from a parking lot. There's not really a wrong time to see it, but it's especially showstopping at golden hour, when the setting sun washes over the sandstone, casting a fiery orange light.

◉ A visit to Horseshoe Bend can easily be combined with Antelope Canyon; both are located near Page.

Marvel at the Grand Canyon

To experience the Grand Canyon in all its glory, you've got to get out on the trails. There's the promise of epic hiking wherever you go, but the more accessible South Rim draws the most visitors; here, the Rim Trail unspools for 13 miles (21 km), taking in numerous overlooks. Buried under snow in winter, the wild North Rim sees only a fraction of the crowds but has a number of fantastic trails, the North Kaibab Trail among them. If hiking's not your thing, you needn't miss out: board a shuttle bus to explore the park, kayak the Colorado River, or venture to the Grand Canyon West Skywalk for epic canyon views.

◉ A stop at one of the visitor centers is key; rangers can provide advice, plus maps of driving routes and hiking trails.

Experience Monument Valley

A symbol of the American West, the towering rocks of Monument Valley have set the scene for countless movies, TV shows, and commercials. And they're just as impressive in real life as they are on screen. With names like the Three Sisters, the Gossips, the Totem Pole, and the Mittens, the distinctive mesas and buttes soar above the plain—and you can see them all on a 17-mile (28-km) scenic drive. For an even better experience of the valley, sign up for a guided tour with a Navajo guide. You're sure to hear stories (both mystical and historical) even more incredible than those told by Hollywood.

◉ The official tour booth is open 8am–5pm daily; check navajonationparks.org/navajo-tribal-parks/monument-valley for information.

Stop off in Flagstaff

Imagine Arizona and cacti-studded deserts and epic red rockscapes surely come to mind. Flagstaff, knitted into the San Francisco Peaks, offers an altogether different escape. This mountain city began life in the late 1800s as a railroad and lumber town, and its place on the map was cemented in 1926, when the now legendary Route 66 was laid through its heart. A century on, Mother Road travelers still pour into the town, drawn by nostalgic motels and diners. And Flagstaff has another claim to fame: the dwarf planet Pluto was discovered here at the world-class Lowell Observatory, where visitors can see the very telescope first used to look upon it.

◉ The Lowell Observatory can be visited every day except Tue and holidays (lowell.edu).

Get outdoors in Saguaro National Park

Saguaro National Park frames the city of Tucson in a vast, cacti-studded tapestry of Sonoran desert scrub. As the name suggests, the heroes here are the towering saguaro, a type of cactus that can grow to around 50 ft (15 m) tall—the tallest ever recorded, outside the park, was a huge 78 ft (24 m). Scenic drives cut through the park, but to really appreciate this desert backcountry, you need to hit the trails. Look out for great horned owls, deer, and even elusive bobcats as you trek through forests of saguaros, barrel cactus, and palo verde.

⦿ A popular way to explore is along the 0.5-mile (0.8-km) Desert Discovery Nature Trail; for information on this and other routes visit nps.gov/sagu.

Taste Sonoran cuisine in Tucson

If you want to taste the flavors of Arizona, come to Tucson. This city's culinary scene is firmly grounded in the sunbaked Sonoran Desert, a surprisingly fertile land where the likes of tepary beans, squash, and chiltepin chile have been cultivated for millennia. Tucson is a border town at heart, too, and restaurants serving tamales, mole, and mesquite-grilled carne asada take influence from neighboring Mexico. All things considered, it's no surprise that Tucson became the U.S.'s first UNESCO Creative City of Gastronomy, in 2015. Feeling hungry? Look out for *birria* tacos and Sonoran-style hot dogs (and leave room for a prickly pear margarita at sunset).

⦿ Dive in during the annual Sonoran Restaurant Week, usually in Sep (sonoranrestaurantweek.com).

Hike Camelback Mountain

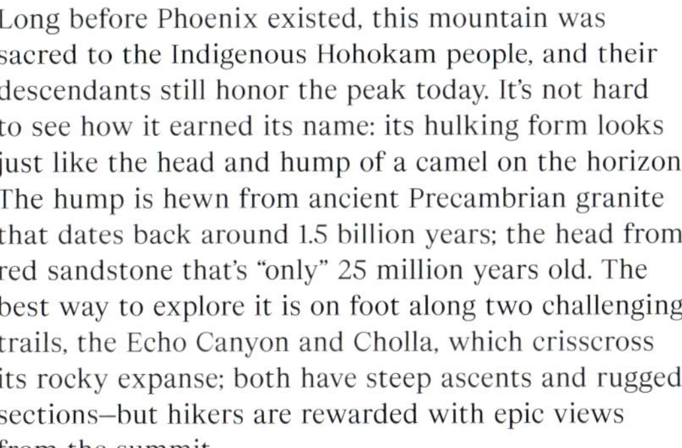

Long before Phoenix existed, this mountain was sacred to the Indigenous Hohokam people, and their descendants still honor the peak today. It's not hard to see how it earned its name: its hulking form looks just like the head and hump of a camel on the horizon. The hump is hewn from ancient Precambrian granite that dates back around 1.5 billion years; the head from red sandstone that's "only" 25 million years old. The best way to explore it is on foot along two challenging trails, the Echo Canyon and Cholla, which crisscross its rocky expanse; both have steep ascents and rugged sections—but hikers are rewarded with epic views from the summit.

⦿ It's important to be prepared for these trails; visit climbcamelback.com for more information.

See cliff dwellings at Walnut Canyon National Monument

Just a short drive east of Flagstaff is Walnut Canyon, a deep fissure in the seemingly boundless plateau that reveals evidence of a Pre-Columbian culture. This gorge was once the home of the Indigenous Singua people, who are thought to have first settled here in around 600 C.E. They left behind intricate cliff dwellings, carved out of limestone and mortar, which survive in a series of ruins today. Muster the energy for the mile- (1.6-km-) long Island Trail, an arduous hike that drops down about 185 ft (56 m), revealing 25 of these ancient cliff dwellings. The views are well worth the exertion.

⦿ Located just 8.5 miles (13.5 km) out of Flagstaff, the canyon is open daily; note, there's an entry fee.

Museum hop in Phoenix

The desert heat can be fierce, so cool off in Phoenix's museums. The Phoenix Art Museum is home to Latin American artworks, Western-themed landscapes, and pieces by European greats like Monet. The Thorne Rooms are a highlight here—these miniature models of period rooms were the brainchild of artist Narcissa Niblack Thorne. The Heard Museum celebrates Arizona's Indigenous history and culture; its exhibits include handwoven baskets, beadwork, and pottery crafted by peoples including the Hopi, Navajo, and Apache. For something more offbeat, the world's largest musical instrument museum calls Phoenix home, too.

◉ The Phoenix Art Museum opens Wed–Sun (phxart.org); the Heard Museum opens daily, except in summer (heard.org/plan).

Stay in a dude ranch

The spirit of the Old West lives on in Arizona's dude ranches, where cattle are put to work and overnight guests are welcomed. Set on wide tracts of scenic land, from cactus-strewn desert flats to mountain-fringed valleys, they pair outdoor adventures with rustic (or rustic-luxe) lodgings dressed in dark wood and Western art. Days here are usually spent on horseback, with guests picking their way through mesquite-strewn backcountry, or crossing creeks and meadows. When you're not in the saddle, you might try your hand at archery or axe-throwing or—if you're in a more upscale spot—relax your weary muscles in a hot tub.

◉ To find a dude ranch in Arizona, check out duderanch.org/find-a-ranch.

When to visit

Save for a few high-country escapes, Arizona is blisteringly hot in the summer. Time your trip for spring or fall, when the temperatures are more comfortable. If you're a skier, Flagstaff's slopes are best from November through March.

See art and design in Scottsdale

Arizona's rippling deserts and epic rockscapes steal the spotlight, but the state has some serious artistic clout, too. This comes to the fore in Scottsdale, a desert city presided over by the McDowell Mountains. The star is Taliesin West, the winter retreat of revered American architect Frank Lloyd Wright. In keeping with Wright's philosophy, the low-slung, clean-lined complex was crafted from the desert itself, using rocks, sand, and gravel gathered from the surrounding landscape—a technique he termed desert masonry. Beyond Wright's masterpiece, neat-as-a-button Old Town Scottsdale brims with fine art galleries and artists' studios, while striking Western landscape paintings hang in Western Spirit: Museum of the West.

◉ Enjoy the best of the city's art scene at the annual Celebration of Fine Art show (celebrateart.com).

Embrace your spiritual side in Sedona

Spend even a short while in Sedona and you'll soon understand why its red rocks have become synonymous with spirituality. These fiery landscapes have a certain aura, first revered by the region's Indigenous peoples, and much later embraced by New Age hippies. Today the rock-swaddled town remains a hotspot for spiritual healers and their supporters, with striking natural wonders such as Bell Rock and Cathedral Rock famed as epicenters of energetic activity. At the famed vortex sites, you might stumble upon a yoga class or a healing circle in full swing. Best to come with an open mind and lean into Sedona's spirit.

◉ To embrace the spiritual energy of Sedona, head to the annual Sedona Yoga Festival in spring (sedonayogafestival.com).

The Natural State

You might say the Natural State possesses a quieter beauty than some of its neighbors farther west: picture ancient rivers twisting through deep-cut valleys, waterfalls tumbling into tree-shaded hollows, and mountains unfurling in lush, forest-cloaked ripples. It's the kind of place that invites you to slow down, with days spent simply taking in the view, soaking in hot springs, or paddling on the water. And doesn't that sound appealing?

STATE MOTTO The People Rule

STATE FLOWER Apple blossom

STATE ANIMAL Western honeybee, white-tailed deer

STATE BIRD Mockingbird

FUN FACT The annual World Championship Duck Calling Contest in Arkansas is the longest-running duck-calling contest in history, having first started in 1936 with just 17 contestants.

Paddle on the Buffalo National River

Rising as a trickle in the Boston Mountains, the Buffalo National River runs wild for some 135 miles (217 km), tumbling through the Ozarks in riffles and bends. In 1972, the free-flowing waterway became the first in the country to earn National River status. Today it remains one of the few U.S. rivers not to have been dammed, its waters free to curl through limestone canyons and valleys thick with oak and hickory. Of course, the best way to experience it is by getting out on the water. Paddling excursions range from mellow, meandering floats to high-adrenaline trips tackling rapids and white water.

◉ Excursions along this mighty river vary greatly and preparation is key; for up-to-date information on closures and tours, visit nps.gov/buff/planyourvisit/paddling.htm.

Spot big cats at Turpentine Creek Wildlife Refuge

A big-cat sanctuary is probably the last thing you'd expect to stumble across in the Ozarks. Yet, just outside Eureka Springs, nonprofit Turpentine Creek has given refuge to rescued animals since 1992. It began with Don and Hilda Jackson, a well-meaning couple who were asked to take in a lion cub that their friend could no longer care for. They did their best to raise it, and soon more pleas for help followed. From those makeshift beginnings grew Turpentine Creek, now an accredited sanctuary that is home to more than 120 lions, tigers, and other once-neglected creatures.

◉ Visitors can see the animals in their natural habitats, while a tram tour through the site reveals more about the sanctuary's stories.

When to visit

Forget fall in New England; Arkansas is just as gorgeous in September and October, and lacks leaf-peeping crowds. If you're wanting to get outside and explore the Natural State, spring's milder temperatures are ideal for hiking and biking.

Marvel at masterpieces at Crystal Bridges

Northwest Arkansas is Walmart country. The retail giant was born in the little town of Rogers in 1962, the idea of businessman Sam Walton. And it was Sam's daughter Alice who spearheaded the creation of the Crystal Bridges Museum of American Art. The museum, opened in 2011, is a work of art itself, its shell-like pavilions knitted into the Ozarks, but it's what's inside that draws the crowds: the collection offers a snapshot of American creativity, featuring artists such as Norman Rockwell and Georgia O'Keeffe. It's a true sanctuary of American art in a surprising corner of Arkansas.

◉ The museum is open Wed–Mon (closed Tue); visit crystalbridges.org to plan your visit.

Maneuver through the bike trails of Northwest Arkansas

For adventures on two wheels, look no further than the Ozarks. This pocket of northwest Arkansas has become a haven for mountain biking; dozens of trails have been laid here, and now some 500 miles (805 km) of track curl through, joining up small-town communities, and beating along craggy ridgelines, over creeks, and beneath cathedral-like oak and hickory canopies. Bentonville is right in the middle of this burgeoning biking scene, with paved trails like the Razorback Regional Greenway slipping through downtown before vanishing into the wooded folds of the Ozarks.

◉ Discover the best trails in Northwest Arkansas at northwestarkansas.org/mountain-bike-trails.

Step back in time at Plum Bayou Mounds

Journey into the past at this sprawling archeological state park, where an ancient Indigenous culture left an incredible mark on the Arkansas landscape. For 500 years, between 650 and 1050 C.E., the Plum Bayou people flourished here, shaping an elaborate complex of earthen mounds that still rise from the landscape today. Walk the trails that wind between 18 surviving mounds, which are thought to have once been used for ceremonies, gatherings, and funerals. End your journey in the visitor center where exhibits and artifacts bring the Plum Bayou people's profound story to life.

◉ The Plum Bayou Mounds site is closed on Mon and Tue; visit arkansasstateparks.com for more details.

Delve into the past at Fort Smith National Historic Site

Echoes of a bygone era reverberate at Fort Smith National Historic Site, home to the remains of two frontier-era forts. The first was built in 1817 to mediate between the Indigenous Osage people and the Cherokee, who were moving west as settlers encroached. A second fort from the 1830s became a permanent U.S. outpost on the border of "Indian Territory." During this time, thousands of Indigenous peoples were forcibly relocated on what became known as the Trail of Tears. Today, visitors can see the old foundations, reconstructed barracks, and exhibits that tell this somber story.

◉ The site is open 9am–5pm daily, while the park is open sunrise–sunset (nps.gov/fosm/index.htm).

Dig for treasure at the Crater of Diamonds State Park

If Lady Luck's on your side, you could leave Arkansas richer than when you arrived. Crater of Diamonds State Park sprawls across the rugged, eroded surface of an ancient volcanic crater, where the coarse earth hides precious minerals like quartz, amethyst, and even the occasional diamond. Here, you can take what you can find: this is the only place on the planet where you can dig for diamonds at the source and keep the spoils of your labor. Even better? The park provides all the tools you might need, so all you need to bring is a prospector's spirit.

◉ You can try your luck year-round; the park is open 8am–5pm daily (arkansasstateparks.com).

Soak in Hot Springs National Park

Forget what you think you know about the national parks of the U.S. In Arkansas, you won't find the dramatic terrains of Yellowstone or the canyons of Zion. Instead, you'll discover the country's first federally protected piece of land, a place set aside in 1832 to safeguard a different kind of wonder: hot springs. Much of the action is focused on Bathhouse Row, a string of handsome early 20th-century bathhouses that either remain as spas or have been repurposed as museums. There are scenic overlooks and hiking trails here, too, the latter the perfect way to work your muscles before a rewarding soak.

◉ The park is free to enter and open 9am–5pm daily, apart from holidays; for more information, visit nps.gov/hosp.

Visit Mount Magazine State Park

Part of the thickly forested Ouachita Mountains, Mount Magazine rises to 2,753 ft (839 m) above sea level—the highest point in Arkansas—and offers stellar views across the Arkansas River Valley. Archeological finds suggest that humans traded here as early as 9500 B.C.E.; millennia later, tourists came from the mid-1800s, lured by the cool mountain climate and dramatic scenery. Not much has changed: people still arrive to walk the park's trails and go horseback riding in the backcountry. Want to test your nerve? Mount Magazine is a great place for climbing and hang gliding.

◉ Opening times usually vary between the peak and off-peak seasons (arkansasstateparks.com).

Experience history in Little Rock

Though a thoroughly modern city, Arkansas' capital, Little Rock, is rooted in history. For one, it played a pivotal role in the Civil Rights movement: in 1957 nine Black students (later known as the Little Rock Nine) entered Central High School under the watch of federal troops, leading the U.S. Supreme Court to declare that segregated schools were unconstitutional. Today that landmark moment is recalled at the Little Rock Central High School National Historic Site. Presidential history runs through the city, too: the 42nd president was born here, and his life is chronicled at the William J. Clinton Presidential Library and Museum.

◉ Little Rock is no relic; calm riverside trails, modern craft breweries, and busy farmers' markets round out the visitor experience.

Chase legends in Petit Jean State Park

Rising above the Arkansas River Valley, the rugged Petit Jean Mountain is bound to a legend of a young French woman named Adrienne Dumont. As the story goes, Dumont's fiancé set out to explore the "New World" in the 18th century. When her pleas to join him were refused, Dumont disguised herself as a cabin boy—called Petit Jean—and set sail. On arriving, she was awestruck by the beauty of the valley and its mountain, but her time here was short. Falling ill, Dumont revealed her true identity and asked to be buried atop the mountain. Today, Petit Jean's Gravesite is the park's most popular overlook.

◉ Nearby is the spectacular Cedar Falls; tackle a steep hike to see it or drink it in from a dedicated overlook.

The Golden State

California has it all: metropolises like LA and San Francisco; natural wonders, from the redwood forests to broiling Death Valley; and the plush wineries of Napa. Colonized by the Spanish in the 18th century, it was the 1848 Gold Rush that triggered a horde of fortune-seekers, later earning it the nickname the Golden State. Today, it's less about gold and more about chasing opportunity. So what are you waiting for? Your California dream is around the corner.

STATE MOTTO Eureka

STATE FLOWER California poppy

STATE ANIMAL California grizzly bear

STATE BIRD California quail

FUN FACT Fitness is a serious business in California, so it's no surprise that it's the only state to have hosted both the Summer Olympics (1932, 1984, and the upcoming 2028 Games) and Winter Olympics (1960).

Hike through Yosemite National Park

"It is by far the grandest of all the special temples of Nature I was ever permitted to enter," wrote naturalist John Muir of Yosemite–and it's hard to disagree. Set foot in the U.S.'s joint-third created national park and you'll find high snowy peaks, towering redwoods, plunging waterfalls, and staggering cliff faces. Trails crisscross the park, from gentle walks through meadows to the all-day trek up the granite monolith of Half Dome, its summit reached via a dizzying steel-cable staircase carefully hooked onto the rock's curving back. From the top, the valley unfurls before you, in all its breathtaking beauty.

◉ Yosemite National Park's visitor center is open 9am–5pm daily. The park gets very busy in summer: at peak times you need to make an advance reservation to visit (see nps.gov/yose).

Look up at coastal redwoods

Towering above the northern California coast, some 300 ft (90 m) high and with trunks as wide as a subway car (you can drive through some of them), coastal redwoods are the world's tallest trees. The best place to see these ancient giants is Redwood National and State Parks and Humboldt Redwoods State Park–the latter includes the serpentine Avenue of the Giants, weaving for 32 miles (52 km) through sky scraping woods. Park up and explore: hiking in the early morning, there's a fresh scent of pine in the air, and plenty of wildlife around, too–Roosevelt elk, salmon and trout in the rivers, and all sorts of birds singing high above.

◉ Redwood National and State Parks (nps.gov/redw) have five visitor centers, open year-round (9am–5pm daily in summer). You'll need your own transportation to explore.

When to visit

May through September bring scorching temperatures to the desert, but stick to the north and coast and you'll see the state at its best. November through April is the time to ski Sierra Nevada's slopes, or gaze up at Death Valley's dark skies.

Ski the High Sierras

Winter-wonderland scenery, mild temperatures, and reliably good snow await in California's High Sierras from November–and that's just the start. The ski resorts of Homewood, Palisades, and Heavenly are some of North America's most stunning, offering views of the jagged peaks of the High Sierras and shimmering waters of Lake Tahoe. Beyond the slopes and scenery there's après-ski magic: snowshoe tours, ice rinks, stargazing events, zip-line rides, cozy fire pits, and s'mores galore. Whether you're carving powder or just soaking up the vibes, California's ski scene is pure alpine gold.

◉ For ski resorts, check out Heavenly (skiheavenly.com), Homewood (skihomewood.com), and Palisades Tahoe (palisadestahoe.com).

SAN FRANCISCO SAN FRANCISCO SAN FRANCISCO SAN FRANCISCO

TOP 5

RIDE A CABLE CAR
These antique trolleys rattle up and down the city's hills, offering sensational views.

BIKE ACROSS THE GOLDEN GATE BRIDGE
Get a different view of SF by crossing this iconic bridge.

VISIT FISHERMAN'S WHARF
It's touristy, but who doesn't love steaming crab shacks and honking sea lions?

TOUR ALCATRAZ ISLAND
America's most notorious prison is preserved for tours (accessed by boat only).

EXPLORE GOLDEN GATE PARK
Blossom-smothered gardens, mind-blowing art and science museums, Dutch windmills, and a herd of buffalo await.

Leave your heart in San Francisco

Lofty skyscrapers, pretty painted houses, and gorgeous views of the bay: San Francisco is one of America's most enchanting cities. Its iconic cable cars may ease the climb up the city's famously steep hills, but San Francisco's soul is best felt on foot–in its bustling markets, through buzzy Chinatown (the country's oldest), and in the energy and joy of the Castro, one of the nation's most prominent LGBTQ+ neighborhoods. And when the fog rolls in under the Golden Gate Bridge and envelops everything in mist, simply while away the hours reading the works of Beat poets in the cafés and bookstores of North Beach.

◉ The California Welcome Center on Pier 39 (Fisherman's Wharf) is open 9am–8pm daily.

Taste California's world-famous wines in Napa and Sonoma

It's a wonderful way to spend an afternoon: sipping crisp Sauvignon Blanc, Chardonnay, or Zinfandel, surrounded by rolling hills smothered in vines. Producing over 80 percent of American vino, California is a wine powerhouse. Napa has some 400 wineries, which include the Gothic "Rhine House" of Beringer and Persian-style Darioush. Sonoma, meanwhile, has a similar number, including grand Buena Vista Winery and Spanish Colonial Bartholomew Park. Want to go a little deeper? Then seek out the lesser-visited vineyards of Santa Ynez Valley, Paso Robles, and the Russian River.

◉ Without a car? Ride the Napa Valley Wine Trolley (napavalleywinetrolley.com) or join a tour.

Step back in time in Monterey

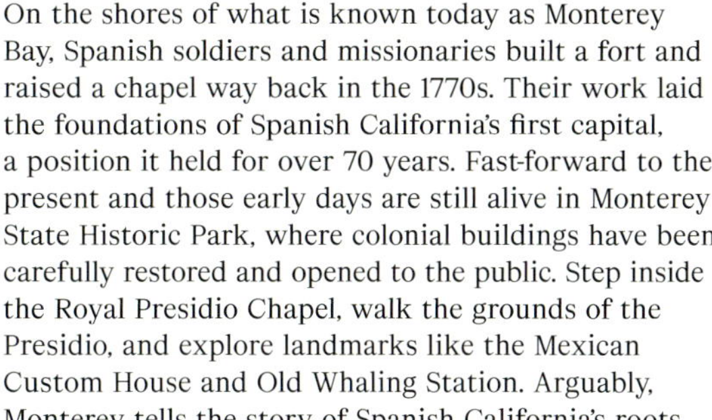

On the shores of what is known today as Monterey Bay, Spanish soldiers and missionaries built a fort and raised a chapel way back in the 1770s. Their work laid the foundations of Spanish California's first capital, a position it held for over 70 years. Fast-forward to the present and those early days are still alive in Monterey State Historic Park, where colonial buildings have been carefully restored and opened to the public. Step inside the Royal Presidio Chapel, walk the grounds of the Presidio, and explore landmarks like the Mexican Custom House and Old Whaling Station. Arguably, Monterey tells the story of Spanish California's roots better than anywhere else.

◉ Get tickets and tour information at the Custom House (adjacent to Old Fisherman's Wharf, Monterey).

Drive Route 66 through the Mojave Desert

Route 66 is the ultimate American road trip, and it saves one of its most beautiful stretches for California. In the Mojave Desert, 130 miles (210 km) of the Mother Road remain, a ribbon of asphalt threading through a vast landscape of sand, sky, and creosote bush. It carries road-trippers past scenes straight out of a movie set—ghost towns, kitschy diners, and long-abandoned gas stations—but the real star here is the desert itself. Cinematic in scope, it's the perfect warm-up act before the final approach to the road's end, over a hundred miles away on the Pacific Coast.

◉ Pick up the Mojave section of Route 66 in Barstow; route66ca.org is a useful planning tool.

Lounge Palm Springs

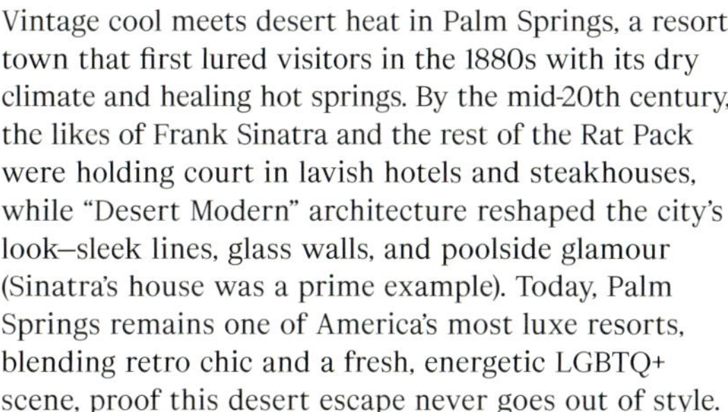

Vintage cool meets desert heat in Palm Springs, a resort town that first lured visitors in the 1880s with its dry climate and healing hot springs. By the mid-20th century, the likes of Frank Sinatra and the rest of the Rat Pack were holding court in lavish hotels and steakhouses, while "Desert Modern" architecture reshaped the city's look—sleek lines, glass walls, and poolside glamour (Sinatra's house was a prime example). Today, Palm Springs remains one of America's most luxe resorts, blending retro chic and a fresh, energetic LGBTQ+ scene, proof this desert escape never goes out of style.

◉ Palm Springs Visitor Information Center (visitpalmsprings.com) is open 10am–5pm daily. For Desert Modernism, see PS Architecture Tours (psarchitecturetours.com) or visit during Modernism Week (modernismweek.com).

Soak up the sun in San Diego

Laid-back and endlessly fun, "Sun" Diego feels like a huge, sun-drenched playground. So, where do you begin? A stroll around tranquil Balboa Park, crammed with gorgeous Spanish Revival buildings, is a must, perhaps followed by an exploration of the historic homes and cantinas of Old Town, where Mexican food stalls and music spill into the streets beside historic buildings. Or make for the dazzling beaches between Coronado and La Jolla, or the seaside amusements at Belmont Park. However you let loose, end your day with a beverage in the buzzing Gaslamp Quarter, and enjoy the downtown vibes.

◉ Visit San Diego has an information center at 996-B N. Harbor Drive, Downtown San Diego (sandiego.org), open 10am–4pm daily.

Spot whales off the Pacific coast

Nothing beats seeing whales in the wild: the spout of vapor, the thunderous crash of a tail on the waves, the shadow of a giant gliding beneath your boat. And California is one of the world's best places to see them. Gray whales migrate south from their summer feeding grounds near Alaska to their winter breeding grounds off Baja California (usually mid-December to April), while in summer humpbacks and even blue whales appear offshore. Adding to the spectacle year-round are dolphins, orcas, and sea lions. All in all, an unforgettable experience.

◉ Coastal tours include All Aboard Adventures in Fort Bragg (allaboardadventures.com); Monterey Bay Whale Watch (gowhales.com); and San Francisco Whale Tours (sanfranciscowhaletours.com).

Explore the otherworldly Death Valley National Park

Part of Death Valley National Park, Badwater Basin is the lowest point in North America, and one of its most surreal landscapes. Here, the desert floor is carpeted in salt crystals, which has cracked into vast geometric shapes that shimmer in the sun. The deeper you walk, the more alien the landscape becomes. There is absolute silence—nothing seems alive. And it's hot, one of the hottest places on earth, making exploring after dark all the more enticing. Indeed, this scorched wilderness saves its greatest spectacle for night, when stars flood the desert sky.

◉ Death Valley National Park (nps.gov/deva) is open year-round, but you really need your own transportation to visit.

Drive the Pacific Coast Highway

Weaving between San Diego and Seattle for some 1,650 miles (2,655 km), the Pacific Coast Highway is the stuff of classic road-trip dreams. The stretch from LA to San Francisco is most rewarding: heading north, the glittering ocean appears almost as soon as you leave the city. Stop in Santa Barbara for Spanish history, palm-lined beaches, and wine tasting, and in San Simeon to watch elephant seals sprawled on the sand. Farther on, the road snakes through Big Sur, its jagged-edged cliffs, isolated beaches, and soaring redwood forests an obvious highlight. So, hop in a car—preferably a convertible—and hit the open road.

◉ Wildfires and landslides can close parts of the road: visit roads.dot.ca.gov for the latest conditions.

LOS ANGELES LOS ANGELES LOS ANGELES LOS ANGELES

TOP 5

BEACH SCENES

Stroll between Santa Monica and Venice Beach for iconic coastal views.

THE GETTY CENTER

Admire art by the likes of Rembrandt and Van Gogh within this impressive Modernist structure.

TOUR HOLLYWOOD

Visit the Walk of Fame, the TCL Chinese Theatre, and the Hollywood Museum.

TAKE A STUDIO TOUR

Take your pick of movie legends: Warner Bros, Paramount, Sony, and Universal Studios.

VISIT DISNEYLAND

The original theme park is still going strong.

Get under the skin of Los Angeles

Los Angeles may be synonymous with the movies, with its iconic Hollywood sign, Walk of Fame, and studio tours, but there's far more to discover here. Spread across 500 sq miles (1,294 sq km) is a patchwork of vibrant neighborhoods, from historic El Pueblo to Little Tokyo, hip Echo Park to lively Westwood, all with their own distinct identities. Out west, LA shows off its beachside spirit: surfers and skateboarders in Malibu, bodybuilders at Venice's Muscle Beach, and musicians lighting up the Sunset Strip. Whatever your vibe, you'll find it here.

Visitor centers are scattered across town (discoverlosangeles.com). LA's Metrorail and buses are a good way to get around (metro.net).

The Centennial State

When it comes to outdoor playgrounds, Colorado has something for every adventurer. Plunging canyons, snow-smothered slopes, and huge sand dunes have long been the preserve of thrill-seekers. At the heart of it all are the Rocky Mountains, where most of the state's soaring peaks can be found piercing the state's blue skies. Beneath these lofty heights stretch lush plains to the east and dry deserts in the south. Thirsty for your next thrill? You'll find it in Colorado.

STATE MOTTO Nothing Without the Deity

STATE FLOWER Columbine

STATE ANIMAL Rocky Mountain bighorn sheep

STATE BIRD Lark bunting

FUN FACT Colorado has the highest average elevation of any state in the U.S., with an average altitude of about 6,800 ft (2,050 m) above sea level.

Drive the Mount Blue Sky Scenic Byway

Highways slice through the Rockies like giant roller-coasters. And the most exhilarating? That's the 49-mile- (79-km-) long Mount Blue Sky Scenic Byway. Topping out at a dizzying 14,140 ft (4,310 m), this is North America's highest paved road. Start your engine at Idaho Springs, before delving into spruce forests and hurtling back up into alpine tundra. Mesmerizing panoramas unfold at every switchback, not to mention shaggy, jumping mountain goats. The road ends just below the summit—but the journey continues. It's a short scramble to reach the top of Mount Blue Sky itself, where all of Colorado sprawls before you and you feel like you're on top of the world.

◉ Reservations are required to drive the highway (recreation.gov); the road is normally open late May–early Sep.

Spend a weekend in Denver

Amazingly, Colorado's "Mile High City" really does reach the hefty height of 1 mile, or 5,280 ft (1,609 m). Glittering skyscrapers dominate its downtown skyline, with the majestic peaks of the Front Range standing proud just beyond. And the city's lofty heights don't end here—Denver is a veritable giant in terms of art. Spend a morning exploring the Art District—home to 30 art galleries and studios—or the whopping Denver Art Museum, before enjoying the city's burgeoning craft beer scene in the River North Art District (also known as RiNo). And after that? There's no better base for a mountain adventure.

◉ Visit Denver (denver.org) operates an information desk at Union Station (9am–4pm daily) and at the Colorado Convention Center (during events only).

Take a walk on the wild side in Rocky Mountain National Park

Herds of elk and mule deer graze in meadows; pudgy yellow-bellied marmots dart across sunlit trails; and is that a moose lumbering through distant trees? Rocky Mountain National Park is a wildlife wonderland, which 66 species of mammals alone call home and where 280 bird species flit by. There are plenty of places from which to spot them from the park's more than 350 miles (560 km) of trails. Get up early and you may even be lucky enough to see a black bear ambling along, or a mountain lion padding through the scrub—just make sure to keep your distance if you do.

◉ Most visitors drive around the park, but free shuttle buses connect Estes Park Visitor Center with the main sights.

When to visit

Colorado is all about the great outdoors, so the best time to visit depends on your interest. Want to hike or cycle? The Rocky Mountains are temperate in summer. Looking to ski? Resorts are best enjoyed December through March.

Ski Aspen, Vail, and Telluride

When it comes to skiing and snowboarding, Colorado is number one. Thanks to high altitudes, its resorts open earlier and close later than anywhere else in the country, with thousands of acres of pristine powder. Three of the best are Aspen, Vail, and Telluride, so take your pick. Chic Aspen has a well-earned reputation for exclusivity and posh apres-ski, while across the White River National Forest lies vast Vail, a behemoth with 275 trails and 32 lifts. To the southwest, Telluride's 19th-century mining-town charm adds character to its top-notch facilities. Whichever you choose, you're guaranteed great après-ski—each resort delivers high-end shopping, lively bars, and excellent dining. And who knows, you might spot a celebrity or two.

◉ Check aspensnowmass.com for Aspen; vail.com for Vail; and tellurideskiresort.com for Telluride.

Admire Cliff Palace in Mesa Verde

Reaching this historic site might be a challenge (you'll tackle uneven stone steps and wooden ladders), but there's little question it's worth it. The Cliff Palace is perhaps the most stunningly complete example of Ancestral Puebloan architecture and the centerpiece of Mesa Verde National Park. This complex of sandstone courtyards and rounded towers was built between 1190 and 1280 C.E., though it was mysteriously abandoned around 1300. You'll explore all manner of alcoves and warrens of tiny rooms, led by a friendly ranger bringing the place to life with stories of the Puebloans who once called this place home.

◉ The park is open year-round, but entry to all cliff dwellings is via pre-reserved ranger-led tours only (May–late Oct; recreation.gov).

Travel along the historic Durango and Silverton Railroad

In the late 19th century, Colorado's formidable mountain ranges were finally conquered by the railroad, slicing through valleys and passes like narrow ribbons of iron. Today the Durango and Silverton Narrow Gauge Railroad preserves some of the most captivating routes, its smoky steam trains nodding to a time gone by. The Scenic Round Trip Silverton Train is a nine-hour adventure beginning in Durango, taking scenic turns past snowy peaks, jagged canyon walls, and glittering white water, to reach Silverton, a weathered mining town where Wyatt Earp wouldn't look out of place. Then it's back to Durango—and to the 21st century.

◉ The train runs May–Oct; see durangotrain.com for other trains on the railroad.

Try Colorado's craft beers

Sipping a crisp brew among steel brewing tanks or outside with views of snowcapped mountains—there's something about an evening at a Colorado taproom. The local craft beer revolution began in 1979, using the local Rocky Mountain spring water and hop-growing industry. Boulder Beer Co. became the first craft brewery in Colorado since Prohibition that year, and Denver's Wynkoop Brewing opened its first brewpub nine years later. Both companies are still going strong, alongside newer stalwarts like New Belgium Brewing, Odell, and Left Hand Brewing. No matter where you end up, you're sure to find stellar views, tasty beers, and good company.

◉ For more on Colorado's beer industry, check out coloradobeer.org or coloradobrewerylist.com.

Take in the view atop Pikes Peak

Towering over Colorado Springs at 14,000 ft (4,267 m), Pikes Peak is one of Colorado's iconic "fourteeners"—and one you don't have to climb to conquer. For a more leisurely route, hop on the historic Pikes Peak Cog Railway, which has been chugging along the mountain since 1891. The 90-minute ride winds through alpine forests and rocky slopes before reaching the summit. Prefer to drive? Prepare for thrilling hairpin turns and stunning views, plus the freedom to stop and take photos along the way. Whichever means you take, bundle up: it's chilly at the summit, but the views are second to none.

◉ The Cog Railway runs year-round; for tickets visit cograilway.com; the base station is at 515 Ruxton Avenue, Manitou Springs (parking is $20).

Museum-hop in Colorado Springs

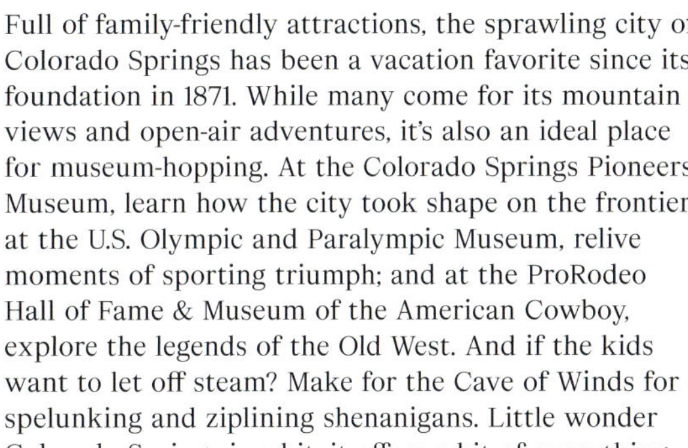

Full of family-friendly attractions, the sprawling city of Colorado Springs has been a vacation favorite since its foundation in 1871. While many come for its mountain views and open-air adventures, it's also an ideal place for museum-hopping. At the Colorado Springs Pioneers Museum, learn how the city took shape on the frontier; at the U.S. Olympic and Paralympic Museum, relive moments of sporting triumph; and at the ProRodeo Hall of Fame & Museum of the American Cowboy, explore the legends of the Old West. And if the kids want to let off steam? Make for the Cave of Winds for spelunking and ziplining shenanigans. Little wonder Colorado Springs is a hit—it offers a bit of everything.

◉ The Visit Colorado Springs Visitor Information Center is open 8:30am–5pm on weekdays (visitcos.com).

Journey through a gorge

Rust-red canyon walls close in as you journey deep into one of Colorado's most spectacular chasms and through some of the state's most tantalizing scenery. This is the luxurious Royal Gorge Route Railroad, a stunning two-hour ride from Cañon City to Parkdale and back. Cut through the rock in the 1870s, the historic track hugs the edge of the Arkansas River; along the way, look out for white-water rafters and blue herons below, and eagles soaring above. Just before reaching the turnaround, the train zips under the rickety Royal Gorge Bridge, the world's highest timber-decked suspension bridge, stretched like a tightrope across the sky.

◉ Book tickets online at royalgorgeroute.com; trains depart at 9am, 12:30pm, 3:30pm, and 6:30pm daily.

See Colorado National Monument

At Colorado National Monument, 200 million years of wind and water have sculpted a desert gallery of spires, domes, arches, and cliffs in vivid reds, purples, and oranges. The best way to take it all in is along Rim Rock Drive, a twisting 23-mile (37-km) route that climbs high above the canyons and links a string of spectacular overlooks with the visitor center at the north end, just outside the town of Grand Junction. Stop often—the views are too good to rush—and stretch your legs on a walk, perhaps. Some trails drop to the canyon floor, revealing the landscape's raw beauty up close.

◉ You'll need your own transportation to visit; the area's east and west entrances are easily accessible from I-70 outside Grand Junction.

The Constitution State

Sure, history anchors Connecticut–America's first constitutional document was produced here, in 1639, after all. But this bewitching state has a few surprises tucked up its sleeve. Take Southwestern Connecticut, which feels so close to New York City that it's practically a suburb. Add the homes of icons like Mark Twain and Katharine Hepburn, a famous pizza joint in Mystic, and an idyllic coastline, and you'll soon be falling head over heels for this little gem of a state.

STATE MOTTO He Who Transplanted Still Sustains

STATE FLOWER Mountain laurel

STATE ANIMAL Sperm whale

STATE BIRD American robin

FUN FACT The world's first nuclear-powered submarine was built in Groton, Connecticut. The USS *Nautilus* (SSN-571) was also the first submarine to complete a submerged journey to the North Pole, in 1958.

Eat pizza in Mystic

Though it's been decades since the movie came out, plenty of folks still visit the charming port town of Mystic for its pizza joint, made famous by Julia Roberts and friends in *Mystic Pizza*. But while the slices at Mystic Pizza are pretty good, there's plenty more to this place than just 1980s nostalgia. Indie stores, cafés, and galleries line the streets in the old downtown, in what was a major shipbuilding hub in the 18th and 19th centuries. The town's maritime past is preserved at the Mystic Seaport Museum, its restored stores, timber taverns, and clapboard workshops re-creating the golden age of sail. But when it's time to eat, there's always that famous pizza place–and a "little slice of heaven."

◉ Mystic (thisismystic.com) is served by Amtrak trains between New York City and Boston.

Learn about Eugene O'Neill at Monte Cristo Cottage

In 1936, Eugene O'Neill became America's only Nobel Prize–winning playwright and, though he drifted between France, New York City, and California, it was Connecticut that influenced much of his writing. His family spent many summers in New London between the 1880s and 1920; the old cottage they purchased is named in honor of Eugene's father, a theater actor known for playing the title role in *The Count of Monte Cristo*. Today the house serves as a museum, which fans of *Long Day's Journey into Night* may find strangely familiar–O'Neill set his most famous play in a house based on this family home.

◉ Monte Cristo Cottage is at 325 Pequot Avenue, New London; for opening times, check theoneill.org/mcc.

When to visit

Like its fellow New England neighbors, inland Connecticut explodes with the colors of fall in October and November. But consider visiting in summer, when the coast is especially inviting, and the water a lovely temperature for swimming.

Grab a roll from Abbott's Lobster

Lobster is boiled fresh in giant pots, its shell cracked open to reveal sweet, pink meat, which is swiftly stuffed between toasted buns. A touch of melted butter, coleslaw, and potato chips are added, and that's it: the classic New England lobster roll. Served up and down the coast, the version knocked out at Abbott's Lobster, just outside Mystic, is one of Connecticut's best, serving a quarter pound of pure lobster meat. Local institution Abbott's has been a favorite since 1947, today plating up stuffed clams, clam chowder, oysters, mussels, shrimp, crab, and corn on the cob, plus the famous lobster roll. Sound good? Pick up a lobster fork and dig in.

◉ Abbott's Lobster is at 117 Pearl Street, Noank (abbotts-lobster.com). It's only open during lobster season, from Memorial Day to Columbus Day.

See modernism in New Canaan

A sculptural glass and black-steel box stands in the middle of a manicured garden. Look closer and you'll see: it's not a sculpture, but a house. Connecticut isn't all clapboard, shingle, and white colonial churches, and nowhere is this more true than in New Canaan. Between the 1940s and 1960s, this rural town became something of a proving ground for the mid-century modernist visions of the Harvard Five: architects and designers Philip Johnson, Marcel Breuer, Landis Gores, John M. Johansen, and Eliot Noyes. Johnson's Glass House is the most famous example; it's hard not to be impressed by this pared-down living space.

◉ The Glass House is open mid-Apr–mid-Dec for guided tours (theglasshouse.org).

Boat around the Thimble Islands

Like fairy-tale stepping stones across the Long Island Sound, the Thimble Islands are an enchanting sight–tiny outcrops of pink granite, topped with trees and ornate Victorian clapboard mansions. More than 20 of these islands are inhabited today and most are strictly off-limits to the public, but local boats from the nearby village of Stony Creek cruise the archipelago. Horse Island is the biggest, while Money Island is the busiest, with over 30 homes, and arguably the most accurately named. Tempted to buy? The smallest islets of the Thimble Islands go for around $700,000, but you'll need a cool $20 million for a bigger one.

◉ For tours, head to Thimble Islands Cruise at the Town Dock in Stony Creek (1 Indian Point Road; thimbleislandcruise.com).

Step back in time in Hartford

Founded by English settlers in 1635, Hartford's history runs deep–and so, too, do its literary roots. The novelist Harriet Beecher Stowe lived here in the late 1800s, as did Mark Twain, just next door. Both former homes are today preserved as museums, where visitors can uncover the lives of these literary giants. Meanwhile, over in the Wadsworth Atheneum Museum of Art, the world's largest collection of 19th-century Hudson River School paintings can be enjoyed. Strolling through the city's many historic sites and museums, it's easy to be transported back to the Hartford of yesteryear.

◉ For information on the Mark Twain House and Museum visit marktwainhouse.org; for the Harriet Beecher Stowe Center, see harrietbeecherstowecenter.org.

Get to know Katharine Hepburn

Progressive, independent, and one of Hollywood's greatest actors, Connecticut-born Katharine Hepburn remains a cultural icon. Her family purchased a summer home in Old Saybrook around 1913 when she was just a child, and it was here that she retired to in 1997. One of America's first colonial towns, Old Saybrook is proud of the connection and, in 2009, the Katharine Hepburn Cultural Arts Center (otherwise simply called "The Kate") opened in her honor, inside the old town hall. Stop by to enjoy a live show in the center's theater, or explore the exhibits that chronicle Hepburn's life with personal items, outfits, and her own paintings.

◉ The Katharine Hepburn Cultural Arts Center is open 10am–4pm Tue–Fri (plus noon–4pm Sat & Sun in Jul & Aug).

Discover historic art colonies

In the late 19th century, young American painters came to Connecticut seeking the bucolic scenery that had inspired the French Impressionists–only closer to New York's art markets. They turned farmhouses into studios and created lively art colonies, and you can tour the places where the movement took root today. Weir Farm National Historical Park preserves the home of J. Alden Weir; in Greenwich, the Bush-Holley House recalls the Cos Cob Art Colony; and in the town of Old Lyme, the Florence Griswold Museum marks the Old Lyme Art Colony. Here, American Impressionism found a home–leaving an arts scene that still thrives today.

◉ For Weir Farm National Historical Park, see nps.gov/wefa; for Bush-Holley House, check out greenwichhistory.org.

Source antique gems

Distressed wooden tables, oak chairs, 1960s lampshades, rusty anchors, whalebone carvings, Victorian dolls, and enough pewter to sink a cruise ship–you'll find just about everything in the antiques paradise of rural Connecticut. It's best to start in Woodbury, a small town justly known as the "antiques capital of Connecticut," thanks to the glut of shops punctuating its main street. Then it's on to the former industrial town of Kent, a 40-minute drive northwest, where factories have given way to galleries and vintage emporiums. Who knows, maybe you'll find a lost treasure tucked between the bric-a-brac.

◉ For antiquing in Woodbury, see antiqueswoodbury.com. For information on visiting Kent, see kentct.com.

Sate your hunger, and hunger to learn, in New Haven

Almost everyone has heard of Yale, the Ivy League school that calls New Haven home. Founded in 1701, its leafy campus dominates the coastal city, with its pristine lawns, cozy bookstores, and lively student cafés and bars. Stop by the Yale Center for British Art to see works by Turner, Hogarth, and Constable, or visit the Yale Peabody Museum. After taking in all that culture, head into central New Haven for "apizza," the local thin-crust specialty with Neapolitan roots but beloved here. Yale's hallowed halls may be for the privileged few, but New Haven's diners and pizza joints are open to all.

◉ The New Haven Visitor Center is at 351 Long Wharf Drive, just off I-95 exit 46 (visitnewhaven.com).

The First State

Small it may be, but Delaware packs a punch. This historical heavyweight was the first state to ratify the U.S. Constitution, and windows to this significant past are found in its cobblestoned colonial towns and cities. Not that it's all history: a booming craft beer scene, abundant orchards, and blissful sandy beaches tempt those wanting some rest and relaxation. Craving an idyllic escape that's off the tourist trail? Look no further than Delaware.

STATE MOTTO Liberty and Independence

STATE FLOWER Peach blossom

STATE ANIMAL Gray fox

STATE BIRD Blue hen chicken

FUN FACT Every spring, Delaware Bay sees the world's largest gathering of horseshoe crabs coming ashore to lay their eggs on the state's sandy beaches. The event also attracts thousands of migratory birds.

Get to know the capital of Dover

Named after the English port town (despite being nowhere near the sea), Dover became the capital of Delaware in 1777, when British troops threatened the former state capital, New Castle, during the Revolutionary War. Like its namesake, Dover sidestepped heavy industrialization, and its old red-brick center remains happily intact. The best parts fall under the First State Heritage Park, and almost every landmark is a stroll away. Check out the elegant Old State House, explore colonial art at the Biggs Museum of American Art, and step inside John Bell House, Dover's oldest wooden home. Then, it's on to Spence's Bazaar, part Amish produce mart, part flea market (added bonus: there's no statewide sales tax in Delaware).

◉ The welcome center at the First State Heritage Park offers free parking and information about sites. Most sites within the park are free to enter.

Soak up history in New Castle

Quiet cobbled streets, red-brick houses, and colonial churches with neat white spires: welcome to New Castle, Delaware's first capital. The town lost its capital status to Dover in 1777, and it's something of a time capsule. Start in the heart of town, at Historic Green, shaded by the stately New Castle Court House and its distinctive cupola. The museums here are housed in historic homes, like the 17th century Dutch House, a cute little cottage with cherry-red window frames and doors, and the grand Amstel House. Complete your tour with a hearty meal at Jessop's Tavern. Chowder, Dutch pot roast, or a mountainous shepherd's pie topped with mash–comfort food with a colonial flavor.

◉ Check out newcastlehistory.org for museum information. Buses trundle between New Castle and nearby towns, though it's faster to drive.

Go peach-picking

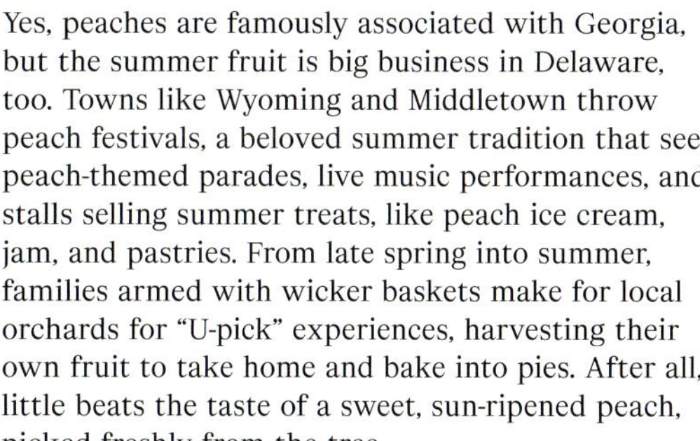

Yes, peaches are famously associated with Georgia, but the summer fruit is big business in Delaware, too. Towns like Wyoming and Middletown throw peach festivals, a beloved summer tradition that sees peach-themed parades, live music performances, and stalls selling summer treats, like peach ice cream, jam, and pastries. From late spring into summer, families armed with wicker baskets make for local orchards for "U-pick" experiences, harvesting their own fruit to take home and bake into pies. After all, little beats the taste of a sweet, sun-ripened peach, picked freshly from the tree.

◉ Find out more about the Olde Tyme Peach Festival at middletownpeachfestival.com. Want to pick-your-own? Bennett's (bennettorchards.com) and Fifers (fifers.com) are both popular options.

Promenade around the Du Pont mansions

You've probably heard of the Carnegies and the Vanderbilts. But have you heard of the Du Ponts? This Gilded Age dynasty made its millions producing gunpowder here in Delaware. The best way to get to know the family? Have a stroll around their former homes, starting with Hagley Museum. After moving from France, this was the Du Ponts' first home in America and a relatively modest house. Later generations built even bigger estates, like the dusty-pink and highly ornate Nemours Mansion, but the crown jewel is Winterthur: a 175-room palace that houses one of the world's biggest collection of American decorative arts.

◉ Each of the Du Pont properties requires a ticket. You can visit all three in one day, though they're best enjoyed over a weekend, when you can take your time exploring the houses and grounds.

Spend a day in lovely Lewes

Set along a natural harbor where the Delaware Bay meets the Atlantic, Lewes is one of the state's prettiest coastal towns—a postcard of tree-lined streets, blooming window boxes, and sailboats bobbing on the water. Founded by Dutch colonists, it later fell under British rule, and traces of both are still felt today. Start at the Zwaanendael Museum to dive into the town's layered past, then wander through the Historic Lewes Town Campus, where nine preserved buildings bring the 18th and 19th centuries to life. Be sure to stop in at the Sussex Tavern at the Stockley Street House for a mug of grog, just like the forefathers drank.

◉ The Lewes Chamber of Commerce is a gold mine of information about attractions, events, and festivals in the town (leweschamber.com).

Sip craft beer

A small state with an insatiable thirst for beer, Delaware started its beer revolution in the 1990s, when brewpub Dogfish Head opened in Rehoboth Beach. The state now has 60 brewpubs (and counting), found in converted warehouses studded with gleaming steel vats, or on picture-perfect shorelines. Sip on drinks like berry-flavored sour beers at Revelation Brewing in Rehoboth Beach, chill with Crooked Hammock's crystalline beach lager in Middletown, dive into some wild brews at Wilmington Brew Works, or savor superb IPAs at Dewey Beer Co., on Dewey Beach. Wherever you end up, the beer is sure to be matched by good vibes all around.

◉ You'll find all the state's breweries (plus wineries and cideries) listed at debrewtrail.com—handy for creating your own brewery tour.

When to visit

Delaware's breezy beaches are best enjoyed from July through September, though exploring inland is more comfortable in spring or fall, when it's less humid. It's surprisingly cold (and even snowy) from November through March, though hotels are notably cheaper.

Unwind on secluded beaches

Forget Florida's crowded beaches: Delaware's Atlantic coast is one of the East Coast's best-kept secrets. Vacationers from D.C. flock to Rehoboth Beach, making merry in its boardwalk amusement arcades, feasting on freshly caught seafood, and letting their hair down in the town's LGBTQ+ venues. But the real treasure lies to the south, in Delaware Seashore State Park. Here, a 6.5-mile (10.5-km) sandy spit stretches all the way to Maryland, fringed by dunes where finding your own quiet stretch of beach is guaranteed. Dolphins play offshore as the sun sets, and nearby campgrounds make it easy to enjoy the moonlit waves beneath a sky full of stars. Could life be better?

◉ It's free to access Delaware Seashore State Park but parking costs around $10 a day.

The Sunshine State

Florida's nickname is no accident: the state practically runs on near year-round good vibes and glorious rays. And when it comes to serving up thrills and spills, this place *delivers*. This is where larger-than-life theme parks launch you skyward, where you can explore sunken shipwrecks, paddle alongside manatees, and marvel at rockets that have landed on the moon. Adventure is mandatory in Florida. With all this on offer, it's time to get down to Florida.

STATE MOTTO In God We Trust

STATE FLOWER Orange blossom

STATE ANIMAL Florida panther

STATE BIRD Mockingbird

FUN FACT Florida is known as the "Lightning Capital of the U.S." due to its high number of thunderstorms. On average, the state experiences anything from 70 to 100 storm days every year.

Travel back in time in Pensacola

Pensacola is known as the "City of the Five Flags." Why? Over time, the flags of Spain, France, Britain, the Confederacy, and the United States have each flown above this Gulf Coast port. That layered past comes alive in the Historic Pensacola Village, where centuries-old buildings tell stories of the early European settlers who traded control of the region. Meanwhile, at the Pensacola Museum of History, exhibits trace Florida's Indigenous heritage and the city's role through shifting empires. And out on Santa Rosa Island, Fort Pickens stands by the sea, a 19th-century stronghold whose Union defense during the Civil War secured this strategic harbor for good.

◉ It's worth purchasing a Historic Pensacola Pass for access to multiple museums and heritage buildings. For extra tidbits and insights, join a walking tour with Emerald Coast Tours (emeraldcoasttours.net).

Clown around in Sarasota

Step right up! Prepare to be amazed by Sarasota, a Gulf Coast city with big-top energy. Circus king and art collector John Ringling put this place on the map when he moved in, in the roaring 1920s. His winter retreat of Ca' d'Zan is the main act, an opulent Italianate-style mansion with 56 rooms, all intended for entertaining—you've got to see it to believe it. Then it's on to the John and Mable Ringling Museum of Art, home to the showman's spectacular art collection, and the Circus Museum, where exhibits range from props, costumes, and wagons, to hands-on activities. Dare to test your mettle as an acrobat? Behold: a tightrope stands ready for the brave and willing.

◉ Time your visit for one of Sarasota's major cultural events, like the ballet season (Oct–May) or the Winter Opera Festival (typically January/February).

Camp on Perdido Key State Park

Of course the Sunshine State is awash with beaches, but those on Perdido Key are extra special. Far from the thronging crowds and dizzying theme parks of Orlando, this slender barrier island has a 16-mile (26-km) sweep of deserted sands preserved as a state park, part of the Gulf Islands National Seashore. Access to the island is via boat only, with camping permitted in a backcountry section of the National Seashore. And what a gorgeous setting to spend a night. Rolling dunes shelter sea oats, the emerald Gulf stretches towards the horizon, and, at night, stars emerge in the inky sky. The cherry on the top: lapping waves provide the soundtrack for a blissful night's sleep.

◉ Camping spots are on a sandy stretch about a half-mile (0.8 km) east of Johnson Beach, only accessible by boat.

Drift across the waters of Florida's springs

Florida's freshwater springs are windows to the wild. Beneath the emerald surface, you'll find an aquatic ballet of sunbathing turtles and the slow-motion movement of manatees, which migrate to the springs' warm waters every winter. Want to get closer to these underwater residents? Organized snorkeling and kayaking experiences are your ticket to a close-up encounter. Head to the peninsula's northwest for a pilgrimage to Crystal River and the famous Three Sisters Springs, the only place where you can legally swim with manatees. After something more chilled? Grab a tube and drift down the currents of Ginnie Springs.

◉ Explorida's guided snorkeling tours follow strict wildlife interaction rules, and educate visitors on how to observe manatees responsibly without disturbing their natural behavior (explorida.com).

Feel the magic in Walt Disney World® Resort

Whether you're young, or just young at heart, a whirl through Walt Disney World® Resort never loses its magic. When Walt Disney bought a stretch of Florida swampland in the 1960s, he dreamed of something bigger than his first California park–of theme parks, hotels, and even an "experimental city of the future." That idea evolved into today's EPCOT®, and the dream keeps expanding. One moment you're waving at princesses by Cinderella Castle, the next you're gliding over global landmarks on Soarin' Around the World, or watching extravagant Broadway-style performances in Animal Kingdom's *Festival of the Lion King* show. Decades on, Walt's vision still feels boundless–and still makes believers of us all.

◉ Stay in a vacation rental in nearby Kissimmee, a short drive away from the resort in Orlando, for more space, less crowds, and easy access.

When to visit

Summer's humidity means hurricanes, so avoid visiting June through August. Mid-April through May brings great weather without the Spring Break crowds, while September through November sees temperate weather and cheaper rates.

Visit Universal Orlando Resort™

Back in the day, Universal gifted us some of the most iconic flicks–*Jurassic Park*, *Men in Black*, *E.T.* Then, in 1990, the studio opened a playground for movie fans to step behind the scenes onto movie lots. The original working sets may have packed up their trailers, but the spirit of film and fantasy lives on in the form of blockbuster rides, epic shows, and characterful parades. The drama is spread over four theme parks, each offering an escape from reality: Universal Studios Florida, Islands of Adventure, water park Volcano Bay, and the newest member, Epic Universe. Today's schedule? Board the Hogwarts™ Express before being launched skyward on the Hulk Coaster, and hurtled back to earth in time for the Bourne Stuntacular. Same again tomorrow?

◉ Download the Universal Orlando app to check ride wait times, use the interactive map to navigate between parks, order food ahead at restaurants, and join virtual lines for popular attractions.

Reach for the stars at Cape Canaveral and Merritt Island

Few places bring the past and future of spaceflight together quite like Cape Canaveral. Since the 1950s, rockets have launched from this stretch of Florida's Atlantic coast, carrying astronauts, satellites, and probes into outer space. Just across the water, on Merritt Island, the excellent Kennedy Space Center brings that legacy to life with exhibits, hands-on training simulators, and even astronaut meet-and-greets. There's also an impressive collection of early rockets, including the now-retired Saturn V that carried astronauts to the moon. Guided tours also venture across to the Cape itself, where weathered launchpads recall triumphs and tragedies–and where rockets still lift into the skies with earth-shaking power.

◉ Cape Canaveral rocket launch schedules are listed on the Kennedy Space Center website (kennedyspacecenter.com). Arrive early to secure a prime viewing spot.

Spend a day roaming through St. Augustine

Founded by the Spanish in 1565, St. Augustine stands as one of the country's oldest continuously inhabited cities, and it wears its centuries with pride. Towering over the waterfront, the formidable Castillo de San Marcos fortress once guarded the city against pirates and the ever-shifting tides of colonial power. Today its museum breathes life into the stories of the Timucua people–the Indigenous community who thrived here long before European settlers arrived, and whose culture was devastated by disease and conflict. Exploring the city's cobblestone streets, you'll find charming 18th-century balconied buildings that have been transformed into lively wine bars and restaurants. Pull up a chair–this is the perfect spot to end the day, a glass in hand.

◉ Visit in winter for the Nights of Lights festival, which sees millions of twinkling bulbs illuminate St. Augustine's historic streets for Christmas (Nov–Jan).

Paddle around the edge of Everglades National Park

You've heard of the Everglades, but have you heard of the Ten Thousand Islands? This mosaic of mangrove islets and peaceful waterways fringes the northwestern edge of the national park, and the best way to explore, and come face-to-face with the waterway's many residents, is by kayak. You'll pass roseate spoonbills sifting the shallows for fish, and dolphins breaking the water's surface in playful arcs. In summer–if you're lucky–you might spot endangered sea turtles hauling themselves up onto sandy keys to dig nests and lay eggs, and, beneath the water's calm surface, manatees drifting lazily on beds of seagrass.

◉ Various operators offer paddling tours that strike out from Marco Island, near the park. A good choice is Kayak Marco Island (kayakmarco.com), which offers tours focused on the local wildlife and ecology.

MIAMI TOP 5

ART DECO DISTRICT
Meander around the Art Deco District in sand-fringed South Beach.

LITTLE HAVANA
Feast on traditional Cuban sandwiches and enjoy live music along Calle Ocho.

WYNWOOD
One of Miami's most creative districts, Wynwood has a wealth of open-air street art, breweries, and rooftop bars.

BOTANICAL GARDENS
See palms, mangroves, and other native Floridian flora at Miami Beach Botanical Garden.

DESIGN DISTRICT
Browse sleek galleries and high-end boutiques in this chic Miami neighborhood.

Get your art and design fix in Miami

A kaleidoscope of pastel-washed Art Deco buildings and glittering high-rises, Miami feels like one big art gallery. Take South Beach, the epicenter of the city's retro style, where neon-lit hotels and restaurants sit beside soft golden sands and swaying palm trees. Then you've got the mainland: Wynwood turns warehouse walls into a technicolor display, and street artists are constantly adding finishing touches to fresh masterpieces. Up in the Design District, forget boring white cubes—cutting-edge galleries elbow for space with high-end fashion houses, creating a fancy-meets-street style that spills out onto the sidewalk.

◉ The Miami Design Preservation League offers guided tours of the city's Art Deco sights (mdpl.org).

Let your hair down on Key West's Duval Street

Fun and freewheeling Key West has tempted many: it was here that Ernest Hemingway partied, Harry S. Truman wintered, and Tennessee Williams is thought to have written some of *A Streetcar Named Desire*. At the city's heart is Duval Street, a mile-long artery that cuts straight across the island, sweeping from the cool waters of the Gulf of Mexico to the vast Atlantic Ocean. It's a colorful parade of beach bars, quirky boutiques, and cafés plating up the island's famous Key lime pie. Take it all in, pausing for a sundowner at Sloppy Joe's Bar, a down-to-earth joint that's been mixing frozen piña coladas since the 1930s.

◉ Don't miss the nightly Sunset Celebration at Mallory Square, where crowds gather to toast the day's end with live music and street performers.

Dive into Biscayne National Park

Tucked into the northernmost point of the Florida Keys is Biscayne National Park, home to the northern tip of the world's third-longest coral-reef tract. On the water's surface, you'll spot Stiltsville, a quirky cluster of raised houses that once played host to a shadier side of history: bootleggers used them during Prohibition for throwing raucous gambling parties. Beneath the waves, shipwrecks tell the dramatic stories of Spanish conquistadors and pirates who fell victim to turbulent seas. These ghostly vessels are now habitats for juvenile parrotfish and spiny lobsters. This rich mix of natural and humanmade wonders makes the park ideal for divers; look up the Maritime Heritage Trail, an impressive underwater route linking six wrecks.

◉ Book a guided dive trip with operators like Biscayne National Park Institute (biscaynenationalparkinstitute.org).

The Peach State

The American story—past, present, and future—is told in Georgia. Tales from the Civil War and the fight for Civil Rights are swapped over buttery biscuits and peach-laden plates, and history is woven into every brick and beam. Beyond the historic charm of Savannah and the state's soupy swamplands, Georgia pulses with modern energy, seen in its iconic music scene, towering corporate ambition, and the state capital of Atlanta—surely one of the most dynamic cities in the U.S. today.

STATE MOTTO Wisdom, Justice, Moderation

STATE FLOWER Cherokee rose

STATE ANIMAL White-tailed deer

STATE BIRD Brown thrasher

FUN FACT The world's most famous soft drink, Coca-Cola, was invented in the state capital of Atlanta in 1886. Pharmacist and creator John Pemberton sold the drink's patent just before his death for $300.

Island hop around the Golden Isles

Cross the causeway from the city of Brunswick and you'll find soft-sand beaches, picturesque lighthouses, and moss-draped trees. Welcome to the Golden Isles, four islands named after the landscape's golden marshes—and the buried treasure, of course. The Spanish certainly sought riches on the islands of St. Simons, Little St. Simons, Jekyll, and Sea Island in the 16th century. St. Simons is the largest and most developed island. Whale watch from the pier, stroll through the colorful coastal villages, or nosh on shrimp and grits at a sidewalk café. For untouched beauty, take the ferry to Little St. Simons, a pristine paradise offering a glimpse of how the Spanish saw the coast. Here, nature is the real treasure.

◉ St. Simons, Jekyll, and Sea island are less than an hour's drive from each other. Little St. Simons is accessed by boat only.

Go ghost-hunting in Savannah

Ancient live oak trees and colonial mansions aren't the only relics of the past in historic Savannah—this is one of the most haunted cities in the U.S., or so they say. Take, for example, Wright Square, where the ghost of Alice Riley is said to wander through the place of her execution, or the 17Hundred90 Restaurant, the atmospheric hangout of boyish specter Thaddeus, who likes to leave pennies for guests to find on tables or at the bar. Whether you're a believer or a skeptic, you're sure to find your new favorite haunt among one of Savannah's top-notch restaurants, charming inns, or spirited bars.

◉ If you're looking for a spirit guide during your stay in Savannah, there are various ghost tours available, plus less spooky and more lively food and bike tours. Find out more at visitsavannah.com.

Spot a gator at the Okefenokee Swamp

The Okefenokee Swamp (try saying that three times fast) is the nation's largest blackwater swamp—a forest wetland where the water is steeped in peat and dark in color, like a pitcher of sweet tea. Spanning nearly half a million acres, the ancient swamp is home to more than 10,000 alligators. Those brave enough can take a self-guided kayak tour through the swamp's twists and turns. Navigate around cypress trees that tower against the glassy water, float through a lily-pad garden, or paddle down a murky canal, where gators sunbathe like they own the place—because, frankly, they do.

◉ Okefenokee Adventures is the official concession of the Okefenokee National Wildlife Refuge, and offers boat rentals and guided tours (okeswamp.org).

Gorge on Georgian peaches

Peach everything—ice cream, cobbler, even wine—takes over farmers' markets and restaurants between May and September. It was actually Franciscan monks who introduced the crop to Georgia in the 1500s, and it quickly took root in the state's fertile and sun-warmed soil, giving Georgia the moniker of the "Peach State." Farms like Pearson, Dickey, or Southern Belle are great to add to your itinerary if you want to see how peaches are grown. But hitting the highway, where vintage pickup trucks haul the latest harvest and roadside stands sling jars of fresh preserves, is an especially sweet way to get a taste of Georgia's famous fruit.

◉ Some orchards, like Southern Belle Farm (southernbellefarm.com), let you pick your own peaches. Less inclined toward manual labor? Never fear, prepicked baskets are also available.

When to visit

Summer is peach season, when the fruit is picked, sold at farm stands, and celebrated at festivals, like June's Georgia Peach Festival. The state is milder in shoulder seasons, with spring bringing bonus events like June's Atlanta Film Festival.

Listen to live music in Athens

What do R.E.M., Widespread Panic, and The B-52s have in common? They all got their start in Athens, a college town with a penchant for indie rock music. Athens' music scene took off in the 1980s, when it played an instrumental role in shaping the new wave and alt-rock genres. Catch a punk show at the 40 Watt Club—one of the nation's most iconic music venues—or head to the Georgia Theatre to see a national act and admire the space's Art Deco architecture. Up-and-coming bands continue to feed off Athens' creative spirit, so get ready to discover your new favorite tune.

The Athens Music Walk of Fame spans a two-block area of downtown and pays tribute to the town's most prominent venues and artists. Follow the route at visitathensga.com.

Watch a light show at Stone Mountain

Just outside Atlanta, a granite monolith known as Stone Mountain rises up by nearly 1,700 ft (515 m), its face engraved with a relief of Confederate soldiers—a memorial that divides Georgians. At the mountain's base sits, somewhat incongruously, an amusement park, complete with mini golf, zip lines, train rides, and a sky ride to the mountain's summit. But it's after sunset on summer nights that the fun really begins. This is when families armed with coolers settle down on picnic blankets around the amusement park to gasp and bop along as a light show, set to music, is projected on the mountain face.

The amusement park is open year-round, but the light show only takes place May through August.

Visit the Allman Brothers Band Museum in Macon

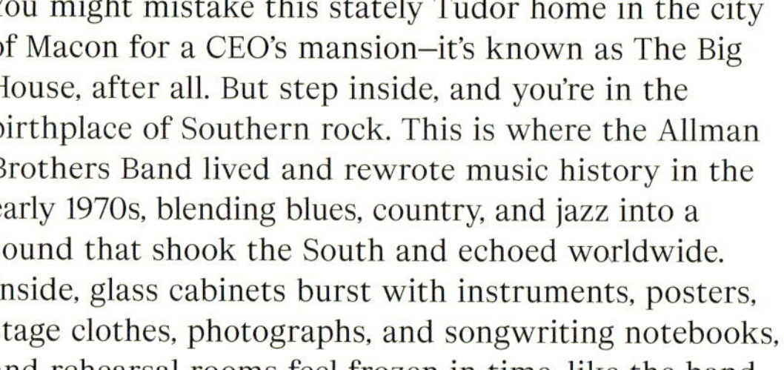

You might mistake this stately Tudor home in the city of Macon for a CEO's mansion—it's known as The Big House, after all. But step inside, and you're in the birthplace of Southern rock. This is where the Allman Brothers Band lived and rewrote music history in the early 1970s, blending blues, country, and jazz into a sound that shook the South and echoed worldwide. Inside, glass cabinets burst with instruments, posters, stage clothes, photographs, and songwriting notebooks, and rehearsal rooms feel frozen in time, like the band is coming back to jam at any moment.

"The Big House" museum is open mid-morning–early evening Thu–Sun. Check online for special exhibitions (thebighousemuseum.com).

ATLANTA TOP 5

WORLD OF COCA-COLA
Sample classic and new flavors of the world's most famous beverage at this museum.

HIGH MUSEUM OF ART
Explore one of the Southeast's largest galleries, housing African and American folk art.

POLARIS
Get a 360-degree view of the downtown skyline in this spinning rooftop restaurant.

MARTIN LUTHER KING JR. HISTORIC PARK
Get to know the Civil Rights leader at his childhood home and family church.

THE ATLANTA BRAVES
Watch the Atlanta Braves—the baseball club has been adopted as the home team of the South.

Experience Atlanta's unwavering spirit

Significantly hit in the Civil War, Atlanta earned its nickname of the "Phoenix City," rising from the ashes and transforming itself into a center of industry (it's here that corporate giants like CNN and Coca-Cola have their headquarters). But Atlanta's true soul is found beyond the boardrooms in neighborhoods like Little Five Points, where vintage stores and street art celebrate the city's remarkable past and character. Don't miss a stroll around the Beltline, a 22-mile (35-km) network of old railroad corridors that—in true Atlanta style—has been repurposed as leafy urban parks and paths, ideal for soaking up Atlanta's unstoppable energy.

Atlanta's Hartsfield-Jackson airport is the busiest in the world, so it's very well connected. In spite of traffic, driving around the city (or getting a cab) is the best way to get around Atlanta.

The Aloha State

Aloha! And welcome to America's ultimate escape. Carved by fire and defined by water, the Hawaiian archipelago dates back millennia, and yet its islands and islets collectively form the youngest state. It feels oceans apart from the U.S., and that's precisely because it is: a chain of eight main islands (it has 137 islands and atolls in total) scattered across the Pacific. Nature's handiwork is truly spectacular: sandy beaches, emerald jungles, and active volcanoes. Where to start?

STATE MOTTO The Life of the Land is Perpetuated in Righteousness

STATE FLOWER Yellow hibiscus

STATE FISH Humuhumunukunukuāpua'a (reef triggerfish)

STATE BIRD Hawaiian goose

FUN FACT Some 2,000 miles (3,218 km) from mainland U.S., and nearly 4,000 miles (6,437 km) from Japan, the state of Hawaii is the world's most isolated populated land mass.

Hike around the Nā Pali Coast on Kaua'i

Serrated cliffs in bright shades of green, orange, and rust-red: it looks like something from prehistoric times, so it's little wonder that the cinematic scenery of Kaua'i was used for the filming of 1993's *Jurassic Park*. Experience the drama for yourself by hiking around the Nā Pali Coast, an untamed wilderness on the north shore of the island. The Kalalau Trail is a popular choice, though it's not for the faint of heart. This 22-mile (35-km) round-trip hugs teetering sea cliffs, crosses rushing streams, and runs through lush valleys. Your reward? Setting up camp on paradise-like Kalalau Beach and sleeping beneath a backdrop of stars.

◉ Permits are needed for camping and hiking beyond the Nā Pali Coast's Hanakapiai Valley. Trails can be slippery and exposed, so pack sturdy shoes and plenty of water. Never underestimate the changing weather.

Surf on O‘ahu’s North Shore

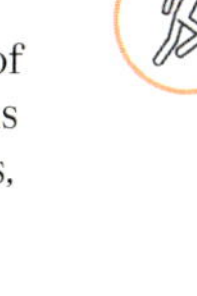

For surfers, this is the holy land of surfing, a stretch of coastline where, in winter, waves swell into mountains of water and break with ferocious power. For decades, the world’s best surfers have tested their nerve on O‘ahu’s North Shore, riding barrels as wide as train tunnels and drops that feel near vertical. It’s no playground for beginners, but watching from the sand is an adrenaline rush in itself. In summer, the giant swells fade and the water calms into glassy stretches of clear, swimmable water. Always wanted to try surfing? This is the time to master the shore’s gently rolling waves, though be warned: the beach attracts sunbathers so you’ll have an audience. Enjoy the ride.

◉ Winter is strictly for pros, so come in the summer months if you’re looking to surf. Surf schools like North Shore Oahu Surf School will help you master the season’s gentler breaks.

When to visit

Both spring and fall hit the sweet spot of warm temperatures and affordable prices, plus you’ll miss the crowds that summer attracts. If possible, come for Lei Day (May 1), a tradition that celebrates the floral garlands with parades and music.

Enjoy Honolulu’s highlights

The state capital of Honolulu, on the island of O‘ahu, sits between turquoise ocean and the rugged slopes of the Koolau Range. Long before the city became the state’s political hub, these fertile coastal plains were home to Indigenous Hawaiian communities. Their heritage is celebrated at the Iolani Palace—the only royal palace in the U.S.—and the Bernice Pauahi Bishop Museum, a trove of Pacific artifacts. Looking to escape the city? Hike to the summit of Diamond Head, an extinct volcano with sweeping views across Waikīkī Beach, considered the birthplace of modern surfing, or chase the mist to Mānoa Falls, where a 150-ft- (45-m-) high waterfall makes for a cool retreat.

◉ Reserve ahead for Iolani Palace tours and start Diamond Head hikes early to beat the heat and crowds. Both charge small entrance fees.

Contemplate the Garden of the Gods on Lāna‘i

A land steeped in legend, the Garden of the Gods (or Keahiakawelo), on Lāna‘i, is truly otherworldly. Shaped by centuries of erosion, its rock towers, craggy spires, and ridges are more akin to Utah's canyonlands than the tropical Aloha State. According to Hawaiian lore, two powerful priests from Lāna‘i and Moloka‘i once competed to see who could keep a fire burning on their island for the longest. To feed his blaze, the Lāna‘i priest used all the land's vegetation, leaving behind this barren, rock-strewn expanse. Come see the ancient rock garden for yourself at sunset, when the light makes this place feel even more magical.

◉ The site is reached via a rough, unpaved road so a 4WD is strongly recommended. Bring water, and remember to leave no trace.

Spot marine life around Molokini Crater, near Maui

Just a short boat ride from Maui's south shore lies Molokini Crater, the sickle-shaped rim of a submerged volcano. Thanks to the crater's sheltered interior, schools of fish thrive, creating a natural aquarium that's protected by a marine reserve. Around 250 species of fish—from the state triggerfish to reef sharks—flicker among the crater's brightly colored coral gardens. And the water is so crystal clear that visibility can extend beyond 100 ft (30 m). Divers plunge into the deep, while snorkelers linger around the surface, watching the marine life flit by like scenes from an underwater movie.

◉ Guided boat trips depart from Maalaea and Kīhei harbors, often combining snorkeling with a stop at a cluster of reefs called Turtle Town. All the necessary gear is supplied.

Explore Haleakalā National Park

Many national parks are historic, but this one is truly ancient: scientists estimate that Haleakalā is about one million years old. Its name means "house of the sun," and if you reach the highest point in the park (Pu'u 'Ula'ula, or Red Hill), at 10,025 ft (3,055 m), it certainly feels as though you could touch the sun. A primitive world of volcanic cinder cones and cloud-wreathed peaks, the park also has a lush side, best seen on the Pipiwai Trail. This 4-mile (6.5-km) round-trip reveals some of the park's great wonders, like bamboo forests and ancient banyan trees. The trail's star attraction? That'll be the Waimoku Falls, a breathtaking 400-ft (122-m) waterfall that cascades down a sheer lava wall.

◉ The Pipiwai Trail is popular, so arrive early to secure parking; there's a fee to enter Haleakalā National Park.

See glowing lava at Hawai'i Volcanoes National Park

Few places capture the raw power of nature like the Big Island's Hawai'i Volcanoes National Park. Two of the world's most active volcanoes, Kīlauea and Mauna Loa, continue to shape the land, their molten streams making new landscapes. For Hawaiians, this land is sacred: Kīlauea is home to Pele, the fiery goddess, whose temper is both feared and revered. Across the park, petroglyphs etched into hardened lava reveal how generations lived in balance with this restless place–drive through the park's lava fields and you'll feel it too, the sense that the island is still coming to life beneath your feet.

◉ Check eruption updates on the NPS website before you go, as some areas close during volcanic activity (nps.gov).

Snorkel off Two Step Beach

On the Big Island's Kona Coast, Two Step Beach (or Honaunau Bay) is as inviting as it sounds. It's named for the lava ledges that swimmers use as natural steps, pushing off into the water with ease. This natural entry point leads snorkelers to reefs teeming with life: sea urchins, parrotfish, and even the occasional spinner dolphin. Green sea turtles are regulars here, too, gliding through mirror-clear waters or hauling themselves onto the same sun-warmed rocks that you pushed off from. When dry land calls again, the shores themselves are a stunning sight to dry off on; the sweeps of black lava contrast dramatically with the aqua-blue ocean.

◉ The lava ledges, or steps, are uneven so water shoes help. The bay is also part of a protected marine life conservation district, so (as usual) no touching or feeding the wildlife.

Drive through cowboy country, from Hāwī to Waimea

Head inland from the lush, artsy town of Hāwī to North Hawai'i, where *paniolo* (Hawaiian cowboys) have wrangled cattle since the 1800s. This stretch of road climbs past pastures edged with bright jacaranda trees, affording wide views over the Kohala Coast, and, on clear days, the looming, cloud-shrouded peaks of Mauna Kea and Mauna Loa. The ranching town of Waimea keeps the cowboy spirit alive with saddle shops and farmers' markets–you might even catch a glimpse of a *paniolo* on horseback. The journey offers a smack of the American West, yet it's still unmistakably Hawaiian.

◉ Consider a guided tour of historic Parker Ranch, in Waimea, one of the largest cattle ranches in the U.S.

While away a day at Kīholo Bay

The Big Island has no shortage of paradise-like retreats, but Kīholo Bay is arguably the most wildly beautiful. No wonder, then, that it was favored by Hawaiian royalty; King Kamehameha even had a huge fishpond built here, in the early 1800s, to keep the good people of Hawai'i well fed, and traces of its walls can still be seen today. Turquoise waters shimmer against the bay's black-lava shore, where sea turtles sunbathe on rocks and bodysurfers hurl themselves into the Pacific's pull. Want to join them? You can strike out from a number of sandy entry points, though the most powerful currents are best left to the experienced.

◉ There is limited parking near the bay; the parking gate closes early on some public holidays, so check the times.

Drive the jaw-dropping Road to Hāna, on Maui

Carving a path along Maui's North Shore, the Road to Hāna is both thrilling and treacherous. The legendary route threads through jungles of palm and eucalyptus trees, over tight bridges, and around 60 razor-sharp switchbacks for 64 miles (103 km), eventually reaching the remote settlement of Hāna. On the one side, you'll spot locals selling the fruits of the land at roadside stands, and waterfalls tumbling into thick vegetation; on the other, the Pacific Ocean looms large. Built in the 1920s to link East Maui's sugar plantations with the rest of the island, the road became a lifeline for the remote community of Hāna. Today, travelers tackle those tight hairpin turns for the scenery and kudos as much as the destination.

◉ Traveling with a tour helps ease congestion and means you won't have to negotiate the long and winding road. Tour company Hāna & Beyond is family-run, and offers cultural storytelling and scenic stop-offs.

The Gem State

Idaho runs on extremes. It's a land of towering peaks, dense forests, and mysterious lava fields–all waiting for exploration and adventure. And nature runs wild here, too. Eagles own the skies, trout dart through the waters, and gemstones glint beneath the earth. And yet, amid this wilderness, cities like Boise thrive, pumping out art and culture in the shadow of the state's rugged mountains. In summary? All manner of treasure awaits in the Gem State.

STATE MOTTO Let it be Perpetual

STATE FLOWER Mock orange

STATE ANIMAL Cutthroat trout

STATE BIRD Mountain bluebird

FUN FACT Artist Emma Edwards Green is the only woman ever to have designed a state seal. Her 1891 design for the Idaho state seal was replaced in the 1950s, but her artwork is still shown on the state flag.

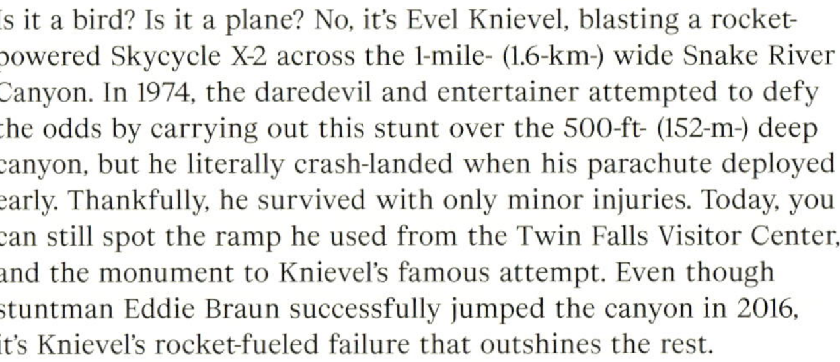

Marvel at Snake River Canyon

Is it a bird? Is it a plane? No, it's Evel Knievel, blasting a rocket-powered Skycycle X-2 across the 1-mile- (1.6-km-) wide Snake River Canyon. In 1974, the daredevil and entertainer attempted to defy the odds by carrying out this stunt over the 500-ft- (152-m-) deep canyon, but he literally crash-landed when his parachute deployed early. Thankfully, he survived with only minor injuries. Today, you can still spot the ramp he used from the Twin Falls Visitor Center, and the monument to Knievel's famous attempt. Even though stuntman Eddie Braun successfully jumped the canyon in 2016, it's Knievel's rocket-fueled failure that outshines the rest.

◉ The jump site is on private property, but it's clearly visible from the Twin Falls Visitor Center (2015 Neilsen Point Place), which is adjacent to the monument on the Perrine Memorial Bridge.

Explore Hemingway's Ketchum

One of America's most famous writers, Ernest Hemingway first showed up in Sun Valley in 1939, and was instantly charmed. The author of *The Old Man and the Sea* spent his last, tumultuous years in nearby Ketchum before his suicide in 1961. While his house isn't open for tours, you can chase his ghost to his favorite watering holes—classic spots like the Casino Bar are still pouring stiff drinks. Want more history? The Wood River Museum offers the full breakdown of his time here. Better yet, grab a copy of one of his books, find a shady spot, and start reading.

◉ Fans can visit the Hemingway Memorial and his grave in the Ketchum Cemetery.

Cruise along the Ponderosa Pine Scenic Byway

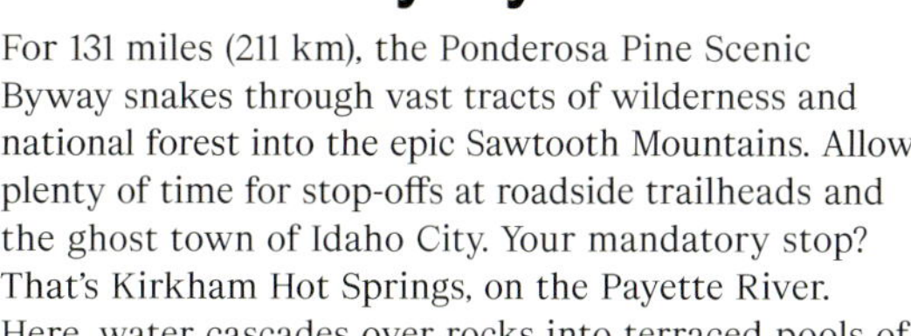

For 131 miles (211 km), the Ponderosa Pine Scenic Byway snakes through vast tracts of wilderness and national forest into the epic Sawtooth Mountains. Allow plenty of time for stop-offs at roadside trailheads and the ghost town of Idaho City. Your mandatory stop? That's Kirkham Hot Springs, on the Payette River. Here, water cascades over rocks into terraced pools of various temperatures, so you can find your Goldilocks pool for a relaxing soak before returning to the road.

◉ If you're visiting Kirkham Hot Springs you'll need your swimsuit and $5 in cash to pay for parking.

Gawk at the otherworldly Craters of the Moon National Monument and Preserve

Stark, untamed, and utterly primeval. Craters of the Moon earns its name—and its fame—from its savage, lunar-like scenery (NASA even used the area for Apollo astronaut training). It encompasses a colossal lava field that blankets a jaw-dropping 600 sq miles (1,554 sq km) of Idaho, and was forged by volcanic eruptions over the last 15,000 years (thankfully, the park hasn't seen an eruption in a couple thousand years). The scenic 7-mile (11-km) Loop Road is a great way to see this epic landscape, as is a hike along the North Crater Trail or into the craggy woodland of Devils Orchard.

◉ To explore the preserve's underground world, check ahead whether the numerous lava tube caves are open (they sometimes close to protect wildlife); you'll need to get a free cave permit from the visitor center to enter.

Go white-water rafting on the Salmon River

Little do people realize that Idaho is home to countless recreational rivers, with plenty of miles of pure wild water full of opportunities for water adventures. Of all the state's white water, the Salmon River is the undisputed favorite. Nicknamed the "River of No Return," the Salmon is an impressive stretch, with numerous thrilling rapids, sandy beaches, deep canyons, and stunning scenery. Spend a day paddling its powerful currents, or sign up for an overnight expedition. Prefer a more laid-back adventure? There are lots of peaceful riverbanks with trails for hiking, and the river is a legendary spot for fishers looking for a quiet afternoon.

◉ Numerous outfitters guide rafting trips on the Salmon River and its tributaries. See the full directory at idahosalmonriver.org.

Marvel at the Teton Range from the Teton Scenic Byway

With its jagged silver peaks looming large over Idaho and neighboring Wyoming, the Teton Range is magnificent. You can, of course, get to know Grand Teton and its smaller siblings within the national park, but the Teton Scenic Byway is tough to beat. This breathtaking 68-mile (109-km) drive writhes around "the quiet side" of the mountains, delivering a gorgeous panorama around every bend of the road. And when it's time to stretch your legs, the byway grants access to numerous trails, including the 30-mile (48-km) Ashton-Tetonia Trail, which follows a former railroad line. It's a gentle route, ideal for uninterrupted views of the Tetons.

◉ The Teton Scenic Byway is well connected, with gas, food, and lodging available at numerous towns along the route.

See bald eagles soaring over Lake Coeur d'Alene

Celebrities and CEOs have quietly snapped up homes along the over 100 miles (160 km) of Lake Coeur d'Alene's shoreline, tempted by its serene sparkling waters and lovely mountain views. But they aren't the only ones who call this area home. Every fall, kokanee salmon flood the waters upriver to spawn and, right on cue, dozens of bald eagles wheel overhead, on the hunt for their annual feast. Seeing these majestic birds gather in droves is arguably the state's greatest wildlife spectacle. In December, you can catch sight of hundreds of bald eagles on any given day, particularly around Wolf Lodge Bay.

◉ Recommended viewing spots include Higgins Point, Mineral Ridge Boat Ramp, and Mineral Ridge Trailhead.

When to visit

Sure, summer is a great time to explore the mountains. But there's something special about Idaho in winter: ski resorts are smothered in crisp snow and lower elevations are pleasant–ideal for a stroll and feeling like you have the place to yourself.

Get to know Boise

Cut through by the Boise River and sitting in the foothills of the Boise Mountains, Idaho's cool capital (and largest city) blends fresh mountain air with creative urban energy. Named by French trappers for its "boisé," or "wooded," river, this so-called "City of Trees" is as green as it is cultured. Cyclists and walkers wind along the 29-mile (47-km) Boise River Greenbelt, a pathway connecting city parks, while in the center of town, streets feature fine museums and galleries. The Boise Art Museum anchors the city's creative core, and nearby Freak Alley Gallery–a technicolor open-air showcase by some 200 artists–turns an ordinary alley into the northwest's largest outdoor gallery. In Boise, you don't have to choose between nature and culture.

◉ Most sights are accessible from downtown Boise (visit boise.com), though you can rent a bike with apps like Lime.

The Prairie State

Chicago dominates any discussion of Illinois. The city is a true dynamo, home to contemporary art, the country's first skyscraper, and legendary musicians. Leave Chicagoland behind, though, and you'll find wholesome farming communities, historic sites, and the tranquil prairies for which the state is known. You'll also discover the legacies of Illinoisans who've left their mark, whether through quests to embellish their homes or campaigns that changed the course of history.

STATE MOTTO State Sovereignty, National Union

STATE FLOWER Common blue violet

STATE ANIMAL White-tailed deer

STATE BIRD Northern cardinal

FUN FACT From pumpkin-spiced hot drinks to homemade pumpkin pie, the bright gourd is a fall staple—and Illinois is the country's top producer. Its output is the highest of any U.S. state by far.

Hit the trails in the Garden of the Gods

Much of Illinois' terrain is tabletop-flat and covered in cornfields, but down in the Ohio River Valley things get varied. Within Shawnee National Forest is the Garden of the Gods, where sandstone bluffs rising out of the surrounding terrain have been eroded into distinct shapes over the course of 300 million years. There are 5.5 miles (9 km) of trails to hike in the Garden area, including the can't-miss Observation Trail, which links some of the most evocative rock formations, like Camel Rock and Devil's Smokestack. Come in the fall, and from the top of the bluffs you'll be treated to divine views of colorful foliage stretching to the horizon.

◉ The Shawnee National Forest has some great campsites, including the Pharaoh Campground in the Garden of the Gods area (fs.usda.gov/r09/shawnee). Sites can't be reserved.

Go big in Casey

Nowhere else takes the American truism that bigger is better quite as seriously as Casey. This town of fewer than 3,000 people is home to a dozen Guinness World Record–holding objects, including the world's largest wind chimes (54 ft / 16.5 m tall), largest pitchfork (60 ft / 18.3 m long), and largest rocking chair, a 56-ft- (17.1-m-) tall, 46,200-lb (20,956-kg) behemoth. More than 20 other giant-but-not-quite-world-record objects are found around town, most within walking distance of each other. Incredibly, they're all the work of one person, Jim Bolin, who began his epic project in 2011 to draw visitors to his hometown.

◉ Some of Casey's supersized objects are interactive: ride the world's largest seesaw or mail a postcard from inside the world's largest mailbox.

CHICAGO TOP 5

ARCHITECTURAL HIGHLIGHTS
Take a Chicago Architecture Center (CAC) boat tour to enjoy the city's varied structures.

CULINARY HOLY TRINITY
Dive into deep-dish pizza, Chicago-style hot dogs, and Italian beef sandwiches.

WRIGLEY FIELD
Watch a Cubs baseball game at this storied stadium.

WILLIS TOWER SKYDECK
Enjoy the Chicago skyline from the Willis Tower Skydeck, atop what was once the world's tallest building.

ART INSTITUTE OF CHICAGO
See world-famous artworks by the likes of Grant Wood and Edward Hopper.

Check out Chicago

When the writer Norman Mailer dubbed Chicago "the great American city," he may have actually been underselling it. Rising from the shores of Lake Michigan, this metropolis of nearly 3 million people measures up against any major city in the world for art, food, and sheer urban energy. There's something for everyone in Chi-town—blues clubs, Michelin-starred restaurants, star-spawning comedy clubs, and world-class museums make up this city's cultural fabric. With so much to enjoy, you won't want to leave.

◉ Visit Choose Chicago, the city's official tourism organization, at choosechicago.com. For information on how to get around town, visit transitchicago.com.

Explore Abraham Lincoln's legacy

Central Illinois is known as the "Land of Lincoln," in tribute to the 16th president of the United States, who called the state home for a time. Lincoln lived in Springfield before moving into the White House, and the city's Lincoln Home National Historic Site preserves his old neighborhood and home. Walk the hallways Lincoln once did, taking in the parlor where he debated current events and the desk where he wrote his speeches. Round out your visit with stops at the Abraham Lincoln Presidential Library and Museum, where you can see a version of the Gettysburg Address written by hand, and the Lincoln Tomb, where the former president is buried.

◉ For the Lincoln Home National Historic Site Visitor Center see nps.gov/liho/index.htm; for the Abraham Lincoln Presidential Library and Museum, visit presidentlincoln.illinois.gov.

When to visit

Summer is generally the best time to visit Illinois, especially if you're Chicago-bound–parks spring to life and festivals like Lollapalooza and Taste of Chicago take place. If you're heading to southern Illinois, though, spring or fall are ideal.

Time travel at the Midewin National Tallgrass Prairie

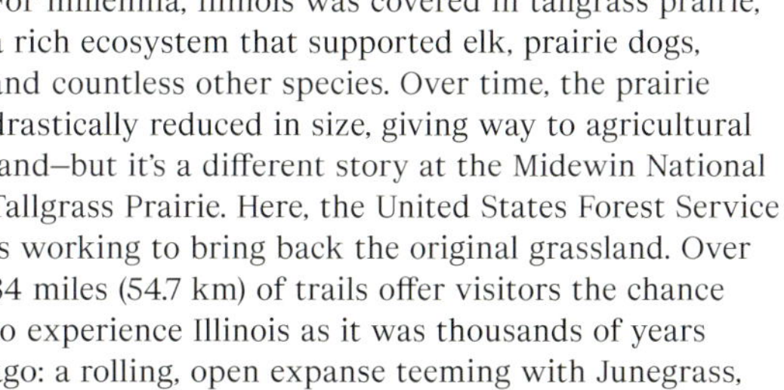

For millennia, Illinois was covered in tallgrass prairie, a rich ecosystem that supported elk, prairie dogs, and countless other species. Over time, the prairie drastically reduced in size, giving way to agricultural land–but it's a different story at the Midewin National Tallgrass Prairie. Here, the United States Forest Service is working to bring back the original grassland. Over 34 miles (54.7 km) of trails offer visitors the chance to experience Illinois as it was thousands of years ago: a rolling, open expanse teeming with Junegrass, Sullivant's coneflower, and little bluestem. It's the perfect place to get lost in nature and time.

◉ Parking is available at the Welcome Center and trailheads. Entry is free, and trails are open 4am–5pm.

Discover a lost civilization at Cahokia

It may lack the name recognition of Machu Picchu or Chichén Itzá, but Cahokia was no less important in the Indigenous history of the Americas. Established in what is now southwestern Illinois around 700 C.E., the settlement grew to become a major political, religious, and economic center by the 12th century. It was abandoned soon after that, with some 120 earthen mounds and a lingering sense of mystery left behind. Today, you can explore 72 of the remaining mounds at the Cahokia Mounds State Historic Site and climb to the top of the 100-ft (30.5-m) Monks Mound, where the city's leader lived.

⦿ The Cahokia Mounds are open from dawn to dusk, and entry is free (cahokiamounds.org). The site is best accessed by car from St. Louis, Missouri, 10 miles (16 km) away.

Find Zen at the Anderson Japanese Gardens

When the Rockford businessman John Anderson decided he wanted a Japanese garden in his backyard, he didn't take matters into his own hands—he hired a former Garden Society of Japan landscape director. Beginning in 1978, Kurisu Hoichi created what would become one of the finest Japanese gardens in North America, a serene expanse of shrubs, moss-covered rocks, and traditional dry gardens, with their mesmerizing concentric rings. Stroll the winding pathways—past stone lanterns, koi-filled ponds, and small waterfalls—and you'll feel transported to the other side of the Pacific.

◉ Anderson Japanese Gardens holds classes for visitors who want to experience traditional Japanese practices, from *sumi-e* ink painting to *ikebana* flower arrangement.

Take a stroll through Galena

Not many places can match the small-town charm of Galena. Set on the Galena River in the rolling hills of northwestern Illinois, the town grew as a lead mining settlement in the 1820s, and it feels like little has changed since. Take a walk down Main Street, where some 140 stone-and-brick buildings date back to the mid-19th century, and revel in the timeless atmosphere as you stop off at quaint independent bookshops, bakeries, and restaurants—you won't find any chain stores here. Indulge in the past even more with a visit to the former home of president and key Civil War figure Ulysses S. Grant, an impressive brick Italianate structure across the river from downtown.

◉ October is an especially fun time to visit Galena, when the town hosts its popular Halloween parade and festival (visitgalena.org).

The Hoosier State

Indiana may be known for its endless cornfields, but there's more to the Hoosier State than that. To the north, towering dunes rise along Lake Michigan; to the south, wooded hills roll toward the Ohio River. All have inspired writers, nurtured presidents, and fueled some of the world's most famous motor races. Whether you come for small-town charm or the roar of the Speedway, Indiana invites you to explore what makes it quietly unforgettable.

STATE MOTTO The Crossroads of America

STATE FLOWER Peony

STATE INSECT Say's firefly

STATE BIRD Northern cardinal

FUN FACT Indiana has a town named Santa Claus, home to year-round Christmas-themed attractions. Its post office receives thousands of letters to Santa during the holidays, with a team of "elves" replying to each one.

Spend time in the capital of Indianapolis

"What people like about me is Indianapolis," said novelist Kurt Vonnegut, who grew up in Indiana's capital city. Founded on the White River in 1821, this place offers a range of attractions: as well as a small museum dedicated to Vonnegut, there's Children's Museum, and a State Museum (the proud owner of Abraham Lincoln's signed wooden mallet of 1829). It's especially good for art, too. Newfields is home to one of the largest collections of Turner paintings outside Britain, while the Eiteljorg Museum showcases works by Georgia O'Keeffe, among others. After all that, head to the Garage Food Hall for snacks, or authentic German Rathskeller restaurant and Kellerbar Bierhall in the building designed by Vonnegut's grandfather, no less.

◉ Downtown is very walkable, but the city's IndyGo bus service also runs over 30 fixed routes from its downtown transportation hub.

Celebrate the Indy 500

Crossing the finish line in his zippy Marmon Wasp racer, at a mind-bending average speed of 74.6mph (120 km/h), Ray Harroun was proclaimed the winner of the first Indy 500 in 1911. The 500-mile (800-km) race became an immediate annual tradition, held at the Indianapolis Motor Speedway, just outside downtown. One of the world's largest sports complexes, it hosts the NASCAR Brickyard 400 in July, as well as the Indy 500 in May. Can't make it for a race? You can still view exhibits and memorabilia at the on-site museum and tour the grounds. Don't miss the Victory Podium, stained with milk—the traditional drink chugged by winning racers since 1936.

◉ The Indianapolis Motor Speedway Museum (imsmuseum.org) is open 9am–5pm daily Mar–Oct and 10am–4pm Nov–Feb. Enter the grounds through Gate 2 along 16th Street.

When to visit

May and July see high-speed racing action, and this is also the best time to enjoy the breezes coming off of Lake Michigan in Indiana Dunes National Park. Things cool off in fall, starting in September, with the added bonus of fall foliage.

Soak up history in Vincennes

Vincennes is a small town with a fascinating history. Founded as a fur-trading post in 1732, it was later occupied by the British and saw fierce engagements in the Revolutionary War. The victorious American campaign is commemorated at the George Rogers Clark National Historical Park. Vincennes went on to serve as the capital of the Indiana Territory in 1800–1813, but since virtually nothing of note happened here thereafter, it's been beautifully preserved. There's the original Indiana Territory Capitol (a humble, red-painted clapboard house), the territory's first school, and a print shop. You can also tour Grouseland, the home of the shortest-serving U.S. president, William Henry Harrison.

◉ The George Rogers Clark National Historical Park is open 9am–5pm daily. You'll find the city's tourism bureau in the Elihu Stout Building at 702 Main Street (visitvincennes.org).

Visit the Lincoln Boyhood National Memorial

Though born in Kentucky, Abraham Lincoln spent his formative years in Little Pigeon Creek, an isolated frontier community in the hilly south of Indiana. It was a childhood marked by hardship and tragedy, notably the death of his beloved mother when he was nine. Today, in the leafy grounds that the 16th U.S. president once called home are sites including his mother's grave, and a carefully constructed replica of the family's log cabin. Quiet and seemingly frozen in time, the grounds are an evocative reminder of just how far that young boy managed to climb.

◉ It's free to enter the memorial site. The grounds are open sunrise to dusk year-round; the visitor center opens 9am–noon and 1–3pm Wed–Sun only.

Learn about the Underground Railroad in Fountain City

Pay a visit to the home of Levi and Catharine Coffin, Quakers and committed abolitionists who served as "conductors" on the Underground Railroad–the secret network that helped enslaved people escape the South in the early 19th century on their way to freedom farther north or in Canada. From the outside their house looks deceptively normal, a simple Federal-style brick home built in 1839, but this one has some unusual features. Today you can tour the secret basement kitchen with spring-fed well, a large attic, and cramped storage garrets at the back that all served as hiding places. It's a sobering but ultimately uplifting experience.

◉ The Levi and Catharine Coffin State Historic Site is open 10am–5pm Wed–Sun.

Get to know the city of South Bend

South Bend, or "the Bend" to locals, is defined by two enduring institutions: Studebaker automobiles and the University of Notre Dame. On the city's north side, Notre Dame's storied campus has been the heart of community life since 1842, its Fighting Irish football team a real highlight, drawing fans from across the country every game day. Founded in 1852, Studebaker went on to produce its first classic cars in the early 1900s, marking the start of a century-long automotive legacy now celebrated at the Studebaker National Museum. After exploring all that and more, cap off the day at an Irish pub–Corby's is a favorite local spot.

◉ South Bend Visitor Information Center is at 101 N. Michigan Street. Downtown South Bend is easy to explore on foot, but exploring the surrounding area is easier with a car (visitsouthbend.com).

Explore Indiana Dunes National Park

Indiana isn't completely landlocked. Its northern border takes in a tiny section of the Lake Michigan shore, with some 15 miles (24 km) of it protected within Indiana Dunes National Park. One of the country's lesser-known reserves, it's a real gem, with massive sand dunes; backwaters alive with the likes of kingfishers and warblers; and some 50 miles (80 km) of varied trails, often blazing with wildflowers in the spring. Paths wind along rivers, across grasslands, and through the dunes to the Great Marsh, the realm of coots, green herons, and wood ducks. Want to swim? The park's beaches are often half-empty, even in the summer.

◉ Start your visit at the park's Dorothy Buell Memorial Visitor Center (daily: Jun–Aug 8am–6pm, Sep–May 8:30am–4:30pm; nps.gov/indu), on Indiana State Road 49, between US-20 and I-94.

Discover the story of Gene Stratton-Porter

Nature photographer, conservationist, film producer, novelist: Gene Stratton-Porter was all of these, though she's best known to Hoosiers for her books. Her writing career took root in the 1890s at the distinctive red-and-green Limberlost Cabin (which you can tour today), in Geneva, where the surrounding swamps and forests provided endless inspiration. When the wetlands were drained, she felt compelled to seek a new home and settled on the shores of Sylvan Lake, purchasing a cabin she named Wildflower Woods. This rustic hide-away is especially charming, a testament to the enchanting gardens she dedicated herself to tending.

◉ It's a 1.5-hour drive from Limberlost Cabin to Wildflower Woods, and you'll need to pay admission for both.

The Hawkeye State

Bright-red barns, big blue skies, and swaths of wheatfields with only grain elevators breaking the horizon: welcome to Iowa, the quintessential Midwestern state. It's home to old Mississippi River port towns, mysterious Indigenous mounds, and historic Czech neighborhoods. Beyond the cities lie the state's iconic cornfields, and, while crop circles may be few, science fiction has its place here: Iowa is the future birthplace of Star Trek's Captain James T. Kirk (expected in 2233).

STATE MOTTO Our Liberties We Prize and Our Rights We Will Maintain

STATE FLOWER Wild rose

STATE ANIMAL None

STATE BIRD American goldfinch

FUN FACT Iowa is home to the world's largest truck stop. The record-breaking Iowa 80 Truckstop covers 220 acres (90 ha) of land and includes a movie theater, dentist, and even a barber shop.

Get cultural in the capital Des Moines

Iowa-born Bill Bryson once called Des Moines "the most powerful hypnotic known to man," but that's a bit unfair. Surrounded by hundreds of miles of pancake-flat farmland, Iowa's capital is something of a cultural oasis. From its roots as a fort, it has evolved into a city of steel-and-glass skyscrapers, linked by the Skywalk, a 4-mile (6-km) network of temperature-controlled bridges. Looming over everything is the gold-leafed dome of the Iowa State Capitol, but the real treasure here is the stylish Des Moines Art Center, designed by Eliel Saarinen, I.M. Pei, and Richard Meier. Home to works by the likes of Hopper, O'Keeffe, and Picasso, it's inspiring, beautiful—and definitely not sleep-inducing.

⦿ The visitor information office Catch Des Moines is at 400 Locust Street, in the heart of downtown (8:30am–4:30pm Mon–Fri; catchdesmoines.com).

Dig into Blue Bunny ice cream history in Le Mars

Le Mars is a sure frontrunner for the title of "Ice Cream Capital of the World": this rural Iowa town makes more than 150 million gallons (567 million liters) of the sweet stuff per year. And it's all thanks to Blue Bunny. The ice cream brand has been making frozen treats here since 1925, when former Le Mars milkman Fred H. Wells founded the brand; the name was decided through a "Name that Ice Cream" contest in town a decade later. Today, you can tour the Blue Bunny headquarters, tasting ice cream flavors, racing freezer robots, and learning about the brand's history–all with the sweet scent of freshly baked waffle cones wafting by.

◉ The Wells Visitor Center and Ice Cream Parlor opens 9am–10pm Mon–Sat, noon–10pm Sun (ilovewells.com).

See the Shrine of the Grotto of the Redemption

Rising from the plains of northern Iowa like a stranded piece of coral reef, this Roman Catholic shrine is one of the Midwest's most unexpected sights. Made from seashells, fossils, precious stones, and ancient rocks, it sprawls on the edge of the otherwise workaday farming village of West Bend. German-born Father Paul Dobberstein began building the structure in 1912, creating nine grottoes depicting scenes from the life of Christ. Work continued for the next 40 years, his glittering finds cemented into towers, arches, fountains, and statues of the Virgin Mary. The result is an otherworldly creation that dazzles, whatever your beliefs.

◉ The shrine is open 24 hours a day, but its visitor office is open 8am–4pm Mon–Fri (westbendgrotto.com).

Explore the Effigy Mounds National Monument

As early European settlers trundled west, they dubbed the Great Plains the "great American desert," believing the landscape to be inhospitable. Little did they know that the mounds they passed along the way belonged to Indigenous civilizations centuries ago. More than 200 humanmade hills are preserved as the Effigy Mounds National Monument; the mounds served as circular burial sites, but there are also long, rectangular types likely used for ceremonies, as well as animal-shaped mounds. Rarely busy, the monument offers a place of tranquility; indeed, a number of Indigenous peoples still consider the mounds sacred.

◉ The Effigy Mounds National Monument is open sunrise–dusk daily; Feb–Apr, it's closed Wed and Thu (nps.gov/efmo).

Discover Czech roots in Cedar Rapids

Cedar Rapids is the unlikely spot for one of the largest Czech diasporas in the country. In the 1850s, an early wave of people fleeing revolutions in the Austro-Hungarian Empire arrived in the young city—and the rest is history. See signs of this industrious community in the historic Czech Village neighborhood (and in New Bohemia across the river), and visit the National Czech & Slovak Museum for an extensive collection of Bohemian national costumes. Hungry? Head to Little Bohemia for no-frills Czech beers and—what else?—piping hot goulash with dumplings.

⦿ For more on the Czech Village and New Bohemia areas, visit the-district.org; for Cedar Rapids tourist information, check out tourismcedarrapids.com.

Visit the Amana Colonies

Since the 19th century, this little pocket of eastern Iowa has been home to the Amana Colonies. Founded by German Inspirationalists—a radical Christian sect that believed in communal living—the colonies are made up of seven once self-sufficient villages. Though communal life ended in 1932, these fascinating High German–speaking communities remain, with farming and increasingly tourism pulling in the dollars. Come to explore the pretty clapboard houses, craft shops, and antique B&Bs. There are also traditional restaurants serving family-style meals—the home-cooked schnitzel, *spatzle* (egg noodles), and *kasseler rippchen* (smoked pork with apple sauce) are superb.

⦿ The Amana Colonies Trail is a 17-mile (27-km) loop connecting all seven villages. The visitor center is open 9am–5pm Mon–Sat, 10am–5pm Sun (amanacolonies.com).

Tour the Field of Dreams

The 1989 cinematic hit *Field of Dreams* spurred on the creation of endless T-shirts, bumper stickers, and memes. Its plot centers around an Iowa corn-turned-baseball field that lures in the ghosts of baseball legends. The movie was filmed just outside the city of Dyersville, in the middle of the Iowa Prairies, on a purpose-built set. Abandoned after filming, the location was gradually developed by local families into a real place, and fans of the sport and movie alike have been visiting ever since. Tour the fictional farmhouse, see the legendary baseball field, and who knows—you might even catch a glimpse of the "ghost" sportspeople (played by local actors) in action.

⦿ The field is open sunrise–sunset all year round, while farmhouse tours usually run 10am–3pm daily (fieldofdreamsmoviesite.com).

Get into the college spirit in Iowa City

Once a 19th-century frontier town, Iowa City is now dominated by the University of Iowa, with its 30,000 students making up half of the city's population. Literature is a big focus here, thanks to the university's legendary Iowa Writers' Workshop, which counts famed writers like Eleanor Catton and John Cheever among its alumni and ex-faculty; needless to say, there are some excellent bookstores to explore, including intimate Prairie Lights Books. Sports fans, meanwhile, can catch a college football game–the university's Hawkeyes are beloved across the state.

◉ For Iowa City tourism information, visit thinkiowacity.com. To find out about Iowa Hawkeyes sports events, check out hawkeyesports.com.

When to visit

With so many charming cities and towns, full of restaurants and bookstores, Iowa is best visited from September through November, when the weather is cool and dry. Top tip: avoid the state in May and June, when twisters and flooding are common.

See the Mississippi in Dubuque

Sweeps of flat hinterland are a dime a dozen in Iowa, making river-port cities like Dubuque a rarity. The great Mississippi River has played a key role in this city since its early days: what began as a small mining settlement founded by French-Canadian pioneer Julien Dubuque in the 18th century grew into a booming river depot and logging hub just 100 years later. Take in the river views from the 19th-century Fenelon Place Elevator–one of the world's shortest and steepest funicular railways–cruise downstream on a riverboat tour, or head to the National Mississippi River Museum & Aquarium. You'll be waxing lyrical about "Big Muddy" in no time.

◉ The Dubuque Welcome Center opens 9am–5pm Mon–Sat, 10am–3pm Sun (traveldubuque.com), and the National Mississippi River Museum & Aquarium opens 9am–5pm daily (rivermuseum.org).

The Sunflower State

Blissful prairies, small towns, and field after field of sunflowers: Kansas is pure charm. Slap-bang in the middle of the country, this is the heartland of America, a state forged by agricultural traditions and frontier history. It was here that abolitionists fought skirmishes early in the Civil War, and the legendary aviation pioneer Amelia Earhart was born. Whether you want to walk in the footsteps of groundbreakers, or simply watch the sun set over the fields, Kansas delivers.

STATE MOTTO To the Stars Through Difficulties

STATE FLOWER Wild sunflower

STATE ANIMAL American bison (buffalo)

STATE BIRD Western meadowlark

FUN FACT Some of the state's more unusual laws include a ban on shooting rabbits from motorboats (the state is landlocked, remember), and on serving cherry pie with ice cream on Sundays.

Feel at peace in Tallgrass Prairie National Preserve

Serene and silent, this idyllic prairie dominated the Kansas landscape for millennia, an endless sea of tallgrass watched over by circling bald eagles. But the march of modern development whittled away more than 95 percent of the landscape, and today the Tallgrass Prairie National Preserve protects one of the last remaining patches. A network of trails winds through the preserve, inviting visitors to experience its wide-open beauty up close. For the best view of the prairie's resident bison, lace up your boots and hike the Scenic Overlook Trail, a challenging 6-mile (9.5-km) round-trip.

◉ The preserve is open daily year-round, though the grasses are tallest in fall. The preserve entrance is 2 miles (3 km) north of Strong City.

Follow the yellow brick road at the OZ Museum

"There's no place like home," said Dorothy of her home state, after a tornado ripped her and her beloved dog Toto away to the fantastical land of Oz. Since 2003, the OZ Museum in Wamego has celebrated the legacy of *The Wizard of Oz*, tracing its early beginnings as a children's book by L. Frank Baum, to the 1939 film starring Judy Garland and the Broadway spin-off *Wicked*. Step inside to find props, costumes (hello, ruby slippers), and life-sized sculptures of the Tin Man and Scarecrow. The star of the show? That's the indoor yellow brick road, which is ripe for skipping down, just like Dorothy did with her ragtag gang of friends.

⦿ Plan to visit for a half-day to fully explore the museum, which is open daily (ozmuseum.com).

When to visit

Kansas is best in the second half of the year, after spring and summer's tornado season. Sunflowers bloom from late summer into early fall, when the days are milder and the nights are cool, and the state's prairies look their finest.

Make a flying visit to the Kansas Aviation Museum in Wichita

A temple to all things airplanes, the Kansas Aviation Museum is fittingly housed in a former terminal of the Wichita Municipal Airport. This stunning Art Deco monument served travelers from 1935 to 1954, and today doubles as a museum and popular wedding venue. Exhibit rooms explore the state's aviation history, with vintage photographs, blueprints, and models, and small aircraft fill the historic terminal. Outside, giants like the Lockheed T-33 and a rare Beechcraft Starship 2000 lie scattered across the abandoned runway, all looked over by the old control tower.

⦿ The museum hosts fun events like murder mysteries, paint-and-sip nights, and "Play on a Plane Day," when visitors can board the aircraft (kansasaviationmuseum.org).

Relive Kansas's frontier days in Dodge City

You've seen old westerns on TV; get a taste of reality in Dodge City. A frontier settlement in the second half of the 19th century, Dodge City became notorious for its Wild West antics. The gunfights were deadly, saloons were raucous, and the legends were real (lawman Wyatt Earp lived here for a stint and was involved in various shoot-outs). Though the dust has long settled, Dodge City hasn't forgotten its wicked past. Stories from the city's Wild West days are retold at the Boot Hill Museum, where a re-creation of the Dodge City of the late 1800s sees costumed performers acting out gunfights.

◉ The staged gunfights take place at noon and 6pm May–mid-Aug. Other events include a variety show and a country-style dinner.

Discover the legacy of abolitionist John Brown

Even before the Civil War tore the nation apart, radical abolitionist John Brown fiercely opposed slavery. The Puritan minister first worked peacefully but, after years of defeat, supported violent campaigns, including here in Kansas. The John Brown Museum, in Osawatomie, chronicles the abolitionist's life, displaying personal possessions and memorializing conflicts, like the Battle of Osawatomie, which saw pro-slavers attack the town and kill Brown's son. Brown actually stayed in this very building for 20 months—it was his HQ for organizing antislavery efforts in Kansas. Though tiny, the cabin stands as a monumental testament to Brown's legacy.

◉ Osawatomie's annual Freedom Festival, held in September, honors Brown's legacy with reenactments and performances.

Find cheer in Kansas's iconic sunflower fields

You can't help but smile at the sight: a sea of bright-yellow sunflowers, their open faces turned up to the sky. Eleven types of sunflower grow here in Kansas, largely cultivated for seeds and oils, as well as cut blooms. With some 60,000 acres (24,000 ha) of the crop, the Sunflower State offers endless photo opportunities, particularly in northwestern Kansas, where sunflower fields stretch to the horizon. And if you're passing through Goodland, don't miss The Big Easel, a striking 24-ft (7-m) replica of Vincent van Gogh's famous *Sunflowers*–it's one of the state's most joyful roadside landmarks.

Check out the Kansas Tourism website (travelks.com) for bloom forecasts and visiting hours at fields open for exploration.

The Bluegrass State

If you had to describe Kentucky in two words, you might say horses and whiskey. And it'd be a fair response: it's known for hosting the country's most famous horse race, the Kentucky Derby; and, yes, a whopping 95 percent of the world's bourbon supply is made here. But Kentucky's spirit runs deeper than bluegrass pastures and oak barrels. Beneath its green fields lie ancient caves, along its trails stretch huge gorges, and in its small towns are many tempting bakeries and craft stores.

STATE MOTTO United We Stand, Divided We Fall

STATE FLOWER Goldenrod

STATE ANIMAL Thoroughbred horse

STATE BIRD Northern cardinal

FUN FACT Kentucky is famously the birthplace of Bill Monroe, the pioneer of the bluegrass music genre. This music style was named after the iconic bluegrass of Kentucky's pastures.

Tackle the rocks of Red River Gorge

Want to explore an environment that's been sculpted by both wind and water over millions of years? Then make your way to Red River Gorge, a sandstone landscape found within the Daniel Boone National Forest. The gorge is made up of sheer cliffs, near-vertical rock faces, rock shelters, and more than 100 natural arches–it's rugged and undoubtedly wild, but thankfully there are designated trails and campsites making it easier to navigate. While the gorge is best explored by climbing, hiking, kayaking, and canoeing are other great ways to immerse yourself in all its natural beauty.

◉ The area's Gladie Visitor Center is open 10am–5pm Thu–Sun (fs.usda.gov/r08/danielboone/recreation/gladie-visitor-center). Inside are displays on pioneer history and the ecology of the gorge.

Hit the Kentucky Bourbon Trail

When Europeans arrived in Kentucky in the late 1700s, they stumbled upon the perfect conditions for whiskey making: fertile soil, a moderate climate, and limestone-rich spring water. With their distilling know-how, they laid the foundations for what would become a huge industry; today, Kentucky produces around 95 percent of the world's bourbon. Sample the best along the Kentucky Bourbon Trail, which links more than 60 distilleries and tasting rooms. Legacy brands include Buffalo Trace, the U.S.'s oldest continuously operating distillery–it kept its stills running during Prohibition by producing "medicinal whiskey."

⦿ Book a guided experience with a custom operator such as Mint Julep Tours to sample bourbon from a curated string of distilleries (mintjuleptours.com).

Tour the Kentucky State Capitol and the Old State Capitol

Founded along a shallow crossing in the Kentucky River, the city of Frankfort took shape in the late 1700s and was chosen as the capital in 1792, when the state was still in its infancy. Politics soon found a stage in the Old State Capitol, a Greek Revival structure completed in 1830. But, by the turn of the 20th century, Kentucky wanted something even grander, and so the Beaux-Arts-style Capitol was born. It opened in 1910, complete with a huge dome soaring 212 ft (64 m) high. Together, the buildings tell the civic story of Kentucky, where landmark laws, from bourbon regulations to Civil Rights milestones, were passed.

⦿ The Kentucky State Capitol is at 700 Capital Avenue, and the Old State Capitol is at 300 W. Broadway Street.

Dive into sporting legacies in Louisville

Louisville's sporting pedigree runs deep. It was home to none other than Muhammad Ali, the heavyweight boxer better known as The Greatest. Follow his journey from Cassius Clay, a teenager training in a neighborhood gym, to Ali, a world champion and renowned activist, at the Muhammad Ali Center. But that's not all—this city produces the iconic Louisville Slugger, the baseball bat that's been swung by legends from Babe Ruth to Ken Griffey Jr. A trip to the Louisville Slugger Museum and Factory reveals how the prized bats are made, sculpted from hunks of ash and maple before swinging their way into sporting history.

◉ The Muhammad Ali Center opens Wed–Sun (alicenter.org); the Louisville Slugger Museum and Factory is open daily.

When to visit

Kentucky is truly a four-season destination—think hot, humid summers, chilly winters, wildflower-filled springs, and fall in blazing color. Most visitors come in the milder spring and fall months.

Explore horse-racing heritage

Kentucky is the so-called "Horse Capital of the World," and nowhere is this more apparent than at Louisville's Churchill Downs. On the first Saturday of May, the track fills with cheering crowds, clutching mint juleps and dressed in bright spring finery. This is the Kentucky Derby, the U.S.'s biggest horse race. Even when the track isn't filled with the sound of thundering hooves, it's worth a visit for guided tours of the site and the Kentucky Derby Museum's displays of trophies and jockey silks. Want to see more horses? Then head east to the city of Lexington, where champion thoroughbreds are reared among the lush, bluegrass pastures of historic farms. Here, you can take to the saddle yourself with a horseback-riding lesson or tour.

◉ Tickets for the Kentucky Derby sell out quickly and should be bought in advance (kentuckyderby.com/tickets).

Chase waterfalls in Cumberland Falls State Resort Park

It's not hard to see how this park's namesake cascade earned the moniker "Niagara of the South." Surrounded by forests filled with pine and hemlock, Cumberland Falls plunges for some 68 ft (20 m) in a roar of white water. Back in the 1930s, the Civilian Conservation Corps transformed the surrounding landscape into a resort park, laying down trails, spanning streams with bridges, and building cabins. Fast-forward to today, and the park and falls are still a beloved nature getaway–without the crowds that flock to its northern cousin.

◉ The park's 1930s DuPont Lodge offers a historic place to stay (parks.ky.gov/explore/dupont-lodge-7904).

Get crafty in Paducah

Paducah might just be one of Kentucky's most artistic towns. From the mid-1800s it grew as a textile hub, with the quilts being produced here evolving gradually from overlooked necessities to coveted art pieces. The town boosted its creative reputation in 2000 with its Artist Relocation Program, which encouraged makers to put down roots in the once-forgotten Lower Town neighborhood. Today, the area is thick with studios and galleries belonging to painters, potters, and, of course, quilters. Stop by to watch the artists at work and try your hand at a craft, or drop in to the National Quilt Museum to admire some of Paducah's famous quilts.

◉ To see the best of Paducah's art scene, head to the Lower Town Arts and Music Festival in May (ltamf.com).

Soak up German heritage in Covington

Breweries, bakeries, Gothic church steeples: Covington isn't your typical Southern city. It was founded in the 19th century by German immigrants, who built the city with a nod to their homeland. This heritage lingers in its streets and festivals today, especially in historic MainStrasse Village. Here, colorful brick façades and steep gables echo the Rhineland, while the 100-ft (30-m) Glockenspiel clock tower chimes over the square. Come fall, the German spirit is fully embraced with Oktoberfest, a jamboree of Bavarian music, bratwurst, and, of course, beer.

◉ Covington Oktoberfest takes place a little earlier than you might expect, usually kicking off in September.

Peer into Mammoth Cave

Beneath the rolling hills of central Kentucky lies a big secret: the world's longest discovered cave system, made up of more than 400 miles (640 km) of dark, subterranean passageways. Human history stretches back for thousands of years at Mammoth Cave National Park, when Indigenous peoples mined the caves for minerals, leaving behind petroglyphs and artifacts. European settlers stumbled upon the epic cave system in the late 18th century, when a hunter pursuing a bear found the entrance. Today, the adventurous can uncover these hidden routes on lantern-lit tours through vast chambers, dark passages, and labyrinthine crawlways.

◉ For more information on Mammoth Cave, including details on cave tours available, visit nps.gov/maca.

Stroll through historic Bardstown

Bardstown, laid out in 1780, is one of Kentucky's oldest cities–and, boy, does it show. Countless Federal-style façades and old brick buildings line its boulevards, where today antique shops, bourbon tasting rooms, and family-run restaurants thrive. Distilleries like Willett and Bardstown Bourbon Company keep centuries-old traditions alive, offering tours, tastings, and unique experiences like blending workshops. And for a closer look at this cherished Kentucky spirit, there are few better places than the Oscar Getz Museum of Bourbon History. It's a historic city with a lot of spirit (literally).

◉ Bardstown hosts the annual Kentucky Bourbon Festival in September, when distillers descend on the small town to celebrate the spirit (kybourbonfestival.com).

Visit Abraham Lincoln Birthplace

In Hodgenville, a grand Neo-Classical memorial rises from the Kentucky hills, its marble columns sheltering a humble log cabin that marks Abraham Lincoln's beginnings. Here, in 1809, the future president was born on a small family farm, sustained by the clear waters of Sinking Spring. A short drive away at Knob Creek, the boyhood landscape unfolds further: weathered cabins, split-rail fences, and fertile fields conjure the rough-hewn world of frontier families. Tended today by the National Park Service, these quiet homesteads hint at the modest roots that shaped a man destined to redefine a nation.

◉ The Birthplace Unit and Boyhood Home at Knob Creek Unit are both open daily (nps.gov/abli).

The Pelican State

Every state in the U.S. is unique, but Louisiana is that extra bit so. Its distinctive Cajun and Creole customs, traditions, and flavors were born from a cultural stew—or gumbo, we should say—that draws on the heritage of Indigenous, French, Spanish, and Caribbean communities. The landscape is just as unique, a quilt of soupy swamps, cypress groves, buzzing bayous and long prairies, with pelicans soaring overhead. Ready to taste a culture like no other? Louisiana awaits.

STATE MOTTO Union, Justice, Confidence

STATE FLOWER Magnolia blossom

STATE ANIMAL Louisiana black bear

STATE BIRD Eastern brown pelican

FUN FACT Louisiana is the only state in the U.S. to have parishes instead of counties; this quirk is reflective of the state's Catholic past, when it was under French and Spanish rule.

Get to know the Crawfish Capital

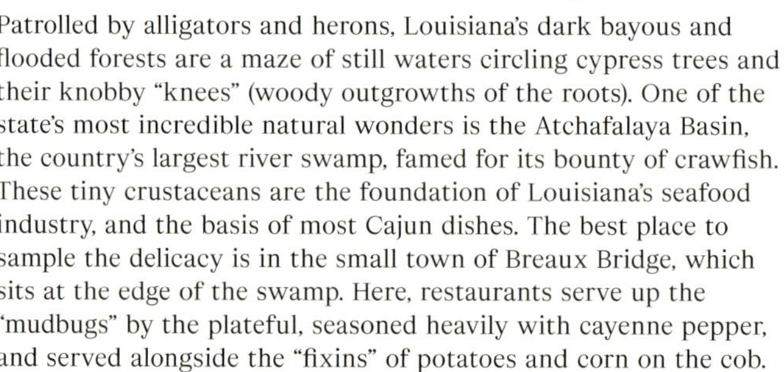

Patrolled by alligators and herons, Louisiana's dark bayous and flooded forests are a maze of still waters circling cypress trees and their knobby "knees" (woody outgrowths of the roots). One of the state's most incredible natural wonders is the Atchafalaya Basin, the country's largest river swamp, famed for its bounty of crawfish. These tiny crustaceans are the foundation of Louisiana's seafood industry, and the basis of most Cajun dishes. The best place to sample the delicacy is in the small town of Breaux Bridge, which sits at the edge of the swamp. Here, restaurants serve up the "mudbugs" by the plateful, seasoned heavily with cayenne pepper, and served alongside the "fixins" of potatoes and corn on the cob.

◉ Get close to the crawfish action and stay at the Bayou Cabins (bayoucabins.com), a cluster of restored cabins situated on Bayou Teche.

Uncover the past at Poverty Point

Louisiana is an old state, but its past goes beyond the more well-known colonial era to a pre-Columbian period that remains, largely, a mystery. And yet: tantalizing pieces of this ancient puzzle have been found, most notably the mounds of Poverty Point. Between 1700 and 1100 B.C.E., Indigenous peoples meticulously moved some 2 million cubic yards (1.5 million cubic m) of soil to create an urban area and ritual site that dwarfed other American human-made structures for two millennia. The concentric mounds and plotted lanes speak to elaborate design sense, in a culture that apparently lacked domesticated animals, or even the wheel.

◉ To make better sense of the mounds (povertypoint.us), join a guided tour.

See art in Shreveport

You've heard of Louisiana, you've heard of Texas, but have you heard of Ark-La-Tex? This region, in northwest Louisiana, is where three states—Arkansas, Louisiana, and Texas—meet to create a one-of-a-kind cultural hub. At the region's heart is Shreveport, a city that combines the *joie de vivre* of Louisiana with the values of Arkansas and swagger of Texas. Alongside its top-notch restaurants, the city has an exciting arts scene, best represented in galleries like the ultra-cool Artspace, a modern art gallery and community center. The largest museum in the city is the R.W. Norton Gallery, a temple to the arts. It's chockablock with works by American artists, like Mary Cassatt and Frederic Remington.

◉ Shreveport's tourist information website has handy information on planning a visit (visitshreveportbossier.org).

When to visit

Ideally, come for carnival season, which runs from January 6 until Mardi Gras (for which the date changes between February and March every year). October through December offers fewer crowds and comfortable temperatures.

Dive into Cajun Country culture

When French-speaking Acadians were exiled from Canada in the 18th century they settled in Louisiana and were dubbed "Cajuns," a term that has become synonymous with the state. Today, real Cajun Country, or Acadiana, is anchored in a region centered around the town of Lafayette. Here you'll find regular live concerts, plenty of dancing, and, perhaps most importantly, *very* good food. And we're not just talking about bowls of traditional gumbo (though that's important, too). Cajun culture is dynamic and constantly evolving. Imagine, Cajun ballads remixed with a heavy dose of electronica, and time-honored dishes being reimagined by up-and-coming chefs.

◉ The Blue Moon Saloon (bluemoonpresents.com), in Lafayette, is one of the best standbys for Cajun shows and lots of dancing. Need to crash? They rent rooms, too.

Say hello to an alligator in the Barataria Preserve

Think of Louisiana, and you may think of alligators—there are over two million statewide. And while you can spot them roaming the canals and waterways of New Orleans, they're more reliably seen in wilder settings like the Barataria Preserve, just a 30-minute drive south of the city. Part of Jean Lafitte National Historic Park, the preserve stretches over 26,000 acres (10,500 ha) of swamp and fecund forest. Boardwalk trails and muddy paths crisscross a series of murky waterways, where flowers bloom in vibrant white and pink, invasive nutria root in the dirt, and gators wink at visitors clomping on dry land.

◉ The preserve is open 9:30am–4:30pm Wed–Sun, all year round (nps.gov/jela/planyourvisit/barataria-preserve.htm).

Eat, drink, cheer, and eat again at an LSU Tailgate

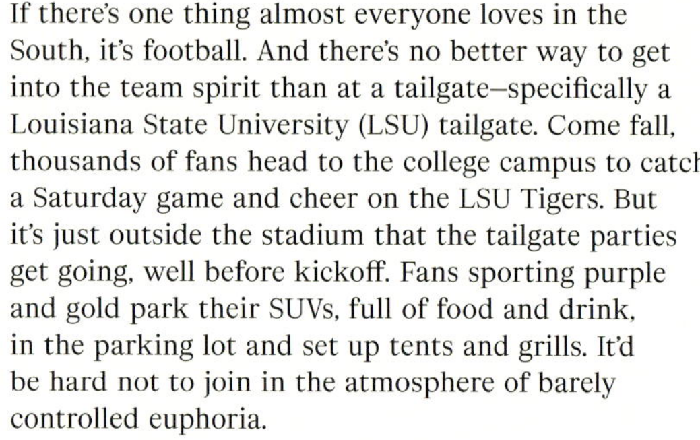

If there's one thing almost everyone loves in the South, it's football. And there's no better way to get into the team spirit than at a tailgate—specifically a Louisiana State University (LSU) tailgate. Come fall, thousands of fans head to the college campus to catch a Saturday game and cheer on the LSU Tigers. But it's just outside the stadium that the tailgate parties get going, well before kickoff. Fans sporting purple and gold park their SUVs, full of food and drink, in the parking lot and set up tents and grills. It'd be hard not to join in the atmosphere of barely controlled euphoria.

◉ Areas like the Parade Grounds are popular for tailgating; see lsusports.net for more information.

Tour the Louisiana coast in Plaquemines Parish

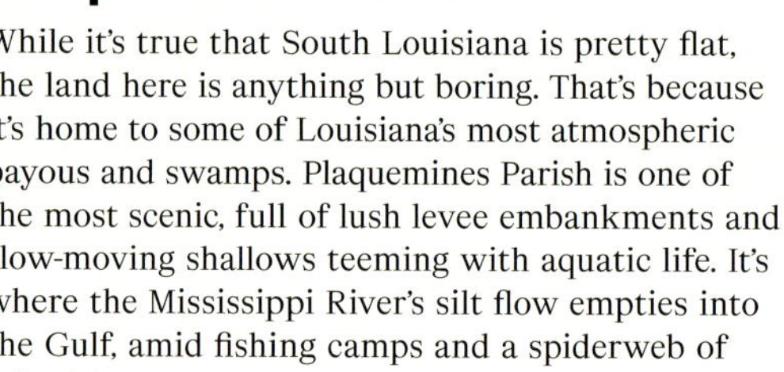

While it's true that South Louisiana is pretty flat, the land here is anything but boring. That's because it's home to some of Louisiana's most atmospheric bayous and swamps. Plaquemines Parish is one of the most scenic, full of lush levee embankments and slow-moving shallows teeming with aquatic life. It's where the Mississippi River's silt flow empties into the Gulf, amid fishing camps and a spiderweb of raised houses. These days, no one visit to the parish area is the same, due to ever-rising water levels that constantly change it.

◉ A guided tour, with an outfitter like Delta Discovery Tours (deltadiscoverytours.com), is essential to understanding the area.

Learn about history at the Whitney Plantation

Louisiana was once at the center of the American slave trade, serving as a refuge for slavers fleeing the Haitian revolt; a major port for boats carrying enslaved people from overseas as part of the transatlantic slave trade; and, later, as the locus of the domestic slave trade. This difficult history is examined at the Whitney Plantation in detail, with the stories of the survivors of the slave trade shared alongside the displays. Within the grounds, which include 16 original structures, are poignant memorials to the people who were enslaved here.

◉ The Whitney Plantation is located about 50 miles (80 km) west of New Orleans; for visitor information, head to whitneyplantation.org.

TOP 5

LIVE MUSIC
Wander the French Quarter or nearby Frenchmen Street for some top-tier live music.

ST. CHARLES AVENUE STREETCAR
Take a ride through town on board a classic streetcar.

FRENCH QUARTER
Historical architecture, art, and nightlife make up this vibrant neighborhood.

PARADES
From Mardi Gras to weekly neighborhood parades, New Orleanians love a procession.

NEW ORLEANS BITES
From po'boy (sandwiches) to gumbo to jambalaya, the homegrown cuisine is iconic.

Let the good times roll in New Orleans

New Orleans is a city with *joie de vivre* at its core. European, Caribbean, and African American influences have shaped a local culture like no other, one that buzzes with energy. Between its sugar-coated beignets, emerald streetcars, and thumping jazz clubs is a city that grooves to the beat of its own drum–and music-filled Bourbon Street is at the heart of all this revelry. Come early spring, the famous street is also where some of the biggest Mardi Gras parades in the world take place. Wherever New Orleanians come from, they always seem to have a certain love: of music, food, tradition, and, at their core, having a good time.

The city's tourist office is at Basin Street Station, open 8:30am–5:30pm daily (neworleans.com).

The Pine Tree State

There are moments when Maine, rearing its craggy mass over the northeastern edge of the U.S., is so beautiful it could be a painting. It's where the Atlantic waves crash into foggy, forest-lined cliffs; thick woods set the scene for black bears and moose; and mountains offer sweeping views. And while it may be home to just one national park, the huge coastal Acadia National Park is impressive—and full of the conifers after which the state is nicknamed.

STATE MOTTO I Lead

STATE FLOWER White pine cone and tassel

STATE ANIMAL Moose

STATE BIRD Chickadee

FUN FACT The iconic ring shape of the modern-day donut was invented in Maine back in the 19th century, when U.S. ship captain Hanson Gregory made a hole in the center of one with a pepper shaker.

Drive along the Bold Coast

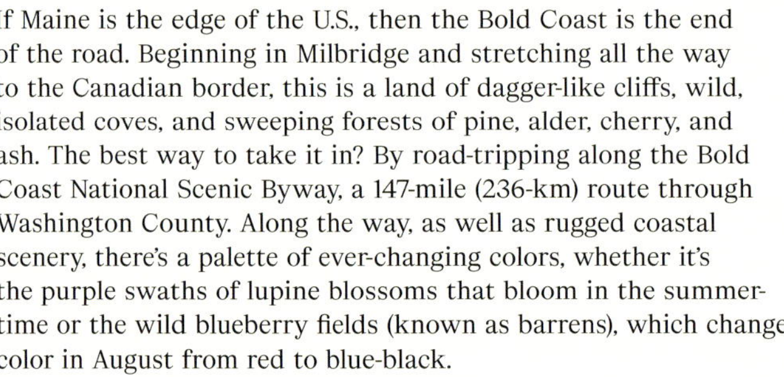

If Maine is the edge of the U.S., then the Bold Coast is the end of the road. Beginning in Milbridge and stretching all the way to the Canadian border, this is a land of dagger-like cliffs, wild, isolated coves, and sweeping forests of pine, alder, cherry, and ash. The best way to take it in? By road-tripping along the Bold Coast National Scenic Byway, a 147-mile (236-km) route through Washington County. Along the way, as well as rugged coastal scenery, there's a palette of ever-changing colors, whether it's the purple swaths of lupine blossoms that bloom in the summertime or the wild blueberry fields (known as barrens), which change color in August from red to blue-black.

◉ For information on the Bold Coast National Scenic Byway, visit downeastacadia.com/road-trips/scenicbyways/boldcoast.

Explore Stephen King's Bangor

Born in Maine, acclaimed author Stephen King set many of his horror-filled stories in the state, including in Bangor. This riverside city was his inspiration for Derry, the fictional town in the 1986 novel *It*; the rusted-red sewer grate on the corner of Jackson and Union streets allegedly inspired the scene where Georgie meets the evil clown Pennywise. King's imagination was also sparked by the city's leafy Mount Hope Cemetery, whose weathered gravestones provided the names for some of his most famous characters (there's one marked "Carrie"). No trip to Bangor would be complete without catching a glimpse of King's old house, an eerie Victorian mansion where he lived for around 40 years—in true King style, the house's wrought-iron fence depicts spiders and bats.

◉ Take a Stephen King-inspired tour of Bangor with SK Tours (sk-tours.com).

Stroll the docks of Rockland

With almost 3,500 miles (5,600 km) of coastline, Maine is tied to the sea. And the city of Rockland in the state's Midcoast region is one of the strongest knots in that rope. Explore the state's oceanic connection along the Harbor Trail, a paved 3.5-mile (5.6-km) route that connects Rockland's working waterfront to one of Maine's most fascinating downtown districts. The trail passes many working commercial fisheries before leading to downtown Rockland, where two impressive art museums—the Farnsworth Art Museum and the Center for Maine Contemporary Art—await. On top of them, you'll find buzzing restaurants, music venues, bars, and stores. In Rockland, there really is as much culture as there is salty air.

◉ For more details on Rockland's Harbor Trail, see mainetrailfinder.com/trails/trail/rockland-harbor-trail.

Get cultural in Brunswick

In many ways, Brunswick is a quintessential Maine town, with plenty of tree-lined streets and a quaint town green. But it's also a small town that punches above its weight culturally. Hear the sound of music in the air? It's likely coming from the Maine State Music Theatre, where world-class Broadway shows are performed. Nearby, the Bowdoin College Museum of Art covers over 5,000 years of art history, while the Peary-MacMillan Arctic Museum contains exhibits dedicated to Arctic exploration, research, and Indigenous peoples. And if you get hungry? There's always "Maine" Street (yes, like the state), lined with restaurants and bars.

◉ To see what's on at the Maine State Music Theatre, check msmt.org. For more information on the Bowdoin College Museum of Art, see bowdoin.edu/art-museum.

Explore the gorges of Gulf Hagas

Many who visit Maine never venture farther than the craggy Atlantic Coast. But those who do veer inland are quickly met with an impressive natural wonder: an unbroken wilderness of primeval forest, within which lies Gulf Hagas. This standout gorge, affectionately dubbed the "Grand Canyon of Maine," is famed for its wild terrain. Eking out like a scar across the North Maine Woods, Gulf Hagas is full of rushing falls, meandering trails, and swift, dark waters. Hikers, adventurers, even skilled kayakers flock here, ready to explore all that this pine-covered area has to offer. It's a true oasis for those who keep the wild close to their hearts.

⦿ Parking is plentiful, but it's also possible to hike here, as Gulf Hagas lies along the Appalachian Trail.

Enjoy a plate of fried clams in Kennebunkport

Oceanside Maine is, unsurprisingly, a seafood haven. Lobster rolls, grilled fish, succulent oysters–you name it, Maine's got it. And if it's clams you're after, then there's no better place than Kennebunkport. Clam chowder might be a staple all over New England, but it's not the only way to enjoy the local mollusk: in Kennebunkport, it's all about fried clams. Make like the summer season tourist crowds and dig into a plate of whole fried clam bellies alongside a freshly squeezed lemonade from a local institution like the Clam Shack, which has been serving up clams since 1968.

⦿ The Clam Shack is open during high season (usually May–Oct); see theclamshack.net for more details.

When to visit

Americans have long escaped to Maine in summer: the weather is gorgeous, and the coastal breeze welcome. Lobster season also starts in June, and runs to early December. Heading to Acadia? The park blooms with wildflowers in spring.

Climb peaks and spot deer in Acadia National Park

Located off the coast on Mount Desert Island, Acadia National Park is New England's only national park–and boy, does it deliver. It's the stomping ground of seasoned hikers, with the uncontested jewel in the crown the smooth peak of Cadillac Mountain. Towering at 1,500 ft (457 m) high, this is the park's highest point, offering up views of countless red cliffs and even more acres of pine forest. Looking for a gentler way to explore? The largely flat, 1.4-mile (2.25-km) Wonderland Trail has views of the rocky coast and the chance to spot deer moving through dappled clearings.

⦿ Acadia National Park is accessible year-round, but the paved roads within are only open mid-Apr–Nov; for more information, check nps.gov/acad.

Delve into all things oysters in Damariscotta

The Main Street of small-town Damariscotta is a postcard-worthy jumble of bookstores, art galleries, and restaurants. But that's not why people flock here. The waters of the Damariscotta River, which rise and fall in time with the Gulf of Maine's tides, is home to plentiful oysters, and some of the best in the nation are harvested right here. Fresh oysters grace the menus of local restaurants, while local oyster farms and harvesters run tours along the watershed, showcasing a quilt of forest and gorgeous, cold rivers. Not keen on oysters? It really is lovely here, and in the town's twin village of Newcastle, just across the river.

◉ To visit the state's oyster farms, head out on the Maine Oyster Trail (maineoystertrail.com).

Get back to nature in Wolfe's Neck Woods State Park

A short drive away from the quaint town of Freeport, this 200-acre (80-ha) state park was gifted to Maine in 1969 by two locals. Today, it's the perfect place to immerse yourself in the outdoors: head off on a hike through forests of white pine and hemlock, try to catch a glimpse of the park's resident ospreys, or simply enjoy a picnic beneath the branches of an oak tree. Another option is to rent a kayak and paddle Casco Bay, admiring the rocky coastline and pausing to see harbor seals pop their heads above the water.

◉ Wolfe's Neck Woods State Park is open year-round 9am–sunset daily. To rent kayaks (mid-Jun to mid-Sep only), visit Wolfe's Neck Center at 184 Burnett Road (wolfesneck.org).

Eat, drink, and be merry in Portland

Unlike Oregon's Portland, Maine's largest city doesn't feel the need to steal the headlines–it just quietly does its own thing. And what it does best is eat and drink: come here to devour seafood dishes, including freshly shucked oysters and indulgent lobster rolls, washed down with a craft beer from one of the city's stellar breweries. Of course, there's more to Portland than simply sating your taste buds. Explore its quaint Old Port, home to cobbled streets and 19th-century warehouses (with plenty of cool indie shops in the latter), and wander through its Arts District, known for its bold street art and the impressive Portland Museum of Art.

◉ The Portland Museum of Art opens 10am–6pm Wed–Sun (to 8pm Fri). For tourist information, see visitportland.com.

The Old Line State

Split in two by the Chesapeake Bay, Maryland balances multiple identities. On one side of the bay, you'll find quiet, deeply rooted rural life; on the other, a cosmopolitan workforce that powers the likes of the U.S. civil service. But this layered identity remains united by a fierce, shared pride, forged by the likes of the legendary "Maryland Line" soldiers, who held their ground during the Revolutionary War to save George Washington's army.

STATE MOTTO Strong Deeds, Gentle Words

STATE FLOWER Black-eyed Susan

STATE CRUSTACEAN Blue crab

STATE BIRD Baltimore oriole

FUN FACT Francis Scott Key wrote the "Star-Spangled Banner", the U.S. national anthem, after he saw the American flag still flying over Fort McHenry following the Battle of Baltimore in 1814.

Wander historic Annapolis

In many ways, Annapolis, with a population barely capping 40,000, feels like a small town, but Maryland's charming capital punches well above its weight. Set on the banks of the pastoral Severn River, the city's elegant streets—all brick rowhouses and narrow alleyways—speak to its past as a one-time colonial capital, a role it assumed in 1694, when it was renamed after the heir to the British throne. Today, a walk round the city's historic district takes in more modern sights, too: students at the U.S. Naval Academy, out for a morning jog; locals enjoying a tall beer in the city's brewpubs; and art galleries lined with watercolors of those bucolic Severn River scenes.

◉ Annapolis (visitannapolis.org) is almost equidistant from the two nearest big cities: Washington, D.C. and Baltimore.

Seek out the good life on the Eastern Shore

Maryland's Eastern Shore is no more than a short 40 miles (64 km) from the outskirts of Washington, D.C., but this rural peninsula feels like a different world. The Eastern Shore remains a land of thin pine forests and huge expanses of marshland, broken up by small towns, some clinging onto life, some charming in the extreme. Easton and St. Michaels are certainly the latter; think maritime museums, cutesy cafés, and wedding-cake homes lining residential blocks that look like they've been lifted straight from a rom-com.

◉ The Eastern Shore is most easily accessed through the Chesapeake Bay Bridge (cbbt.com), itself a bit of an engineering marvel. On weekends, the bridge can get clogged with day-trippers, so plan accordingly.

Get to know Poe in Baltimore

Wet with rain and the Chesapeake fog, Baltimore is a city of docks and sailors and salt. There's a palpable sense of noir in the air—unsurprising, given this was the hometown of Edgar Allan Poe, the influential 19th-century writer who was master of the macabre. Tread the creaky floorboards of the Edgar Allan Poe House and Museum, where he wrote several of his earliest works; thumb through one of his original books at the Central Library; visit his grave at Westminster Hall; or, on a lighter note, catch a Baltimore Ravens game—the football team is named after Poe's most famous poem.

◉ The Edgar Allan Poe House and Museum is on the corner of North Amity (poeinbaltimore.org). Central Library, part of the Enoch Pratt Free Library (prattlibrary.org), is in Mount Vernon. Buy tickets to Ravens games at baltimoreravens.com.

Listen to the birds sing on the battlefield of Antietam

As the dividing state between North and South, Maryland was at the center of several key conflicts during the American Civil War, including the single bloodiest day in U.S. history: the Battle of Antietam (1862). While the Confederates battered the Union Army during the engagement, a potential Southern advance was ultimately reversed–at a combined cost of 23,000 casualties. For all its violent history, today's Antietam, just outside Sharpsburg, is a slice of 19th-century rural beauty, quiet but for the sound of birdsong and studded with cemeteries for the war dead.

◉ Antietam National Battlefield (nps.gov/anti) is about 70 miles (113 km) west of Baltimore and the same distance north of Washington, D.C. The park is open year-round.

Learn about the birth of the Free State in St. Mary's City

Marylanders consider themselves stewards of the U.S.'s reputation for religious tolerance, and a little speck in southern Maryland is the reason why. In St. Mary's City, site of the state's first European-colonizer capital, Catholic refugees passed the Act Concerning Religion –the first law in the Thirteen Colonies that guaranteed free worship (for Christians). This monumental act laid the foundations for the nation's First Amendment, which includes freedom of religion. The tale is told in a living-history museum that stretches across a beautiful scoop of Chesapeake rural riverscapes.

◉ Historic St. Mary's City is open 10am–4pm Tue–Sat (hsmcdigshistory.org); its outdoor exhibits close for winter. Purchase tickets at the visitor center (18751 Hogaboom Lane).

Watch the morning mist burn off Deep Creek Lake

Many outsiders assume Maryland, tied as it is to the Chesapeake Bay, to be a state of flat topography and estuarine waters. But in her northwesternmost corner is a dollop of icy dark water, hemmed in by forested mountains. Folks flock to Deep Creek Lake to swim, fish, and hike, the latter a particularly enjoyable option in the early morning, when a wet woolen blanket of mist smothers the lake. Its location, at the foot of Meadow Mountain and the verdant Appalachians, is appealing in any season, from fall's fiery foliage and winter snowfall to spring blossoms and long summer evenings.

◉ Public access to the lake is managed by Deep Creek Lake State Park (dnr.maryland.gov).

Trace the route of Harriet Tubman's Underground Railroad

The salt marshes and woods of the Maryland Eastern Shore feel like a primeval wilderness, and this Jurassic landscape proved to be an invaluable cover for enslaved people escaping north in the 19th century. The most famous of these runaways was Harriet Tubman, born into plantation life near the town of Cambridge. After liberating herself, she braved some 13 missions as a "conductor" on the Underground Railroad, escorting other escapees through this network of safehouses. Her story (and others) is compellingly told at the Harriet Tubman Underground Railroad National Historical Park, in rural Church Creek.

◉ The Harriet Tubman Underground Railroad National Historical Park (nps.gov/hatu) is part of a route that is replicated in the fascinating Harriet Tubman Underground Railroad Scenic Byway (harriettubmanbyway.org).

When to visit

Summer is the best time to sample Maryland's blue crab and enjoy Chesapeake Bay. If you're visiting Washington D.C., November and December are magical, with events like the National Christmas Tree Lighting and Georgetown GLOW.

Enjoy some coastal fun in Ocean City

For a state that boasts a deceptively long coastline (almost 3,200 miles, or some 5,150 km), Maryland has a surprising lack of traditional sandy beaches. But beside the Atlantic Ocean, the appropriately named Ocean City offers a long and wide stretch of golden sand. Here, you can play beach volleyball shoreside, bodysurf in the waves, or simply stroll along the 1902 boardwalk snacking on saltwater taffy. There's also a huge Ferris wheel, a buzzing arcade, and a ride-filled amusement park–as you'd expect from any beach spot worth its salt.

◉ Ocean City's official website provides up-to-date visitor information (ococean.com). Need something quiet? Head south to the quiet shores of Assateague Island State Park.

LIBRARY OF CONGRESS
Shelves of knowledge meet gorgeous architecture at the largest library in the world.

SMITHSONIAN
The world's largest free museum complex satisfies curiosity for any topic.

14TH STREET
D.C. nightlife hotspots shift, but 14th Street is ever reliable for an evening out.

NATIONAL MALL
A storied site of protests, inaugurations, celebrations, monuments, and memorials.

DUPONT CIRCLE
A mix of diplomats, students, journalists, and policy wonks buzz around this handsome residential neighborhood.

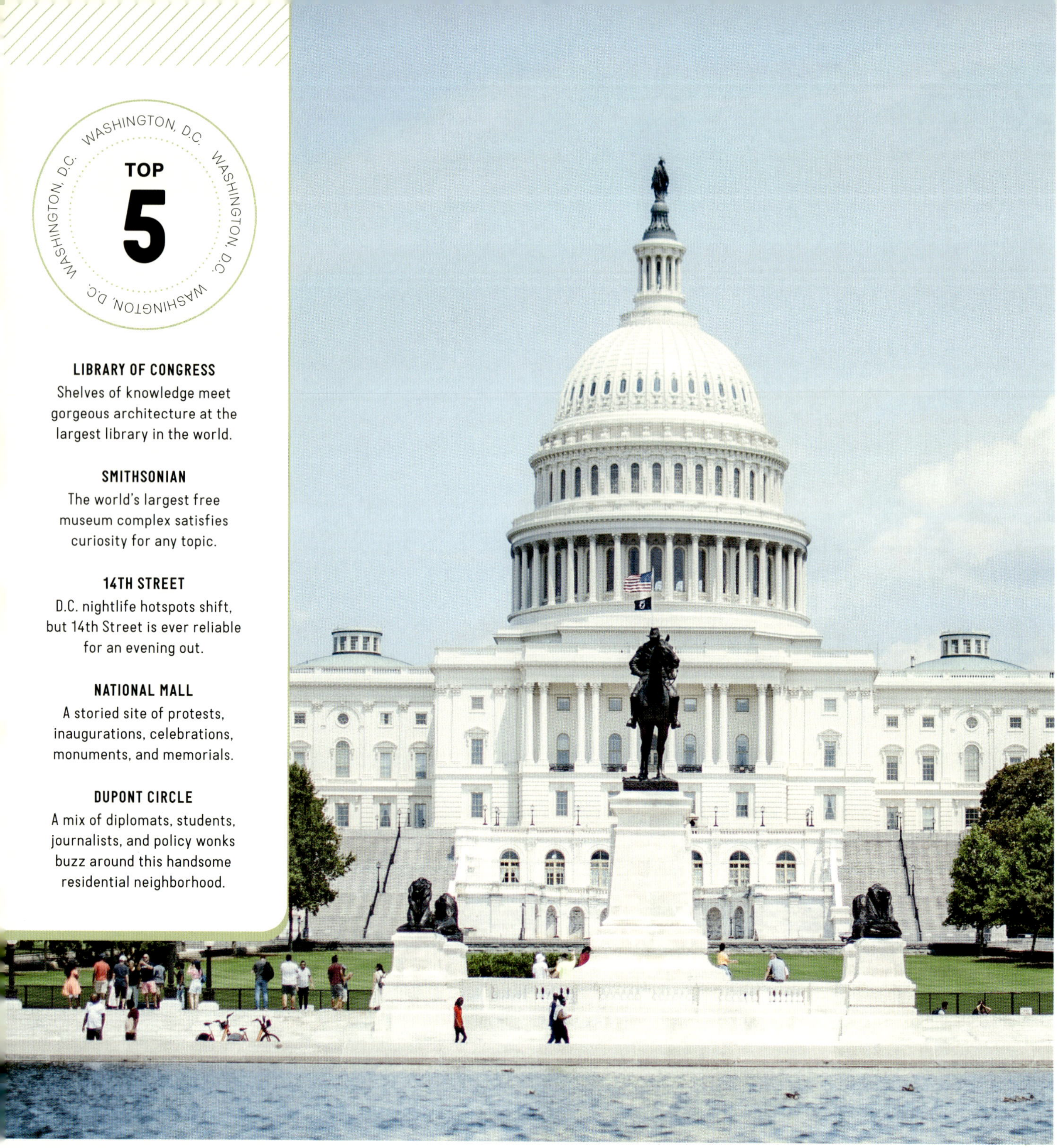

Delve deeper in Washington, D.C.

It's easy to think of Washington, D.C.–a federal district bordering Maryland–as a nonstop highlights reel of marble icons. But this cliché is, well, just that. Yes, the nation's capital contains many of the public motifs of the American experiment, but it's also a place full of creativity, imagination, and downright brilliance. Challenge yourself at thought-provoking museums like the various Smithsonian museums here, taste your way through an impressively global dining scene, and discover a vibrant nightlife culture that paints a D.C. far more colorful than those numerous stony facades.

The official visitor center for the city (washington.org) is at 901 7th Street N.W., open daily 7:30am–4pm. The D.C. Metro system (wmata.com) is efficient and easy to use.

Crabs and coffee on the docks in Crisfield

The Maryland blue crab—*Callinectes sapidus*, the beautiful swimmer—is the celebrated food of the Chesapeake Bay, and, by extension, Maryland itself. Although local fisheries have experienced bouts of feast and famine, the town of Crisfield, deep in the Maryland Eastern Shore, is still inextricably tied to the blue-crab harvest. Feast on crab cake at Gordon's, a cash-only place where "watermen" (independent fishermen) fuel up on coffee and scrapple (peppered pork) sandwiches ahead of a day's fishing on the Bay. Then learn about all things blue crab at the town's J. Millard Tawes Historical Museum.

◉ The J. Millard Tawes Historical Museum (crisfieldheritage.org) is at 3 Ninth Street and open 10am–2pm Tue–Sat.

Sail into the sunset on the Chesapeake Bay

Maryland can make a strong case for being the most irregularly shaped state in the country, and the Chesapeake Bay, which cleaves Maryland in half, is the main culprit. But it's not fair to say that the Bay (and here, it's always "the Bay") is just a crick in the state's crookedness. Chesapeake is the largest estuary in the U.S., 4,480 sq miles (11,600 sq km) of craggy coastlined bay that balances salt water and fresh water. It is also a tide-kissed wilderness and a playground for millions. Sail onto these waters as the sun dips below the low, long horizon, and experience a special laid-back kind of gentle beauty.

◉ Search for "Sailing Tours" at visitmaryland.com, the state's tourism website, for a slew of tours and charters offered across the Chesapeake Bay.

The Bay State

Massachusetts is where modern America was born, and where it learned to think for itself. The Pilgrims landed here, the American Revolution began here, and writers like Emerson, Thoreau, and Alcott created a literary heritage that endures to this day. From movie sets to Fenway Park, clapboard towns to Cape Cod, this is a place full of the hallmarks of the American story. History buffs, this one's for you.

STATE MOTTO By the Sword We Seek Peace, But Peace Only Under Liberty

STATE FLOWER Mayflower

STATE DOG Boston terrier

STATE BIRD Chickadee

FUN FACT Webster in Massachusetts is home to Lake Chaubunagungamaug. Thanks to its impressive moniker, the lake wins the title of longest name for a geographical landform in the U.S.

Visit Martha's Vineyard

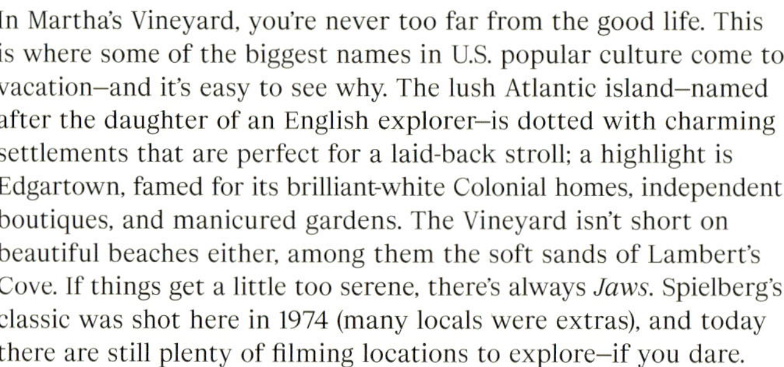

In Martha's Vineyard, you're never too far from the good life. This is where some of the biggest names in U.S. popular culture come to vacation—and it's easy to see why. The lush Atlantic island—named after the daughter of an English explorer—is dotted with charming settlements that are perfect for a laid-back stroll; a highlight is Edgartown, famed for its brilliant-white Colonial homes, independent boutiques, and manicured gardens. The Vineyard isn't short on beautiful beaches either, among them the soft sands of Lambert's Cove. If things get a little too serene, there's always *Jaws*. Spielberg's classic was shot here in 1974 (many locals were extras), and today there are still plenty of filming locations to explore—if you dare.

◉ The visitor center can be found at 24 Beach Street, Vineyard Haven, near the ferry dock (9am–5pm Mon–Fri; mvy.com).

Tour around Cape Cod

A long, hook-shaped peninsula with some 560 miles (900 km) of shoreline, Cape Cod in the summer is quintessential New England—and the best way to see its highlights is on the road. Start at the meandering stretch of Rte.-6A, which runs parallel to the North Shore between Sandwich and Orleans, weaving past beaches, salt marshes, and colonial villages. The beaches become wilder as you pass into the Outer Cape on U.S.-6, where the best sand is protected within Cape Cod National Seashore—be sure to sample the world-famous oysters in Wellfleet along the way. Eventually the road runs out in Provincetown, the salt-washed, historic port and LGBTQ+ resort that feels a world away.

◉ The Cape Cod Welcome Center is open late May–early Oct 9am–5pm daily (capecodchamber.org).

When to visit

Like most of New England, Massachusetts is popular in the fall (October through November), when forests burst with color. The coast is best in the summer (June through September), though this is also the busiest, most expensive time to visit.

Discover Provincetown

Provincetown has always been different. Stranded at the far end of Cape Cod, surrounded by ocean on three sides, it's a bit like an island. Though in many ways a typical New England town—with clapboard cottages, crafty shops, and even some Pilgrim connections—it also has a distinctive edge. For one thing, it's filled with Portuguese bakeries and restaurants, thanks to the large Portuguese fishing community that settled here in the 1860s. For another, it's got a free-thinking attitude, a legacy of the art colony that flourished here in the late 19th century. Today, Provincetown is best known for its welcoming LGBTQ+ community, which has flourished ever since Philip "Phil" Baiona opened Weathering Heights, the town's first openly gay bar, in 1952.

◉ Get more information at the Provincetown Office of Tourism, 330 Commercial Street (ptowntourism.com).

BOSTON TOP 5

PAUL REVERE'S OLD NORTH CHURCH
Boston's oldest church, where lanterns were hung to warn of British troop movements.

BOSTON TEA PARTY SHIPS & MUSEUM
Exhibits and costumed interpreters bring the events of 1773 to life.

FANEUIL MARKETPLACE
Comprises historic Faneuil Hall and Quincy Market.

MUSEUM OF FINE ARTS
Boston's premier gallery, filled with world-class art.

NORTH END
Boston's Little Italy is crammed with bakeries, cafés, and restaurants.

Visit Boston, the "Cradle of Liberty"

New England's biggest city, cultural capital, financial center, and biotechnology hub—Boston is all these things and more, but its history is the real draw. Founded in 1630, central Boston is full of remnants of both its colonial past and the American Revolution, which exploded here in 1775. The Freedom Trail covers key historical sights, ending across the river in Charlestown, where the USS *Constitution* and Bunker Hill Monument recall the fight for independence. It's even got a piece of television history: Cheers in Beacon Hill inspired the 1980s hit TV show—and became the most famous bar in America.

Head to the Boston Common Visitor Center for tourist information, open 8:30am–5pm daily (meetboston.com).

Learn about John F. Kennedy

On a warm afternoon in May 1917, Jack Kennedy, the future 35th president of the United States, was born in Brookline, Massachusetts. After his tragic assassination in 1963, it was his mother, Rose, who helped restore the old family home, open today as the John Fitzgerald Kennedy National Historic Site. Preserved as it was when JFK was born, inside around 20 percent of the artifacts are family originals. It's not all about his start, though; head over to the John F. Kennedy Presidential Library & Museum to learn more about JFK's years as president.

◉ John Fitzgerald Kennedy National Historic Site is open Jun–Oct 10am–5pm Thu–Sun (nps.gov/jofi).

Cheer on the Patriots and the Red Sox

To the infuriation of the rest of the country, Massachusetts–and Boston in particular–has a phenomenally successful sporting record. Ice hockey, basketball, or football, Boston teams seem perennially on top, their shirts worn with pride across the region. Catch the Patriots at Gillette Stadium, where muskets fire after every touchdown, or join the crowd at Fenway Park, singing "Sweet Caroline" as the Red Sox hit a home run. Just remember one thing: never, ever mention the New York Yankees.

◉ The New England Patriots play in Foxborough (patriots.com); the Red Sox play at Fenway Park (mlb.com/redsox).

Grab a bite from a clam shack

Plump, tender, and crunchy: nothing beats a tray of freshly fried belly clams enjoyed by the ocean shore. Clams, along with oysters, lobsters, and scallops, have been fished in Massachusetts Bay for centuries, but it was Lawrence "Chubby" Woodman who first breaded and fried them in 1916. Today Woodman's of Essex remains a classic, serving clams dipped in evaporated milk, coated in corn flour, and fried. It has rivals, mind you: in Ipswich, the Clam Box sees long lines eager to order, while on Cape Cod it's all about Mac's Seafood, with several locations serving richly seasoned clams. Wherever you end up, be sure to add the essential condiment: homemade tartar sauce, drizzled with lemon juice.

◉ Try Woodman's of Essex (woodmans.com), Clam Box (clamboxipswich.com), or Mac's Seafood (macsseafood.com).

Take it easy in the Berkshires

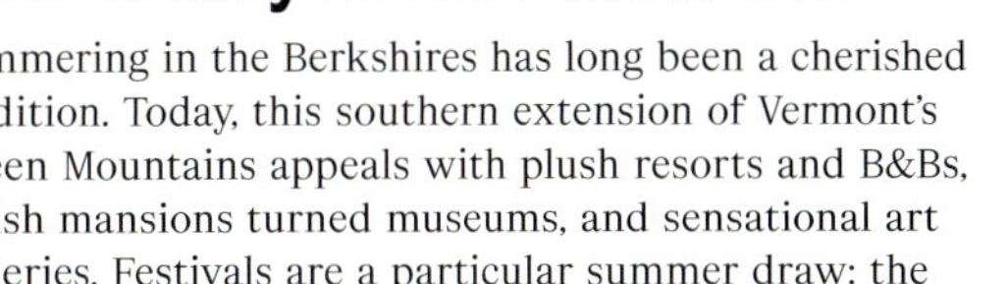

Summering in the Berkshires has long been a cherished tradition. Today, this southern extension of Vermont's Green Mountains appeals with plush resorts and B&Bs, lavish mansions turned museums, and sensational art galleries. Festivals are a particular summer draw: the Boston Symphony performs concerts every July and August weekend at Tanglewood, Jacob's Pillow hosts the country's famous contemporary dance festival, and the Williamstown Theatre Festival and Shakespeare & Company in Lenox ensure plenty of outdoor stage action. Bring a blanket, picnic, and a bottle, and enjoy.

◉ For more on the Berkshires, visit berkshires.org; there's a visitor center in Lenox, open 10am–3pm Mon & Wed–Sat.

Spot a whale in the Atlantic

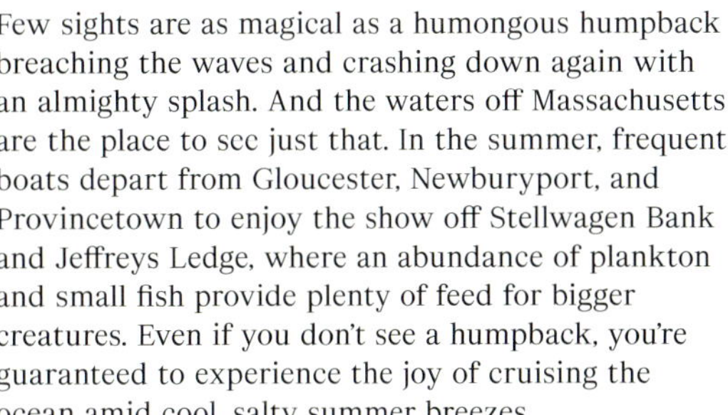

Few sights are as magical as a humongous humpback breaching the waves and crashing down again with an almighty splash. And the waters off Massachusetts are the place to see just that. In the summer, frequent boats depart from Gloucester, Newburyport, and Provincetown to enjoy the show off Stellwagen Bank and Jeffreys Ledge, where an abundance of plankton and small fish provide plenty of feed for bigger creatures. Even if you don't see a humpback, you're guaranteed to experience the joy of cruising the ocean amid cool, salty summer breezes.

◉ Try Provincetown's Whale Watch Dolphin Fleet (whalewatch.com), Gloucester's Cape Ann Whale Watch (seethewhales.com), or Newburyport Whale Watch (newburyportwhalewatch.com).

Uncover witchy history in Salem

Almost everyone has heard of the Salem Witch Trials: a hysteria that gripped the town of Salem in the 1690s, resulting in the execution of 20 innocent people. Today, Salem contains a bewildering profusion of witch museums and hosts "Haunted Happenings," the biggest Halloween celebration in the world. Visit the Witch Dungeon Museum for theatrical reenactments (it's the site of the prison where the accused were locked up), or the Witch House for a bit more history–this was the home of hapless Judge Jonathan Corwin. Beyond these macabre attractions, there's plenty more to see: in the art of the Peabody Essex Museum, and at the lovely old waterfront, there's not a broomstick to be seen.

◉ Salem's visitor information center is open 9am–5pm daily (salem.org).

The Great Lakes State

Bordering four of the five Great Lakes—hence the nickname—Michigan is rich in natural beauty. But it's not all about the pine-covered islands and dense forests that the state boasts in abundance. Michigan's often-overlooked cities are calling, too, from comeback king Detroit, the home of Motown, to Grand Rapids, famous for its craft-beer scene. Whether you kayak below soaring bluffs or sip suds in an urban taproom, it's "Pure Michigan," as they like to say around these parts.

STATE MOTTO If You Seek A Pleasant Peninsula, Look About You

STATE FLOWER Apple blossom

STATE ANIMAL White-tailed deer

STATE BIRD American robin

FUN FACT Michigan is the only state in the U.S. to border four of the five Great Lakes, while Lake Michigan is the only one of the Great Lakes to sit entirely in U.S. territory.

See the water fall at Tahquamenon Falls State Park

In this remote state park in northern Michigan, the Upper Falls roar over a wide shelf in the Tahquamenon River. Akin to a mini Niagara, the falls have carved a gorge here, which today is lined by platforms that offer spectacular views of the amber-hued water plunging downward (the unusual color is thanks to tannins in the surrounding swamps). Downstream, the Lower Falls tumble in a series of gentler cascades around an island (reached by renting a rowboat). The falls are never that busy, but come early to have them all to yourself.

⦿ An entry fee is charged to access the park; see michigan.gov/dnr/buy-and-apply/rec-pp for more details. You'll need your own car to visit.

Take a ferry over to Mackinac Island

John Jacob Astor, once one of the wealthiest men in America, based his fur-trade empire on Mackinac Island in the early 1800s. As you approach by ferry today, this forest-smothered outcrop in choppy Lake Huron feels little changed in the centuries since. Graceful Victorian homes line the harbor, where you can check in to the historic Grand Hotel and shop at venerable Murdick's, which has been selling fudge since 1887. Hike, bike, or horseback ride (motorized vehicles are banned) to appreciate the island's bucolic charms. Snaking through the woods, or along the lakeshore in absolute silence, it's like traveling back in time.

◉ Most visitors arrive by ferry from mainland Michigan (sheplersferry.com or arnoldtransitcompany.com). The Mackinac Island Tourism Bureau is at 7274 Main Street, (mackinacisland.org). Several outlets offer bike rental.

Sip suds in Grand Rapids

No prizes for guessing what Grand Rapids, or "Beer City USA," is best known for. Michigan's booming second city is home to more than 40 microbreweries, which together knock out some of the best ales in the country. Try the Belgian-style ales of Brewery Vivant, the Bavarian beers of Küsterer Brauhaus, and the IPAs of Founders Brewing, who kicked off the city's craft-beer scene in 1997. Pull up a stool and raise a glass to 38th President Gerald Ford—his childhood home was in Grand Rapids and he now lies buried, with wife Betty, at the fascinating Gerald R. Ford Presidential Museum.

◉ Download the Beer City Brewsader app for information on beer-themed experiences, tours, and events. For more information on Grand Rapids, visit experiencegr.com.

Explore Sleeping Bear Dunes

Up on a storm-battered stretch of Lake Michigan's coastline, you'll find gigantic sand dunes, soaring bluffs, and dense strands of beech-maple forest. A National Lakeshore, Sleeping Bear Dunes gets its name from an old Anishinaabe (Ojibwe/Chippewa) legend: two offshore islands (North and South Manitou) are believed to be the tombs of two drowned bear cubs, and the mainland dunes the resting place of the grieving mother bear. The dunes are certainly a big draw, offering the chance to clamber up a 200-ft (61-m) sand pile–and, much more fun, career back down it again. But the real highlight of a visit here is the Pierce Stocking Scenic Drive. This hilly, 7-mile (11-km) loop winds aside the blue waters of Glen Lake, east of the dunes, and past its undulating dunes and shady forests. Stop to take in the drive's iconic view of Lake Michigan, wafted by the cool lake breeze.

◉ Stop in at the Philip A. Hart Visitor Center (8:30am–4:30pm daily; nps.gov/slbe), in the nearby town of Empire, for more information. The village of Glen Arbor, 8 miles (12 km) north of the visitor center, on Hwy-22, is the primary hub for park activities and accommodations.

Enjoy Detroit's revived downtown

Home of automotive giants Chrysler, Ford, and GM, Detroit soared off the back of car manufacturing, earning it the nickname "Motor City." Motown (short for "Motor Town") Records followed, a label that reshaped the music industry. But after the rise came the fall, and Detroit was declared bankrupt in 2013. While parts of the city are still recovering, downtown has been rejuvenated, giving Detroit a mix of old and (very) new that makes it such a fascinating place to visit today. Cool places to explore include the Detroit Institute of Arts, the artsy, community-led Heidelberg Project, and—for a blast of the musical past—the Motown Museum.

◉ Get around the city using the Detroit People Mover (which covers downtown) and the Qline streetcar that connects downtown with the Detroit Institute of Arts.

Explore Ann Arbor and the University of Michigan

Just 40 miles (64 km) west of downtown Detroit, compact Ann Arbor is a totally different world. Progressive, artsy, and with students making up almost half the population, it's been dominated by the University of Michigan since it moved here from Detroit in 1837. Soak up the scholarly atmosphere on a stroll of the leafy campus, which features its own fine-art and archeology museums, then hit downtown itself, anchored by the brightly daubed shops, book-stores, and cafés of Main Street, and home to the city's huge Art Fair in July.

◉ Ann Arbor's tourist office is at 315 W. Huron Street (open office hours Mon–Fri; annarbor.org). Amtrak trains and Greyhound/Megabus services link the city with Detroit.

Spend a day with Henry Ford

Henry Ford founded his eponymous car company in 1903, but it was the introduction of the Model T five years later that revolutionized the world—and helped make him a billionaire. Today, some of the Americana that Ford collected over his lifetime—an astounding 26 million artifacts in total—is displayed at the Henry Ford complex in Dearborn (his birthplace, and still the Ford headquarters today). The complex is also home to the mammoth Museum of American Innovation, crammed with vintage vehicles such as the limousine JFK was shot in and the bus Rosa Parks was riding when she refused to give up her seat (thus launching the modern Civil Rights movement).

◉ The Henry Ford complex, at 20900 Oakwood Boulevard, Dearborn (thehenryford.org), is open 9:30am–5pm daily.

Visit Michigan's Little Bavaria and Holland

Glockenspiels and windmills are more Mitteleuropa than Michigan, but the state's hinterland is a treasure trove of European-themed attractions. In aptly named Holland, founded by Dutch Americans in 1847, you'll find an 18th-century windmill (imported from the Netherlands) and a Dutch-themed theme park, while Frankenmuth is chockful of faux Bavarian architecture and Lutheran churches, a nod to its German founders. This being Michigan, you're never too far from a brewpub (Dutch or Bavarian style) in either.

◉ Holland Visitors Bureau (holland.org) is at 78 E. 8th Street, and Frankenmuth Visitor Center is at 635 S. Main Street (frankenmuth.org); both are open daily.

Experience untamed wilderness at Isle Royale National Park

Ready for a digital detox? Michigan's only national park, Isle Royale occupies an island in the heart of Lake Superior, and is one of the least accessible and least visited parks in America–with no cell phone or wi-fi service to boot. Cars are banned: instead, a network of hiking trails fans out through boreal forest and hills, past swampy lakes, bogs, and abandoned fish shacks. Come prepared for the wilderness–it'll likely be you, some loons, and the occasional grazing moose.

◉ Isle Royale is open April 16 through October 31. The park headquarters (nps.gov/isro) is in Houghton, on the mainland, but two visitor centers operate on the island, at Rock Harbor and at Windigo. Ferries depart Copper Harbor.

When to visit

Although the state's cities are year-round destinations, most of rural Michigan is best enjoyed in summer (June through September), when the sunny weather and warm (ish) water provide optimal conditions for hiking and kayaking.

Kayak the Pictured Rocks National Lakeshore

Over thousands of years, rain, wind, ice, and sun have played nature's sculptors on the arches, columns, and caves of this protected section of Lake Superior. And there's no better way to see their work than on a guided sea-kayak tour. You'll slip under waterfalls, paddle into caves, and even spy a sunken ship, all while gliding across deep-blue waters beneath a spectacular array of sandstone cliffs, daubed in reds, oranges, browns, and whites by minerals. Afterward, enjoy a drink at the Duck Pond Eatery & Beer Garden, arms tired but worldly stresses left far behind.

◉ Sea kayaks are the only kayaks suitable for Lake Superior (see paddlingmichigan.com). Munising Falls (nps.gov/piro) and Grand Sable visitor centers are open 9am–5pm daily.

The North Star State

Minnesota is routinely ranked as one of the best states to live in, recognition that any Minnesotan would acknowledge with a knowing, "Oh, sure, you betcha!" The Twin Cities of Minneapolis and St. Paul are home to vibrant multicultural communities and a culinary scene that other cities look upon with envy. Out of town, things get even better. Vast boreal forests, the mighty Mississippi River, and thousands of glacial lakes make the state a utopia for outdoor adventure.

STATE MOTTO The Star of the North

STATE FLOWER Pink lady's slipper

STATE FISH Walleye

STATE BIRD Common loon

FUN FACT Minnesota's Mall of America, located in the city of Bloomington, is the largest mall in the U.S., covering a whopping total area of 5,600,000 sq ft (520,260 sq m).

Paddle the Boundary Waters Canoe Area Wilderness

Minnesota is nicknamed the Land of 10,000 Lakes. That's actually an undercount, and the erroneous tally is never more apparent than in the Boundary Waters Canoe Area Wilderness, a watery expanse where solid ground seems to be the exception. The main way of getting around here is to paddle and portage, gliding silently past boreal and hardwood forests that are home to moose, beavers, and black bears. Make your way to a remote lodge, or pitch your tent at a lakeshore campsite, where a crackling campfire and a sky full of stars make for a perfectly primeval escape from the world.

◉ If you're not an experienced outdoorsperson, a guided canoe trip is a good way to go. You'll find outfitters in the towns of Ely and Grand Marais.

Rent a houseboat in Voyageurs National Park

The 218,000-acre (88,000-ha) Voyageurs National Park is named for the French-Canadian fur traders who traversed the region in birch-bark canoes in the 18th and 19th centuries. You could do the same, but it's much more fun to partake in the classic Minnesota pastime of renting a houseboat and sailing your mobile abode into the park's remotest reaches. Spend your days in perfect solitude, swimming, fishing, and whizzing down the slides that some houseboats are equipped with. When the sun goes down, lie back and listen to the haunting cries of loons, as the Milky Way peppers the night sky.

Several companies in the towns of International Falls and Crane Lake rent houseboats. For overnight visits, you'll need to get a houseboat permit from recreation.gov.

See eagles soar at the National Eagle Center

Few animal encounters can match the majesty of witnessing a bald eagle soaring through the sky. A perfect combination of grace and power, it's no wonder they're America's national symbol. Among the best places in the country to spot bald (and golden) eagles is along the Mississippi River between Minnesota and Wisconsin. Visit the National Eagle Center in Wabasha to join a guided drive or river cruise to observe the raptors as they hunt for fish or perch in trees along the shore. You can also meet eagles that the center has rescued and rehabilitated from injury.

Tickets for programs and tours at the National Eagle Center are popular and best purchased in advance. See nationaleaglecenter.org for details.

Eat your way through Minneapolis

Minneapolis has emerged as one of the country's most exciting culinary destinations, with many of its top restaurants closely tied to Indigenous and immigrant communities. Owamni, named the United States' best new restaurant in 2022, focuses on Indigenous foodways, using only ingredients that existed on the continent before Europeans arrived. Vinai and Diane's Place has brought Hmong food to national attention for the first time, while Hamdi and Karmel Mall are go-tos for Somali cuisine.

◉ Want to take a deeper dive into Hmong food? St. Paul's HmongTown Marketplace (hmongtownmarketplace.com) is home to nearly 300 vendors.

Pay homage to Prince at Paisley Park

There are great musicians, and then there are geniuses. Prince Rogers Nelson, better known simply as Prince, was the latter. Born in Minneapolis in 1958, over a four-decade career he won seven Grammy awards, was inducted into the Rock & Roll Hall of Fame, and revolutionized what pop music could be through groundbreaking songs like "When Doves Cry" and "Sign O' the Times." Explore Prince's legacy on a tour of Paisley Park, his former home, where you can see old concert wardrobes, instruments, motorcycles, and the studio where he recorded some of his biggest hits.

◉ Paisley Park is located in the Minneapolis suburb of Chanhassen and is open Thu–Mon. Tours start at $75.

When to visit

The easy answer is summer, when the state's plentiful outdoor attractions beckon. But don't sleep on winter. Yes, it's frigid, but Minnesotans embrace the chill with snow-centric events like Minneapolis' Great Northern Festival.

Sweat it out in a sauna

Many Minnesotans trace their ancestry to Scandinavia, so when visiting, why not (warmly) embrace the culture? Saunas can be found across the state, but a few are destinations in themselves. In Minneapolis, the Hewing Hotel has a rooftop sauna and spa pool that overlooks the downtown skyline. In Duluth, you'll get Lake Superior vistas and harborside cold plunges at Cedar and Stone. There are more Great Lake views from Sisu + Löyly's sauna in Grand Marais; or, you can visit its floating sauna on nearby Devil Track Lake. If trees are more your thing, head into the woods outside Finlayson to sweat in sauna cabins and do a bit of forest bathing at Silvae Spiritus.

◉ Find more on the Hewing Hotel at hewinghotel.com, Cedar and Stone at cedarandstonesauna.com, Sisu + Löyly at sisuandloyly.com, and Silvae Spiritus at silvaespiritus.com.

Road trip along the North Shore

For a little bit of everything Minnesota—lakes, cities, forests, small towns—take a road trip along the state's North Shore. From the lively city of Duluth, home to the world's largest freshwater inland port, head north on State Highway 61. The road runs some 150 miles (241 km) to the Canadian border; en route, you'll find small shops selling local maple syrup, docks where iron ore is loaded onto cargo ships, art galleries, lighthouses, a pink stone beach, and waterfalls aplenty. The best part? Once you reach the Canadian border (and Minnesota's tallest waterfall), you get to turn around and do it all again.

◉ Grand Marais makes for a great place to stay on a multi-day trip to the North Shore. The charming town has a notable arts scene and the region's top accommodations and dining.

The Magnolia State

Mississippi hums with history—literally. This is where the blues took shape, in the cotton fields of the Delta, its rhythms echoing across the world. And the state's cultural richness goes beyond music: writers like William Faulkner gave a voice to the South here, while visionary artists along the Gulf Coast captured the state's wild beauty. It's a state best explored slowly: along its backroads, through towns thick with barbecue smoke, and beside the river that has witnessed it all.

STATE MOTTO By Valor and Arms

STATE FLOWER Magnolia

STATE ANIMAL White-tailed deer

STATE BIRD Mockingbird

FUN FACT Thank Mississippi for the teddy bear. Former president Theodore Roosevelt's refusal to shoot a bear on a hunting trip near Onward, Mississippi, inspired the creation of the stuffed toy bears.

Enjoy the Gulf Islands National Seashore

Discover wild coast at its most unspoiled on the Gulf Islands National Seashore, where 160 miles (258 km) of shoreline and barrier islands are preserved. Your excursion begins with a ferry ride from Gulfport to Ship Island. You'll soon spot the 19th-century Fort Massachusetts standing sentinel over the sand. Built to defend the Gulf, its brick walls overlook dunes that offer nesting grounds for terns and plovers. Speaking of nature, look out over the water and you might just see the nose or a flipper of a curious dolphin beside your boat. When your ferry makes it to the island, take your time wandering the boardwalk trails that wind through the salt marshes, where herons fish in the waters and osprey wheel overhead.

◉ Rangers lead free guided tours of Fort Massachusetts on Ship Island, sharing stories of Civil War skirmishes and hurricanes (nps.gov/guis).

Gallery hop along the Mississippi Gulf Coast

Yes, Mississippi's Gulf Coast has beaches and barrier islands, but it's also got a booming art scene. The 30-mile (48-km) stretch between Bay St. Louis and Ocean Springs is particularly creative, with a glut of whimsical art museums, indie galleries, and colorful studios. In Biloxi, the Ohr-O'Keefe Museum of Art celebrates the "Mad Potter" George Ohr, whose experimental ceramics were decades ahead of their time, while in Ocean Springs, the Walter Anderson Museum of Art honors the visionary artist and naturalist who painted everything from pelicans to bayous. Spend a day experiencing the artistic spirit for yourself.

⦿ You can arrange your own walking tour of local galleries, but there are a number of organized art walks across the Gulf Coast towns, including in Ocean Springs and Bay St. Louis.

Drive Mississippi's section of the Natchez Trace Parkway

The Natchez Trace Parkway is more than just a road, it's a journey through time. Tracing the course of an ancient trail that was once walked by Indigenous peoples, the parkway stretches for 444 miles (715 km) from Natchez, Mississippi, to Tennessee *(p208)*. Mississippi claims the longest and most storied stretch of the road, passing through tranquil forests, meadows, and river valleys. Pause to photograph the historic inn Mount Locust, where weary travelers once broke their journeys, before continuing 30 minutes along the road to the Sunken Trace, where countless footsteps have worn a deep gully into the soft earth.

⦿ Stop in at Tupelo's Natchez Trace Parkway Visitor Center, where a short orientation film traces the route's history.

Brush up on your Civil War history in Vicksburg

Perched high on the Mississippi River bluffs, Vicksburg bore witness to one of the Civil War's most pivotal chapters. It was here that the 1863 siege played out, severing Confederate supply lines and giving the Union control of the Mississippi. This story unfolds in the sprawling Vicksburg National Military Park, where visitors can walk through trenches, gaze upon some 1,300 monuments, and explore the ironclad USS *Cairo*, home to a collection of naval relics. Need a change of pace? In the town itself, discover riverfront murals and historic homes, as well as welcoming Southern restaurants that offer a place to rest and reflect.

⦿ Cyclists can pedal along the park's 16-mile (26-km) touring road, winding past monuments and scenic overlooks.

Find culture in the college town of Oxford

Sprouting from the hills of northern Mississippi, Oxford is the land of writer William Faulkner. Start your exploration at Rowan Oak, the white-columned home where he wrote many of his Southern Gothic novels. Wander its trails shaded by towering magnolias—you'll soon see how he found inspiration for his fictional Yoknapatawpha County here. The house itself holds secrets: you'll see his typewriter, and the outline for his novel *A Fable* scribbled in pencil onto the study wall. Away from the house, locals hobnob in the town's galleries and the legendary Square Books store, and University of Mississippi students mingle on campus.

◉ Oxford's Double Decker Arts Festival is held in April, and fills the buzzy Square with live music, local food, and art stalls.

Visit the Mississippi Civil Rights Museum in Jackson

Few museums in the South—or the entire U.S.—are as powerful as this one. Telling the story of the long fight for Civil Rights from Mississippi's perspective, the museum comprises eight galleries that are packed with exhibits, photographs, and oral histories that give voice to those who have risked everything for change. History is traced from slavery and Reconstruction, through the Jim Crow era, which saw radical racial segregation, and to the present day. The central "This Little Light of Mine" gallery plays the Civil Rights anthem on repeat, growing louder and brighter as more visitors gather—a powerful symbol of hope and unity.

◉ Pair your visit with a trip to the Museum of Mississippi History next door for context on the state's complex past.

Pay homage to Elvis in Tupelo

Tupelo is where Elvis Presley's legend began. Born here in 1935, the future King of Rock 'n' Roll grew up in a humble two-room house that still stands, part of the Elvis Presley Birthplace Museum complex. Here, exhibits trace his early years—gospel church visits, small-town performances, and his rise from Tupelo boy to global icon. Visit the Assembly of God Church, where Elvis first sang hymns with his family, and look out for a life-sized bronze statue depicting young Elvis, guitar in hand, with his future cape-draped self. Downtown, Tupelo Hardware still welcomes visitors to the spot where Elvis's mother bought him his first guitar instead of the rifle he wanted, while murals celebrate the King's roots, his face splashed across Tupelo's brick walls.

◉ Each June, the Tupelo Elvis Festival hosts lively street parties and fills downtown with concerts at the Lyric Theatre.

When to visit

Spring and fall bring mild weather, blooming wildflowers, and festival season—from Clarksdale's blues-filled Juke Joint Festival (in April) to Ocean Springs' Peter Anderson Arts and Crafts Festival (in November).

Learn about the blues in the Mississippi Delta

Hear that? That's the sound of a steel guitar, drifting across the Mississippi Delta. It was here that the blues was first born from struggle and slavery. Throughout the 19th century, enslaved African Americans worked the plantations along the Yazoo and Mississippi rivers, and turned shouts and laments into a new form of expression that carried the pain of oppression and the longing for freedom. Today, the Delta is a living museum of this legacy. Experience it in places like Clarksdale, where the Delta Blues Museum and Red's Lounge keep the story of the blues—past and present—alive.

◉ The Mississippi Blues Trail follows more than 200 markers across the state, each celebrating the people and places that shaped the blues, from churches and museums to juke joints.

The Show Me State

Back in the 19th century, Missouri was regarded as somewhere you'd travel through, not to. But not anymore. Today, the "Show Me State" is the linchpin of the Midwest, with historic cities like Jefferson City and St. Louis (home to the iconic Gateway Arch) offering attractions in abundance. And the nickname? It comes from a speech by a congressman in 1899, summarizing that folks from "Missour-uh" are not easily taken in: "I'm from Missouri, and you've got to show me."

STATE MOTTO Let the Welfare of the People Be the Supreme Law

STATE FLOWER Hawthorn blossom

STATE ANIMAL Missouri mule

STATE BIRD Eastern bluebird

FUN FACT The phrase "the best thing since sliced bread" is thanks to Missouri; it was here, in 1928, that the first automatic bread-slicing machine was used by the Chillicothe Baking Company.

Soak up the atmosphere of St. Louis

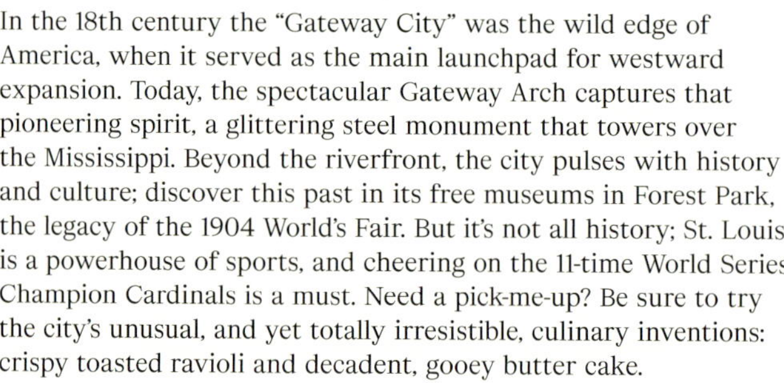

In the 18th century the "Gateway City" was the wild edge of America, when it served as the main launchpad for westward expansion. Today, the spectacular Gateway Arch captures that pioneering spirit, a glittering steel monument that towers over the Mississippi. Beyond the riverfront, the city pulses with history and culture; discover this past in its free museums in Forest Park, the legacy of the 1904 World's Fair. But it's not all history; St. Louis is a powerhouse of sports, and cheering on the 11-time World Series Champion Cardinals is a must. Need a pick-me-up? Be sure to try the city's unusual, and yet totally irresistible, culinary inventions: crispy toasted ravioli and decadent, gooey butter cake.

◉ For more details, visit the Gateway Arch Visitor Center (explorestlouis.com); book tickets for the tram ride to the top of the arch in advance.

Explore Mark Twain's Hannibal

It hasn't changed that much. Red-brick streets still slope down to the muddy expanse of the Mississippi, giant barges cruise past floating logs, and small forest-smothered islands and bayous carve up the main channel. No place influenced Mark Twain as much as his boyhood home of Hannibal. Today, the small town serves as a living memorial to the creator of two of the nation's most beloved fictional characters: Tom Sawyer and Huckleberry Finn. Twain's time in Hannibal is chronicled at the fascinating Mark Twain Boyhood Home & Museum, which includes his modest white clapboard house, plus a reconstruction of the home of Tom Blankenship, Twain's real-life model for Huck.

◉ For an overview of Hannibal, visit visithannibal.com. Find more about the museum at marktwainmuseum.org.

Visit the George Washington Carver National Monument

The life of agricultural scientist George Washington Carver, also known as the "Black Leonardo," soared from unimaginable hardship to triumph. Born enslaved in the early 1860s, he eventually gained a degree and a teaching post at Tuskegee Institute. His genius revolutionized farming and made him famous, with innovations like alternating cotton with sweet potatoes to restore devastated soil. His memorial in Diamond is on the site of his boyhood home; while this structure no longer exists, you can visit replicas of the labs in which he worked and the later Moses Carver house.

◉ The monument is open 9am–5pm daily, except holidays; for more information, visit nps.gov/gwca/index.htm.

When to visit

Missouri's calendar heats up after the summer solstice: August sees the Missouri State Fair, before Kansas City hosts American Royal, a huge barbecue cooking contest, in September, and the colors of fall take over the Ozarks.

Sample barbecue in Kansas City

Barbecue is an art form in Kansas City, Missouri (not to be confused with its twin city across the river in Kansas). Legend has it that one Henry Perry started barbecuing from an outdoor pit in the early 1900s, and the food was so good it launched a city-wide craze. As a major meatpacking center, Kansas City had plenty of fresh meat, and today some 100 barbecue joints thrive, with the scent of ribs smoking over hickory and oak wafting across the city. Arthur Bryant's, which traces its roots to Perry's original spot, is often called the "King of Ribs," but you'll find charred "burnt ends" and more at historic giants like Gates & Sons and modern favorites like Joe's Kansas City Bar-B-Que. There's even a Museum of BBQ to make sense of it all.

◉ The Museum of BBQ opens 10am–6pm daily (midday–5pm Sun); for more information, see museumofbbq.co.

Spend time in Branson and the Ozark Mountains

Fans of country music are in for a treat in Branson, the "Ozark Disneyland." Nestled in Missouri's scenic Ozark Mountains, this lively resort town is famed for its country shows, from the Haygoods family act and Dolly Parton's Stampede to the long-running Shepherd of the Hills Outdoor Drama. Beyond the stage, you'll find zip lines, the Branson Scenic Railway, and lakes perfect for boating. When it's time for peace and quiet, head to the Ozark Trail, where natural springs, crystal-clear streams, and waterfalls wind through woodland that feels a million miles from civilization.

◉ For more information on visiting the city of Branson, check out explorebranson.com; for the Ozark Trail, see ozarktrail.com.

Stop off in Jefferson City, Missouri's capital

Here's a capital city that keeps a secret: tiny Jefferson City, not mighty St. Louis, holds Missouri's governing title. Originally a simple trading post on the Missouri River, it never boomed, and so the city preserves its past beautifully. Stroll through 1850s architecture at the Jefferson Landing State Historic Site or dive into state history at the Missouri State Museum, found under the giant dome of the state capitol building (which was inspired by St. Peter's Basilica in Rome). The artwork inside is noteworthy, especially the detailed *Social History of Missouri* mural by Thomas Hart Benton.

◉ The Visitors Bureau is found at 700 E. Capitol Avenue and is open 8am–5pm Mon–Fri (visit jeffersoncity.com).

Learn about President Truman

Harry S. Truman, Missouri's most famous resident, rose from humble origins to become the 33rd U.S. president. Born in 1884, the farmer's son famously never completed college but was chosen as Franklin D. Roosevelt's vice president in 1945, assuming the presidency soon after. He is chiefly known for making the decision to drop atomic bombs on Japan, and leading the nation through the start of the Cold War. The illuminating Harry S. Truman National Historic Site preserves the stately mansion that became his homebase from 1919 until his death in 1972, and his tumultuous time in office is explored at the nearby Harry S. Truman Presidential Library & Museum, where he and his wife are buried.

◉ For visitor information for the Harry S. Truman National Historic Site, visit nps.gov/hstr. For the Library & Museum see trumanlibrary.gov.

See the little house on the prairie

The TV series *Little House on the Prairie* immortalized a romantic view of 19th-century pioneer life. "Home is the nicest word there is," declares Laura, the show's pigtailed heroine, in the first episode. And this was certainly the view of author Laura Ingalls Wilder, who wrote the beloved books that inspired the series. Based on her own life, the story chronicled Ingalls' childhood in the woods of Wisconsin and the Great Plains of Kansas, but she cherished a simple wood-frame structure most of all: Rocky Ridge Farm, in Mansfield, Missouri. Now a museum, this is where she wrote her beloved books in the 1930s and 40s. Get to know the author by touring her study, see where she wrote the *Little House* series, and read her original handwritten manuscripts.

◉ The Laura Ingalls Wilder Historic Home & Museum is open Mar–mid-Nov (lauraingallswilderhome.com).

Find adventure in Glacier National Park

You'll soon see why Glacier National Park is nicknamed "Crown of the Continent." It's one of Montana's jewels, carved by ice over millennia and unfolding across a playground of sawtoothed peaks, turquoise lakes, and valleys where waterfalls tumble from snowfields. The park's Going-to-the-Sun Road, blasted through the mountains in the 1930s, remains one of America's greatest drives, but you'll need to swap wheels for walking boots and get out onto the trails to properly appreciate Glacier's wildlife. Here, mountain goats skitter across scree, moose wade among lakeside reeds, and grizzlies roam throughout—a reminder that this is true wilderness.

◉ Glacier is Blackfeet country. The Indigenous guides at Sun Tours (suntours.co) lead visitors through the park's epic landscapes, offering insights into Blackfeet history, heritage, and modern culture.

The Treasure State

Mother Nature rules in Montana. The state unfolds under a sky so wide it feels infinite, knitting together snow-crowned peaks, sweeping prairies, and rivers that beat through glacial valleys. Beyond the call of the wild, you might gallery-hop in Bozeman, sip beer in Billings, or bike by the river in Missoula. In essence, this is a state where wilderness and culture are inseparable, making it a hit with just about every kind of visitor.

STATE MOTTO Gold and Silver

STATE FLOWER Bitterroot

STATE ANIMAL Grizzly bear

STATE BIRD Western meadowlark

FUN FACT Montana's name is based on the Spanish word for mountain, *montaña*, based on the name that had been given to the region in which the state is now found by early Spanish explorers.

Make a splash on Flathead Lake

Born of glacial melt at the end of the last Ice Age, Flathead sprawls as the largest natural freshwater lake west of the Mississippi River. Its glassy waters stretch out for some 27 miles (43 km), rimmed with cherry orchards and mountain ridges, and scattered with wildlife-rich islands. The Salish, Kootenai, and Pend d'Oreille peoples have called these shores home for centuries, fishing the depths and traveling by canoe. Today, kayakers paddle to Wild Horse Island, a protected state park known for its–you guessed it–wild horses; sailboats tack into the wind; and swimmers plunge into the cooling waters.

◉ Half a dozen state parks dot Flathead's shoreline and islands, offering parking, picnic spots, and boat launches. Summer is the peak season for swimming and sailing, while shoulder months mean quieter trails.

When to visit

Montana shifts with the seasons. Big Sky's slopes tempt snow fiends in winter, while hikers hit the national parks once the trails thaw in late spring. Summer throws up the Montana Folk Festival near Butte and the Crow Fair near Billings.

Stay on a Montana dude ranch

The hit TV show *Yellowstone* thrust Montana into the spotlight, stirring nostalgia for the West with its rippling rangelands and dramatic cattle-ranch backdrops. A stay at a Montana dude ranch will help you lean into that Wild West fantasy. The tradition stretches back to the late 19th century, when easterners came west seeking the romance of cowboy life. Today, offerings range from working ranches with rustic accommodations to upscale lodgings amid silver screen–worthy landscapes. Top spots include Lone Mountain Ranch and The Resort at Paws Up, where you can ride fence lines with wranglers, take supper by the campfire, and sleep in cabins beneath starry skies.

◉ For the real deal, check the Montana Bunkhouses website (montanaworkingranches.com), which lists working ranches that offer accommodations and activities.

Ski or summer hike at Big Sky Resort

Big Sky certainly lives up to its name, with sprawling slopes and vast horizons that can be explored on all manner of adventures. Opened in the 1970s, the resort has grown into one of America's premier ski destinations, spreading across four mountains and with runs that plunge through powdery bowls and tree-lined glades. In summer, the ski lifts carry hikers and bikers up the slopes instead, whisking them to high meadows crisscrossed with trails. Lone Peak, blanketed in snow in winter and strewn with wildflowers in summer, towers above it all, offering views that bend into Yellowstone and the Tetons.

◉ Big Sky Resort covers more than 5,800 acres (2,350 ha), with 300 named runs and 38 lifts linking everything from beginner greens to double-black chutes. The ski season typically runs from late November through April.

Blend culture and the outdoors in Bozeman

Bozeman began as a frontier supply town in the 1860s, and today it mixes mountain grit with real cultural verve. It's often jokingly nicknamed "Bozeangeles," due to its large number of West Coast transplants and increasingly cosmopolitan vibe. Hip neighborhoods buzz with bookstores and breweries, while beloved institutions like the Museum of the Rockies (famed for its fossils) give the city a cultural heft to rival much larger places. Wilderness is on the doorstep, too–the Gallatin Range rises to the south and Yellowstone is just down the road–a balance that has made Bozeman one of Montana's fastest-growing cities.

◉ Book a few nights at The LARK (larkbozeman.com), reimagined from an old motel and filled with local artwork.

Go wild in Montana's slice of Yellowstone

Just 3 percent of Yellowstone National Park spills into Montana, but boy is it a thrilling sliver. Much like the park's wonder-filled Wyoming swath, Montana's Yellowstone is alive with wildlife, and scattered with thermal wonders. The northern entrance at Gardiner has welcomed travelers since 1903, although Cooke City–Silver Gate is the quieter gateway, where bison graze grassy river valleys and wolves pad through the Lamar Valley at dawn. Crow and Shoshone peoples hunted and traveled these parts long before the park was created in 1872—and now that same land is traced by hikers, bikers, and horseback riders.

◉ West Yellowstone, crammed with restaurants, laid-back hotels, and cabins, is a (very) popular base for exploring the park.

Live the cowboy life on horseback

There's no better way to explore Montana than saddled up on a sure-footed steed, and modern-day riders can still cut the same paths long worn by ranchers and wranglers. Red Lodge's Elk River Outfitters leads rides across sagebrush valleys, cottonwood stands, and creek beds, sharing stories of cattle drives and cowboy traditions rooted in the 19th century. Based out of Big Timber, Absaroka-Beartooth Outfitters beats through wide-open ranch country carved through by the Yellowstone River. Riding in Montana isn't just for leisure—it's a glimpse of a working culture that still shapes the West.

◉ More information on these trips is available at elkriveradventures.com and absarokabeartooth.com.

Visit Little Bighorn Battlefield National Monument

In June 1876, rolling hills near the Little Bighorn River became the site of one of the most famous and tragic clashes of the American West. Here, Lakota, Cheyenne, and Arapaho warriors, led by Sitting Bull and Crazy Horse, defeated Lieutenant Colonel George Custer and the 7th Cavalry. Today, the battlefield is preserved with white headstones marking where soldiers fell and red markers honoring Indigenous warriors. The visitor center and interpretive trails recount both perspectives, acknowledging the profound cost of westward expansion. Looking out over the prairie, you'll sense how history still echoes across this land.

◉ Begin at the visitor center, where exhibits and ranger talks place the battle into context, before walking the trails.

Attend the Crow Fair celebration

Each August, the Apsáalooke (Crow) people host one of the largest powwows in North America. The Crow Fair, first held in 1904, brings together thousands of Apsáalooke community members—along with other Indigenous nations and visitors—to a valley near the Little Bighorn. Tepees rise in colorful rows, horses are paraded in dazzling regalia, and evenings pulse with drumbeats as dancers fill the arena. For the Crow people, it's a reunion and a cultural affirmation; for visitors, it's an open invitation to witness living tradition, and one of Montana's most powerful cultural events.

◉ Enrolled members are admitted free, while everyone else requires a day or weekend pass. You'll also need to buy a separate license if you want to take photos.

Drive the Beartooth Highway

Opened in 1936, the Beartooth Highway is an engineering marvel, hairpinning across alpine tundra and providing views that live up to Montana's "Big Sky Country" nickname. Threading from Red Lodge to Cooke City, it climbs above 10,000 ft (3,050 m), with pullouts revealing serrated peaks, and sweeping valleys carved by glaciers. The road's evocative name comes from a prominent peak in the range, which to the Indigenous Apsáalooke (Crow) people resembled a "Na Piet Say," or "bear's tooth." Today, drivers and motorcyclists trace the same wild spine of the Rockies, the air thinning and horizons widening with each mile.

◉ The Beartooth Highway closes seasonally, so plan your trip carefully. Conditions permitting, the road is open from the Friday of Memorial Day weekend (in May) through mid-October.

See alfresco art at Tippet Rise

Is there a better way to see great art than in the great outdoors? Near the tiny town of Fishtail, a working sheep ranch doubles as one of America's most offbeat art destinations. Tippet Rise Art Center scatters monumental sculptures across its rolling prairie—concrete arcs rise like steeples, and structures woven from branches blend into the bucolic surroundings. A hike here doubles as an arty escape, as you'll come across these whimsical creations on one or another of the ranch's 15 miles (24 km) of trails. Another highlight is the summer concert season: the art-dotted rangeland becomes even more atmospheric as the sound of chamber music reverberates across it.

◉ You'll need to pre-purchase a $10 ticket for admission to the summertime performances. Guided van tours lasting around 2.5 hours bring the artworks into context.

The Cornhusker State

Some might say Nebraska flys under the radar, overshadowed as it often is by neighboring Wyoming and Colorado. But there's no reason it should. Its landscape is surprisingly varied: quiet prairies, scenic rivers, and striking rock formations promise all kinds of outdoor adventure. Add in lively railroad and aerospace attractions, plus some American Midwest spirit, and Nebraska reveals itself as a warm, characterful state well worth your time.

STATE MOTTO Equality Before the Law

STATE FLOWER Goldenrod

STATE ANIMAL White-tailed deer

STATE BIRD Western meadowlark

FUN FACT The World's Largest Time Capsule, weighing 45 tons (41 tonnes) and containing some 5,000 items, was sealed and buried in Nebraska in 1975. It was opened 50 years later, and artifacts are now on display in Seward.

Paddle along the Niobrara National Scenic River

A 76-mile (122-km) stretch of free-flowing, shimmering water, the Niobrara National Scenic River attracts paddlers of all levels. It's fed by Wyoming snowmelt and clear Sandhills springs, and carves a wandering path through northern Nebraska. Whether you choose to ride a tube for a lazy afternoon, paddle a canoe, or navigate a kayak, you're guaranteed incredible views: you'll float past more than 200 waterfalls tumbling into rocky outcroppings, including Smith Falls, the state's highest at 63 ft (19 m). If you're lucky, you might catch sight of a deer drinking from the riverbank.

◉ Check out the river's official website (nps.gov/niob) for a list of outfitters offering guided trips, rentals, and shuttle services.

Walk in the footsteps of pioneers at Chimney Rock

For pioneers heading westward in the 1800s, the lone spire of Chimney Rock served as a punctuation mark on the Oregon Trail. Its presence on the horizon represented progress on this perilous journey and the promise of hope for what awaited ahead. Chimney Rock continues to ignite big feelings as it stands stalwart at 300 ft (91 m), having weathered erosion and lightning. The ancient formation can be seen from the historic site's visitor center, which offers context on the local environment and the rock's cultural significance. But it's worth walking the short trail from the center to get a truly humbling, close-up view, and to feel the weight of those who journeyed through this desolate landscape.

◉ Chimney Rock National Historic Site is 1.5 miles (2.4 km) south of Nebraska State Highway 92, near the town of Bayard. Want to walk the trail? You'll need comfortable shoes.

Hike through Toadstool Geologic Park

Deep within the sprawling Oglala National Grassland is another world: Toadstool Geologic Park. This otherworldly landscape was sculpted by wind and water for millennia, revealing a treasury of exposed fossils and striking rock formations. Named for the many hoodoos that resemble giant mushrooms, these unique "toadstools" formed when softer clay eroded more quickly than the sandstone caps protecting them above. To truly experience this unique geology, plan to hike the 5-mile (8-km) loop trail. Starting and ending at the campground, the path meanders around the formations and trails past prehistoric rhino tracks.

◉ The park is open daily year-round; fees are required for day use and camping. Don't drive the dirt road leading to the park when it's wet, as the mud can be impassable for many vehicles.

Make a splash in Lake McConaughy

Thanks to its reputation as the state's largest body of water, Lake McConaughy has earned the nickname of "Big Mac." And watersports fans are certainly loving it. Spanning 56 sq miles (121 sq km), the lake is a watersports paradise, with swimmers, wakeboarders, and even scuba divers seeking adventure in the waters here. It's also become legendary among anglers, having produced numerous state-record fish. Need a place to crash? With overnight camping allowed on some of its white-sand beaches, you can turn your visit into a real escape.

⦿ Start at the Lake McConaughy Visitor and Water Interpretive Center on Nebraska State Highway 61. Boat rentals are available. Note that camping reservations and fishing licenses are required (outdoornebraska.gov).

Ascend the Golden Spike Tower

You've ridden the rails and seen freight trains hurtle past, but have you ever witnessed hundreds of trains being grouped and "shunted"? You can at sprawling Bailey Yard, in North Platte, the world's largest classification yard. Take the elevator up the Golden Spike Tower where you'll be greeted by bird's-eye views of an astonishing 14,000 railcars being "humped" (or sorted). Skilled crews break down and reassemble over 100 trains daily for the Union Pacific Railroad, the yard's owner and operator. Downstairs, the visitor center offers fascinating exhibits detailing the yard's rich history, along with a gift shop jam-packed with train memorabilia, ideal gifts for the train lover in your life.

⦿ Be sure to visit both the open-air, 7th-floor observation deck, where you'll hear the sounds of the yard, as well as the indoor, 8th-floor deck for 360° views.

Learn about Cold War history

Ready to step into the Cold War's cockpit? From 1948 to 1992, the Strategic Air Command (S.A.C.) was the muscle behind the U.S. Air Force, orchestrating the bomber fleet from its nerve center at Offutt Air Force Base in Nebraska. Today this incredible story lives on at the Strategic Air Command and Aerospace Museum, in nearby Ashland. Here you'll discover the largest collection of Cold War aircraft in the U.S., including a stealthy Lockheed F-117 "Nighthawk," a mighty Boeing B-17 "Flying Fortress," and even cosmic travelers like the Apollo Command Space Module. Want to pilot your own mission? Check out the museum's virtual-reality experience, or visit the planetarium and be launched into deep space.

⦿ The museum is open daily except for major holidays (sacmuseum.org).

Wander the Cowboy Trail

Imagine traversing over 200 wooden bridges, each one offering stellar, panoramic views of the open prairie. This is the Cowboy Recreation and Nature Trail, one of the longest "rails-to-trails" projects in the country. This former railroad line has been brilliantly reimagined as an incredible 200-mile (322-km) route of developed trail. Open to cyclists, pedestrians, and horses (this is cowboy country, after all), the route passes through 30 cities and towns, perfect for resting and refueling. In between these welcoming stops, the experience is pure Nebraska: keep an eye out for spectacular wildlife, including soaring bald eagles and vibrant monarch butterflies, all framed by stunning river scenery and the historic echoes of the old rail line.

◉ The Cowboy Trail connects the towns of Valentine and Norfolk. Cars are not permitted (outdoornebraska.gov).

When to visit

Summer and fall promise the best and most reliable weather, so you can really enjoy the state's outdoor activities before the winter snow and spring thunderstorms set in. September and October are especially lovely, with fewer crowds.

Get to know the city of Omaha

Welcome to Omaha, Nebraska's energetic urban heart, found on the banks of the Missouri River. Forged by a history of frontier commerce, the city was built on the grit of railroads and meatpacking in the mid-1800s, and today that industrious spirit continues to thrive. Locals are proud of the city's lush green parks and world-class attractions, like Omaha's Henry Doorly Zoo and Aquarium, which routinely ranks among the best globally. Housing nearly 1,000 animal species, it famously features the world's largest indoor desert and the largest indoor rainforest. A short, 15-minute drive away, the fascinating Joslyn Castle and Gardens is a magnificent historic home built to resemble a Scottish castle, which now serves as a museum.

◉ Omaha's Henry Doorly Zoo (omahazoo.org) is open daily. Joslyn Castle (joslyncastle.com) offers daily tours.

The Silver State

Just like the entertainers of Las Vegas, Nevada likes to put on a show. The state's cinematic landscapes will have you at the edge of your seat: red-rock canyons and sweeping desert landscapes set the scene, while stars like Tahoe take center stage. Beyond the epic scenery, Nevada has a great cast of characters, from various Indigenous groups to early pioneers and back to the performers of Sin City itself. Wherever you end up, sit back and enjoy the show.

STATE MOTTO All For Our Country

STATE FLOWER Sagebrush

STATE ANIMAL Desert bighorn sheep

STATE BIRD Mountain bluebird

FUN FACT Hosting around 150 to 300 ceremonies a day, Las Vegas is the Wedding Capital of the World. Top spots to tie the knot include the Graceland Wedding Chapel; it held the world's first Elvis-themed ceremony in 1977.

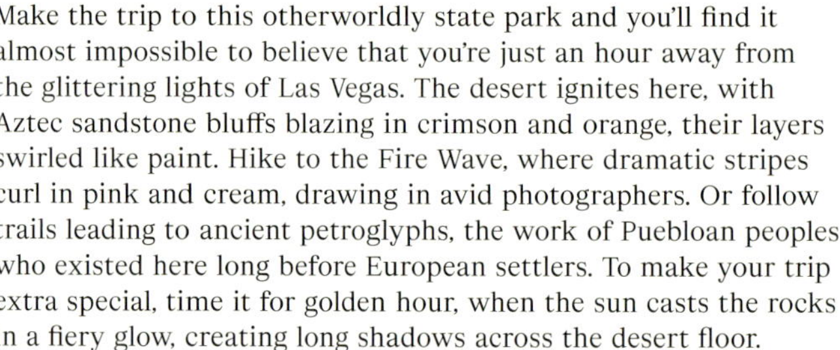

Hike in the Valley of Fire State Park

Make the trip to this otherworldly state park and you'll find it almost impossible to believe that you're just an hour away from the glittering lights of Las Vegas. The desert ignites here, with Aztec sandstone bluffs blazing in crimson and orange, their layers swirled like paint. Hike to the Fire Wave, where dramatic stripes curl in pink and cream, drawing in avid photographers. Or follow trails leading to ancient petroglyphs, the work of Puebloan peoples who existed here long before European settlers. To make your trip extra special, time it for golden hour, when the sun casts the rocks in a fiery glow, creating long shadows across the desert floor.

⦿ The Valley of Fire State Park is open daily, sunrise–sunset; stop by the visitor center to see exhibits about the park's geology and early human history (parks.nv.gov/parks/valley-of-fire).

Stop by an Old Western saloon

Frontier life looms large in Nevada's story. When miners weren't digging for silver or traversing the land, they gathered in saloons–places to swap tales, gamble, and enjoy a drink or two. Several of these watering holes are still around: the Genoa Bar, opened in 1853 in its namesake town, unfolds in a jumble of wooden furniture and curiosities (think vintage photographs, taxidermy, and an antique mirror), where everyone from Mark Twain to presidents including Theodore Roosevelt have stopped by. Over at the Pioneer Saloon in Goodsprings, see the bullet holes in its walls from a historic gunfight. Order a whiskey, lean on the counter, and you'll be part of a tradition as old as Nevada itself.

◉ At Pioneer Saloon, sample a glass of Old Man Liver American Whiskey, a punchy, oaky blend distilled by the owner himself (pioneersaloonnv.com).

When to visit

If you can handle the heat, time your visit for events like Burning Man in late September, or Reno's Hot August Nights, a classic car festival. Otherwise, Nevada's epic state and national parks are best experienced in shoulder seasons.

Drive the Extraterrestrial Highway

Nevada State Route 375, better known as the Extraterrestrial Highway, has more reported U.F.O. sightings than any other road in the entire country. Which makes sense when you consider its unique location, tucked into the remote reaches of south-central Nevada. This far-out highway skirts Area 51, a hush-hush military test site that some believe to be a top-secret laboratory for captured alien spacecraft. What happens behind security fences remains a mystery, but quirky roadside stops lean into the vibe: the Alien Research Center, with its towering silver alien statue; the E.T. Fresh Jerky shop, hawking snacks and souvenirs; and the Little A'Le'Inn diner, serving up "alien burgers."

◉ Give yourself at least half a day for the 98-mile (157-km) drive and fuel up beforehand.

THE STRIP
See the Bellagio Hotel's dancing fountains and the High Roller observation wheel on Sin City's bright Strip.

THE ARTS DISTRICT
Swap neon signs for bright murals, and casino bars for craft breweries in Vegas's creative heart.

WORLD-CLASS SHOWS
Be dazzled by Vegas's stages, from the famous Cirque du Soleil to A-list residencies.

THE NEON MUSEUM
Wander among restored vintage signs in the "neon boneyard."

FREMONT STREET
See the buzzing street where casinos were first opened back in the 1930s.

Indulge in the razzle dazzle of Las Vegas

"Welcome to fabulous Las Vegas": so reads the sign as you cruise into town. Like a shimmering mirage in the Mojave Desert, Vegas emerges from the desert as a big, bold, brash place of promise. Zip past neon signs glowing in the night as you head down The Strip, a 4-mile (6-km) stretch at the heart of the city where resorts, world-class shows, partying crowds, and many 24-hour casinos await. And when the neon glow gets too much, you're only a short drive from the desert's wild side—Red Rock Canyon's ocher cliffs and Valley of Fire's swirling sandstone are both close enough for a half-day escape.

◉ Head to the Visit Las Vegas website for all the information you need before visiting (visitlasvegas.com).

Visit Hoover Dam

Completed in 1936, Hoover Dam was a feat of Depression-era engineering. Its Art Deco towers, concrete curves, and sheer scale symbolized America's might, and it remains an impressive sight. Tours reveal the labyrinth of tunnels and turbines that harnessed the Colorado River, taming floods and powering the Southwest. From the top, you can gaze across the deep blue of Lake Mead, once the world's largest reservoir. You'll also learn how this colossal structure electrified the desert and laid the foundations for modern Las Vegas, powering the neon and casinos that would later define the city.

◉ Descend into the dam's construction tunnels and powerplant on a guided tour, or explore at your own pace from the visitor center (open 9am–5pm daily).

Experience a ghost town

Ghost towns are scattered all across Nevada, eerie reminders of the 19th-century silver and gold rush, which went bust as quickly as it boomed. These days, exploring these old mining towns feels a bit like ghost hunting: picture quiet, dust-choked streets, crumbling facades, a train depot to nowhere. Some of the most intriguing are Pioche, where the supposedly haunted Overland Hotel and Saloon creaks with ghost stories, and Rhyolite, once a bustling gold camp of some 10,000 people. Hear a sound? That's just the echo of pickaxes and pianos—and the people who won (and probably lost) a fortune.

◉ It's free to visit Pioche's Million Dollar Courthouse, though it's only open May–Oct. It's also free to visit haunting Rhyolite, which is managed by the Nevada Bureau of Land Management (blm.gov).

Explore Downtown Ely

If you want to get to know Ely, start with the murals splashed all across downtown—bold snapshots of Indigenous heritage, mining booms, and pioneer grit. They set the tone for a town that lives its history rather than leaving it behind. Take, for example, the Nevada Northern Railway Museum, which brings the mining era to life with steam locomotives that once hauled copper ore across the desert, or the McGill Drugstore Museum, a preserved 20th-century pharmacy, its shelves still lined with remedies and perfumes. Not to be missed is Ely Renaissance Village, where a number of restored historic buildings bring early immigrant stories vividly to life.

◉ Time your visit for Ely's Fire and Ice Festival in January, which features popular events including an ice sculpture competition and snowshoeing.

Take a break at Lake Tahoe

Cradled by the Sierra Nevada, Lake Tahoe straddles the border between Nevada and California. Long before tourism, the Washoe people lived around these waters, fishing and gathering plants in alpine meadows; you can learn more about this heritage at the Nevada State Museum, a short drive east from the shoreline. Today, though, the biggest draw here is the promise of adventure. Summer sees sailing regattas and paddling trips, while, on the shores, hikers trace pine-fringed trails. In winter, snow blankets the peaks above the lake, turning it into a skiing and snowboarding paradise.

◉ For helpful Lake Tahoe visitor information, see the lake's tourism website (visitlaketahoe.com).

See Cathedral Gorge

At first glance, Cathedral Gorge State Park looks like a giant might have sculpted it from clay. Towering spires and narrow slot canyons ripple across the valley, as if shaped by an enormous hand. In truth, it was ancient lakes and relentless rainstorms that carved these formations over millions of years. The Paiute people once gathered plants and hunted in these gullies, and their presence lingers in oral histories touched upon during ranger-led tours. Those same tours lead visitors through the formations, pointing out geological quirks and desert wildlife. Many hikes culminate at Miller Point Overlook, where the ground falls away to reveal sweeping views of Cathedral Gorge's labyrinth of clay peaks.

◉ Check the schedule at the visitor center for free ranger programs (parks.nv.gov/parks/cathedral-gorge).

Uncover the layers of Great Basin National Park

Great Basin is one of America's least-visited national parks—and that's part of its magic. There's beauty both below and above ground here. Beneath the surface, the Lehman Caves form a marble maze of stalactites and vast chambers carved over millennia. Above, the Wheeler Peak Scenic Drive climbs toward an ancient stand of bristlecone pines and sweeping views of Snake Valley. And farther above still, when darkness settles, a sky little touched by light pollution blazes with stars. Remote, raw, and unshowy, the park is one of Nevada's best-kept secrets, and one you may just want to keep all to yourself.

◉ Check the NPS website to plan your visit around the park's astronomy events (nps.gov/grba/index.htm).

Learn about Indigenous heritage at Pyramid Lake

Some 50 miles (80 km) north of Reno, Pyramid Lake glimmers in the desert, watched over by pyramid-shaped tufa formations. For the Pyramid Lake Paiute people, this is ancestral land, central to their stories and traditions. Make a beeline for the Pyramid Lake Museum and Visitor Center to see displays about this heritage, from fishing practices to the 19th-century Pyramid Lake War, an 1860 conflict between the Northern Paiute and U.S. settlers. There are plenty of activities here, too—boat, kayak, or cast for Lahontan cutthroat trout, and get to know the lake as it is today.

◉ Join excursions led by Paiute hosts, like a fishing trip with Kooyooe Pa'a Guides (kooyooepaaguides.com).

Dig into mining history

Step back to the days when silver mining was big business. In Tonopah, the so-called "Queen of the Silver Camps," fortunes were made overnight after silver was struck in 1900. At the Historic Mining Park, you can wander among towering headframes and machinery that once powered the town's boomtime. Not far from Reno, Virginia City rose from the riches of the Comstock Lode, one of the richest silver strikes in American history. At its height, it was a busy city with ornate opera houses and saloons that seemed never to close. Today, you can ride a heritage railroad or poke around museums like the Comstock History Center.

◉ For more information on visiting Tonopah's Historic Mining Park, see tonopahminingpark.com.

Explore the past in Carson City

Nevada's capital might be small, but its past looms large across its historic buildings. Carson City grew on the back of the Comstock Lode silver strike; today, its original Old West spirit is embedded into the city's modern character. To uncover its past, start at the imposing State Capitol, built around 1870 from local sandstone, before delving into the Nevada State Museum. Here, you can learn about the state's natural history, Indigenous cultures, and mining booms and busts. Over at the Nevada State Railroad Museum, locomotives recall the frontier heyday and bring this definitive era to life.

◉ Guided tours of the Capitol must be booked two weeks in advance; walk-in tours are available 10am–3pm Sat.

Drive the "loneliest road in America"

In the 1980s, *Life* magazine dubbed U.S. Route 50 through Nevada "the loneliest road in America." Follow this wonderfully stark highway and you'll soon see why. The road unfurls across wide basins and over empty mountain passes, where ghost towns and sagebrush cling to the margins. Mining towns like Austin, Eureka, and Ely—now welcoming way stations with saloons, hotels, and museums—are strung like beads along otherwise empty stretches. And did you think tumbleweed was an old Western cliché? You might just see it roll across the asphalt here. The loneliest road it might be, but that's hardly a bad thing when your surroundings are this magical.

◉ Fuel stations can be few and far between, so top off your tank (and your snacks) whenever you stop in the small towns along the way.

The Granite State

Nature in New Hampshire reigns supreme: home to the forest-smothered White Mountains, alpine lakes, white-water rivers, and ski resorts, the Granite State offers endless opportunity for an escape into the outdoors. An added bonus? It's got to be the spectacular fall foliage that blazes across the landscapes every year. Among it all are colonial villages and towns, which make the perfect base from which to uncover New Hampshire's scenic best.

STATE MOTTO Live Free or Die

STATE FLOWER Purple lilac

STATE ANIMAL White-tailed deer

STATE BIRD Purple finch

FUN FACT Punctuality is ingrained in the fabric of New Hampshire history. It's where, in Concord, the alarm clock was invented in 1787. It was made for early birds; the only time setting on the alarm was 4am.

Ride along the Conway Scenic Railroad

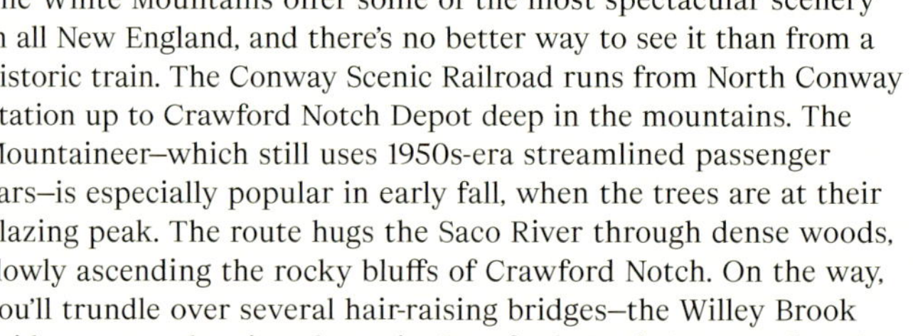

The White Mountains offer some of the most spectacular scenery in all New England, and there's no better way to see it than from a historic train. The Conway Scenic Railroad runs from North Conway Station up to Crawford Notch Depot deep in the mountains. The Mountaineer–which still uses 1950s-era streamlined passenger cars–is especially popular in early fall, when the trees are at their blazing peak. The route hugs the Saco River through dense woods, slowly ascending the rocky bluffs of Crawford Notch. On the way, you'll trundle over several hair-raising bridges–the Willey Brook Bridge over a plunging chasm in Crawford Notch State Park and the curved "Frankenstein Trestle" are especially dramatic.

◉ The Mountaineer runs along the railroad May through November; for more information, visit conwayscenic.com.

Gulp craft beers at Smuttynose Brewing Co. and beyond

New Hampshire's original craft brewery, Smuttynose Brewing Co. has been setting the standard since 1994. Founded in Portsmouth and now based in Hampton, it's home to a welcoming taproom and beer garden serving rotating brews straight off the line. In summer, little beats listening to live music on the patio while sipping your new favorite brew (there's an annual Brewfest in October, too). Smuttynose isn't alone, either: there are over 80 breweries in the state, best discovered on the NH Beer Trail. The good news? It's a small state, so you're never far from a great craft beer.

◉ For the full list of New Hampshire craft brewers and more detail on the NH Beer Trail, see nhbrewers.org.

Sink your teeth into New Hampshire history in Concord

New Hampshire's capital, Concord (pronounced "conquered"), may be small, but it's incredibly rich in history and character. Explore the gold-domed State House, lined with paintings and portraits, and the New Hampshire Historical Society Museum, set in a beautiful Romanesque building. The Pierce Manse, meanwhile, offers a glimpse into the life of Franklin Pierce, the nation's 14th president. And when you've had your fill of history, Concord makes a perfect base for exploring New Hampshire's forests, lakes, and the White Mountains.

◉ The Capitol Region Visitor Center opens 8:30am–5pm Mon–Fri (visitconcord-nh.com).

When to visit

There's really no better time to visit than in fall, though this is inevitably the busiest time. If you're not one for crowds, try summer, when the coast and lakes sparkle, or winter, when skiing and winter sports reign supreme.

Learn about the Shakers at Canterbury Shaker Village

In 1774, Mother Ann Lee made the decision to emigrate from Manchester, England, to America. She wasn't alone—a band of nine Christian followers, who regarded her as the female representation of God, came with her. Lee was the spiritual leader of the Shakers, named for their ecstatic dancing during worship, and for the next 100 years they thrived in New England. Canterbury Shaker Village was established in 1792, one of 19 Shaker communities at the time. The world of Ann Lee and her flock is faithfully reproduced across 25 original and four reconstructed Shaker buildings. Walking through, it's as though no time has passed at all.

◉ Canterbury Shaker Village is open year-round, with tours May–Nov: 10am–4pm daily (shakers.org).

Cruise around Lake Winnipesaukee

Lake Winnipesaukee is massive. It's not only New Hampshire's largest lake, but the third biggest in New England—no mean feat in the heart of the Lakes Region. And a cruise on vintage paddle steamer *MS Mount Washington* is the best way to take it all in. From the water, you'll glimpse islets—there are more than 260, smothered in pine and summer cottages—and the varied wildlife that calls the lake home, from geese to moose. Hop on board from either of the two main lake towns: the busy Weirs Beach resort or historic Wolfeboro. From there, it's smooth cruising.

◉ The Meredith Visitor Information Center is located on 272 Daniel Webster Highway, Route-3 (9am–4pm Mon–Fri); for cruises, see cruisenh.com.

Drive up Mount Washington

Mount Washington is the highest peak in the northeastern U.S., meaning it's best accessed on four wheels (although seasoned hikers also tackle it on foot). Hitting the road also means a trip back in time: the Mount Washington Auto Road follows the original carriage track completed in 1861. The winding 8-mile (13-km) route passes dense hardwood forest on the way to the summit, which stands some 6,288 ft (1,917 m) above sea level. At the 4,000-ft (1,219-m) mark, the road winds above the trees into a bare landscape of windswept tundra, dotted with alpine flowers, before continuing to the peak. Conditions can be dramatic up here, but on a clear day it's possible to enjoy views that stretch all the way to the Atlantic.

◉ The Mount Washington Auto Road is open mid-May–Oct from 9am (closing times vary; see mt-washington.com).

Admire the sculptures at Saint-Gaudens National Historic Park

Augustus Saint-Gaudens was one of America's greatest sculptors, who at one point called these quiet backwoods of New Hampshire home. Best known for his lifelike bronze sculptures, he began spending summers in Cornish in 1885. When he moved here full-time five years later, he also established the Cornish Art Colony, a community of creatives with whom he worked until his death in 1907. Today, his former home makes for a tranquil backdrop to the replicas and castings of his works shown here. Wander the gardens, wooded nature trails, or the grassy lawns, and let the creativity of the art colony take hold.

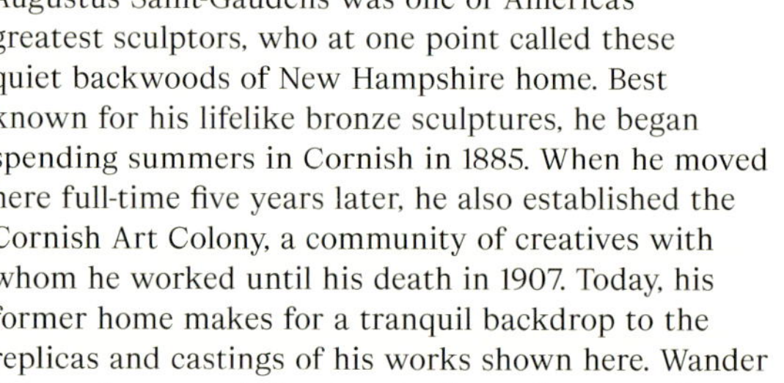

◉ Saint-Gaudens National Historic Park is open late May–Oct: 9am–4:30pm Thu–Mon (nps.gov/saga).

Traverse the White Mountains

A great, granite massif at the heart of the state, the White Mountains are New Hampshire's pride and joy. Full of dense pine forests, shady glades, and calm mountain streams, the area is perfect for some scenic hiking. Some of the easiest trails are in Franconia Notch State Park, while more challenging hikes await in Pinkham Notch and along the Appalachian Trail, which passes through. Among the idyllic scenes, Mount Washington is the crown jewel, reaching towards the sky at 6,288 ft (1,917 m) high. So, what are you waiting for? Your White Mountains adventure awaits.

◉ Visitor information can be found at the White Mountains Visitor Center, at exit 32 off I-93 in North Woodstock on the Kancamagus Highway (visitwhitemountains.com).

The Garden State

With New York City on its doorstep, New Jersey could have played second fiddle, but that's never been its style. This is a state with attitude and ambition. Just take a look at its universities, top-rated in the country; or its world-changing inventions, courtesy of Thomas Edison. And let's not forget the coastline: charming seaside cities, beautiful beaches, and stunning Atlantic views beckon visitors in droves. The best way to describe New Jersey? Small but mighty.

STATE MOTTO Liberty and Prosperity

STATE FLOWER Common blue violet

STATE ANIMAL Horse

STATE BIRD American goldfinch

FUN FACT With more diners per capita than any other U.S. state, New Jersey has been hailed the "Diner Capital of the World." How many are there? Estimates range from 400 to 600.

Roam the Princeton University campus

One of the country's most prestigious institutes of higher education, Princeton University isn't just for academics—it's open for all to explore. Its handsome campus, established in 1756, unfolds as a feast of artful architecture and stunning outdoor spaces. Kick off your visit at the soaring Princeton University Chapel, a masterpiece of Gothic design completed in 1928, though you'd think it had been completed centuries ago. A short walk away is the Princeton University Art Museum, displaying a world-class collection of works that includes everything from ancient Greek statues to paintings by Manet and Gauguin. Finally, rent a canoe or kayak and join Princeton's famed rowing team on Lake Carnegie.

◉ The university's website (princeton.edu) covers these attractions and more, with a map of the campus and other visitor information.

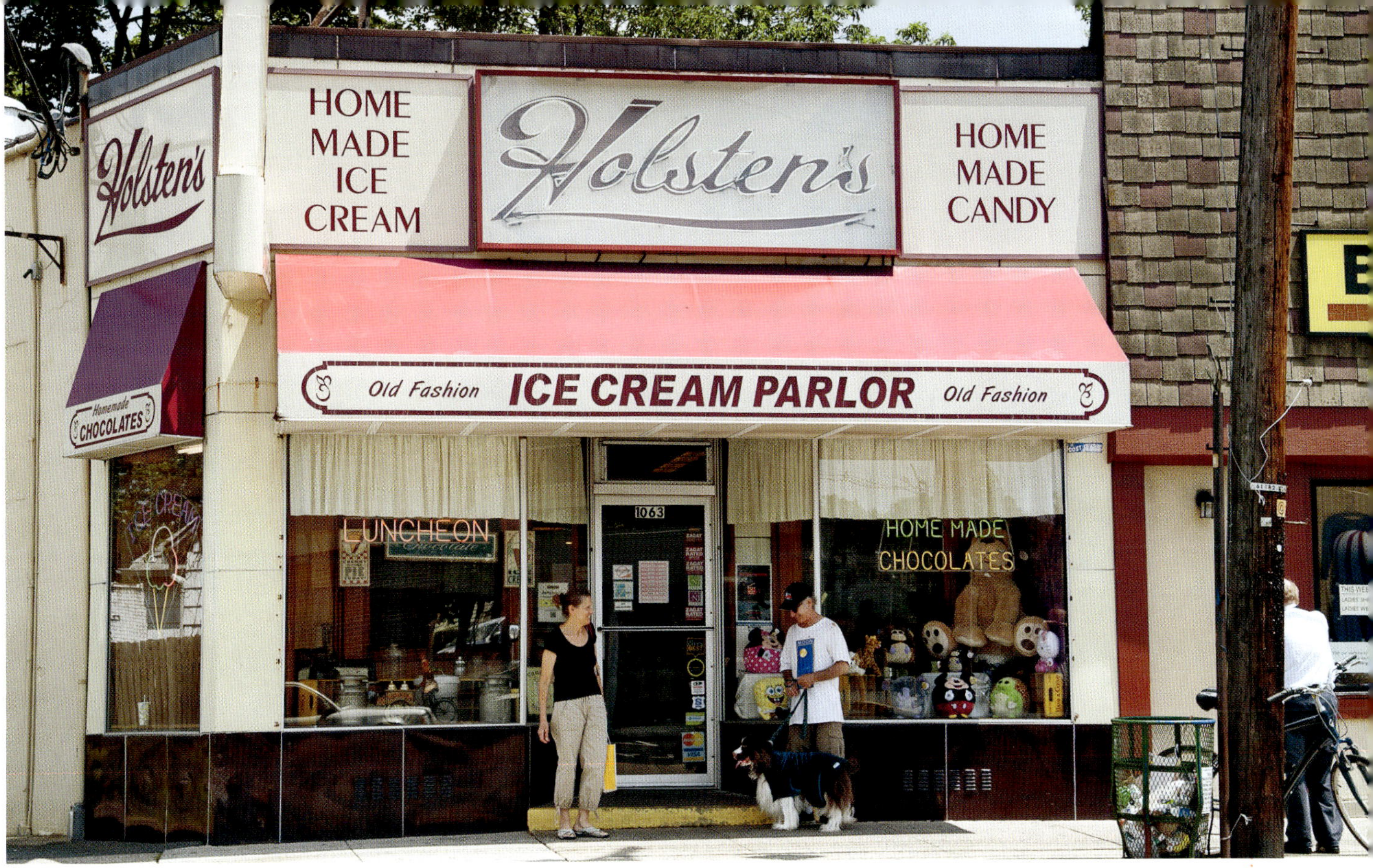

Check out the filming locations for *The Sopranos*

Hailed as one of the greatest television shows in American history, *The Sopranos* captivated viewers from 1999 to 2007 with its tales of mob boss Tony Soprano. At its heart was the state of New Jersey, with many real-life locations forming backdrops. Walk in Tony's footsteps by heading to the town of Elizabeth, where he and his crew would regularly dine in Vesuvio restaurant (now Del Porto), Uncle Junior's House in Newark, the Bada Bing club in Lodi, and, of course, Tony's house in North Caldwell. For the ultimate pilgrimage, munch on a plate of onion rings at Holsten's, the Bloomfield diner immortalized in the show's finale.

◉ Check out sopranos-locations.com for a comprehensive list of filming locations, along with maps and information on the episodes in which they appeared.

Visit the Thomas Edison National Historical Park

The movie camera. Nickel-iron batteries. Sound-recording equipment. What do all of these things have in common? They were all invented by Thomas Edison, and worked on in his lab in West Orange. Now preserved as the Thomas Edison National Historical Park, this redbrick mansion and laboratory were at the center of American innovation from the late 1800s. The site even housed the world's very first movie studio, nicknamed the "Black Maria" for its resemblance to police vans of the time. Access the historic grounds with a visitor pass, and be sure to reserve a place on a tour of Glenmont, the inventor's beautifully preserved home.

◉ Be sure to make a tour reservation on the park's website (nps.gov/edis) well in advance; tours are in high demand and same-day tickets are often not available.

Enjoy the amusements of the Jersey Shore

For more than a century, Americans and tourists alike have been lured by the Jersey Shore's 90 miles (145 km) of sandy beaches, with its promise of sunshine and nostalgic amusements along its boardwalks. Some 20 towns punctuate the coastline, including the city of Margate, where six-story Lucy the Elephant has raised smiles since the 1880s. At the very tip of the shoreline, Cape May Lighthouse rewards those who choose to climb its 199 steps with stellar views of the Atlantic. And no visit is complete without a concert at The Stone Pony, in Asbury Park, where a young Bruce Springsteen launched his legendary career.

◉ Browse New Jersey's tourism website (visitnj.org) for a comprehensive directory of Jersey Shore attractions.

Hike along the Batona Trail in the Pinelands

Known by locals simply as the Pinelands, the New Jersey Pine Barrens is the largest remnant of a forest that once stretched from North Carolina to Canada. Its sandy soil supports a rich tapestry of pine trees, hardy oaks, and thickets of huckleberry shrubs, all of which is protected from the march of development by the Pinelands National Reserve. Explore this unique landscape on the 53-mile (85-km) Batona Trail (short for "back to nature"), on a day's hike. Alternatively, set out on a multiday backpacking trip from the Ong's Hat ghost town in Brendan T. Byrne State Forest, all the way to Bass River State Forest.

◉ The Pinelands Preservation Alliance is a great resource for hiking the Batona Trail (pinelandsalliance.org).

When to visit

Excluding winter, New Jersey enjoys pleasant weather throughout the year. But the best time to visit? That's either spring or fall, when crowds visiting the state's cities and beaches have thinned out.

Learn all about New Jersey's shipbuilding history

Just across the Delaware River from Philadelphia is the city of Camden, known for its maritime legacy. From 1899 to 1968, the colossal New York Shipbuilding Corporation anchored its operations here; its efforts during World War II were nothing short of heroic, transforming the shipyard into the biggest and busiest facility of its kind. To find out all about this unique history, plus shipbuilding techniques and the like, visit the Camden Shipyard & Maritime Museum, housed inside a repurposed church adjacent to the yard.

◉ The Camden Shipyard & Maritime Museum is located at 1912 S. Broadway. Check the website for opening hours (camdenshipyardmuseum.org).

The Land of Enchantment

Known as *Tierra del Encanto* in Spanish, New Mexico certainly has plenty to enchant. Here, vast skies watch over fluted mountains and sweeping mesas, luminous white-sand deserts and vivid blue pools. Such diverse terrain mirrors the state's cultural identity: this is a place where the "Great Houses" of Ancestral Puebloans stand side by side with Indigenous pueblos and Spanish-built towns. And with aliens and Americana adding a bit of quirkiness, it's hard not to be spellbound.

STATE MOTTO It Grows as it Goes

STATE FLOWER Yucca

STATE ANIMAL Black bear

STATE BIRD Greater roadrunner

FUN FACT More than 500 balloons take to the skies every October in the Albuquerque International Balloon Fiesta, the largest ballooning event in the world and (supposedly) the most photographed.

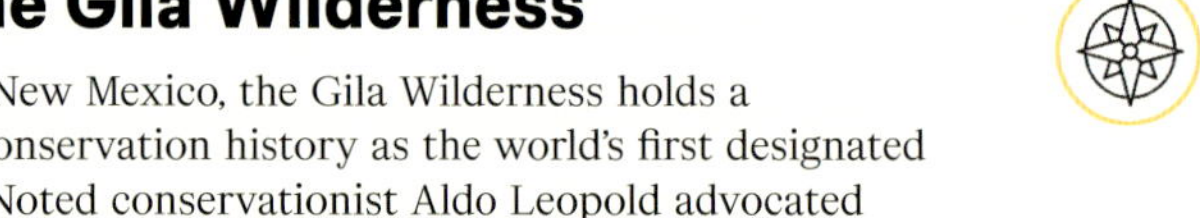

Explore the Gila Wilderness

In southwestern New Mexico, the Gila Wilderness holds a special place in conservation history as the world's first designated wilderness area. Noted conservationist Aldo Leopold advocated for the government to protect the headwaters of the Gila River (which runs from New Mexico through Arizona), and in 1924, roads and other development were banned here for good. The decision preserved more than 560,000 acres (225,000 ha) of untamed country, where three forks of the river flow along the base of the Mogollon Mountains. On the fringe of the wilderness lies the Gila Cliff Dwellings National Monument, the ruins once occupied by Indigenous peoples nearly 1,000 years ago.

◉ Miles upon miles of trails run through the wilderness; for details, visit fs.usda.gov/r03/gila.

Hike the dunes in White Sands National Park

At the heart of the Tularosa Basin, White Sands National Park preserves the world's largest gypsum dunefield. As its name implies, the park's dunes consist of stark white sand. But there's life here, too: grasses, cacti, and the like that stabilize the sand, while jackrabbits, lizards, badgers, foxes, and other hardy creatures have made this harsh climate their home. The Dune Life Nature Trail is a great introduction to this unique ecosystem. You can hike the 1-mile (1.6-km) loop in about an hour by following markers planted in the sand; look closely, and you'll see how the desert springs to life.

◉ The Dune Life Nature Trail is located 2.5 miles (4 km) northwest of the visitor center; for more details, see nps.gov/whsa.

Go underground at Carlsbad Caverns National Park

Beneath the craggy Chihuahuan Desert in far southeastern New Mexico lies one of America's most surprising national parks—almost all of it subterranean. Carlsbad Caverns protects a labyrinthine underworld made up of more than 100 limestone caves dripping with stalactites. There are two ways to get down to the caverns: descend some 750 ft (230 m) by elevator or follow the 1.25-mile (2-km) Natural Entrance Trail to explore this underground fantasyland. From April to October, stay until dusk to watch half a million Brazilian free-tailed bats emerge out of the caves—it's arguably one of the greatest wildlife spectacles on earth.

◉ Timed entry tickets are required to enter the park, and reservations are recommended (nps.gov/cave).

Learn about Pancho Villa's cross-border raid of Columbus

On March 9, 1916, Mexican revolutionary Pancho Villa led an attack on the small border town of Columbus when his militia's supplies were running low. The subsequent battle left 16 Americans dead (and many more Mexicans) and ended in a crushing defeat for Villa, who was driven back to Mexico and drew the ire of President Woodrow Wilson. The U.S. Army entered Mexico but failed to apprehend Villa. Trace the story at the Columbus Depot Museum, which chronicles the raid and its aftermath, and at Pancho Villa State Park, where it all took place.

◉ For opening hours and other such information, visit columbusnewmexicohistoricalsociety.org for the museum, and emnrd.nm.gov for the park.

Explore Albuquerque

With more than 500,000 residents, Albuquerque is New Mexico's largest city. It was established by Spanish explorers in 1706, though it had been inhabited by Indigenous peoples long before that. For a slice of both cultures, see the 24,000 images carved by Indigenous peoples into the rock preserved at Petroglyph National Monument, or visit the preserved Spanish Old Town. Today's Albuquerque is influenced heavily by its past peoples, with wonderfully vibrant arts and food scenes, and almost endless festivals. The highlight? That's got to be October's International Balloon Fiesta, the world's largest hot-air balloon festival.

◉ For more information, check out visitalbuquerque.org. Details on the Petroglyph National Monument can be found at nps.gov/petr.

Get arty in Taos

There are art towns, and then there's Taos. With more than 80 art galleries, it's estimated the northern New Mexico town has more artists per capita than any other community in the U.S. The Taos Society of Artists fostered its reputation in the early 1900s, later attracting visionaries like Georgia O'Keeffe and sparking a creative legacy that thrives today. Explore it all at Taos's three standout art museums: the Harwood Museum of Art, emphasizing Hispanic and contemporary art; the Taos Art Museum, dedicated to the society itself; and the Millicent Rogers Museum, home to a stellar collection of Indigenous art.

For the Harwood Museum of Art, see harwoodmuseum.org; for Taos Art Museum, check out taosartmuseum.org; and for the Millicent Rogers Museum, see millicentrogers.com.

See the creativity of Tinkertown

Tinkertown is no town, but a roadside attraction unlike any other. It's the life's work of the late Ross Ward, who spent 40 years carving figurines and collecting all manner of memorabilia to create this sprawling museum. Inside you'll find a miniature circus, countless antique tools, horseshoes, wedding cake toppers, pencils, and even a sailboat that once circumnavigated the planet. The museum itself is made up of concrete and more than 50,000 glass bottles, arranged to give the structure a homemade feel. The result is a masterwork of folk art that's one of the strangest slices of Americana you can find. Ward's motto was, "I did all this while you were watching TV."

Tinkertown is located on 121 Sandia Crest Road, Sandia Park; the museum is open Apr–Oct Fri-Mon (tinkertown.com).

Visit historic pueblos

New Mexico is home to 19 historic pueblos, active Indigenous communities that are largely open to the public. Each pueblo is its own sovereign nation governed by a different tribe, and many are among the oldest continuously inhabited communities in the country. The pueblos are well known for their artisans, who practice time-tested techniques to make pottery, jewelry, baskets, and other items. Of note are the Acoma pueblo and the Zuni pueblo: the Acoma pueblo lies just west of Albuquerque and is the oldest of the 19, its people having lived here for more than 2,000 years; the Zuni pueblo, meanwhile, near the Arizona–New Mexico border, is known for its traditional dancers and ornate silver and turquoise jewelry.

Albuquerque's Indian Pueblo Cultural Center is a great place to start (indianpueblo.org).

Cool off at the Blue Hole of Santa Rosa

Struggling with the heat? You need Santa Rosa's Blue Hole. Found along Route 66 in eastern New Mexico, this sinkhole, akin to Mexico's cenotes, has been something of an oasis for centuries. All sorts have stopped to cool off in its waters (always a refreshing 62°F / 16.5°C): Indigenous peoples, cowboys, road-trippers, and now scuba divers. Because of its depth, and the fact a spring at the sinkhole's bottom recycles the water every six hours or so, visibility is great, allowing divers to spot fish or peer up at travelers jumping in to wash off the dust of the road. Divers can even get certified here. So go on, it's time to make a splash!

◉ There's a dive center, fishing pond, and snack bar on-site; the Blue Hole is open year-round (visitsantarosanm.com).

See the historic dwellings of Ancestral Puebloans

Ancestral Puebloans (also known as the Anasazi) lived in what is now New Mexico and its neighboring Four Corners states from 700 to 1300 C.E. For hundreds of years, they built communities in huge "Great Houses," some with up to 200 rooms, practiced agriculture, and saw rapid population growth as their culture thrived. Around 700 years ago, a major drought spurred their migration south and east to wetter climates—but some sites remain preserved today. The Aztec Ruins National Monument in Aztec and the Chaco Culture National Historical Park near Bloomfield are both excellent, featuring ruins and restored structures.

◉ See nps.gov/azre for Aztec Ruins National Monument and nps.gov/chcu for Chaco Culture National Historical Park.

Savor the state's green and red chile

Along with an official state bird, flower, and song, New Mexico has an official state question: "Red or green?" It's about chile, essentially a spicy sauce (not the pepper itself) that smothers burritos, enchiladas, and just about everything else. The main ingredient is of course peppers: picked early, they're green and fiery; left to ripen, they turn red, sweeter, and smoky. So, what will it be? Head to Hatch, the self-dubbed "chile capital of the world," where you'll find numerous stores selling chile-infused food products of all kinds. Can't decide? Ask for "Christmas," a mix of both.

◉ In far southwestern New Mexico, the Hatch Chile Festival (hatchchilefestival.com) takes place every Labor Day weekend.

Discover Santa Fe

The oldest continuously inhabited state capital in the U.S., Santa Fe was the first European settlement west of the Mississippi when it was established around a central plaza in 1610. Its Spanish settlers were overthrown by Indigenous peoples in 1680, but Spain reclaimed the city a decade later. Many buildings from that era still stand, including the San Miguel Mission, believed to be the nation's oldest church. All that history is fascinating, but today, it's creativity that defines Santa Fe. The city has a bunch of great galleries, regular art markets in its plaza, and can't-miss attractions like the Georgia O'Keeffe Museum, the Museum of International Folk Art, and the wildly imaginative Meow Wolf. Come for the history, stay for the art.

◉ Discover Santa Fe's website is a great resource for visitors (santafe.org).

When to visit

It may be busy (and hot), but there's little beating the state in June through September, when festivals are in full swing. If you'd rather stay cool, come in winter when hikes are more comfortable and skiing opportunities abound.

Visit Roswell's International UFO Museum and Research Center

As Mulder said on *The X-Files*, "the truth is out there." And maybe it's in Roswell. In June 1947, something crashed on a ranch outside the city. The U.S. Army announced the recovery of a "flying disc," launching a UFO craze that's never really faded. True believers insist it was a flying saucer; skeptics hold it was just a surveillance balloon launched from a nearby airfield. At the International UFO Museum and Research Center, the mystery lives on through exhibits about the incident, plus accounts of later UFO sightings, leaving you to decide for yourself what, exactly, came down that June.

◉ The International UFO Museum and Research Center is located at 114 N. Main Street. (roswellufomuseum.com).

The Empire State

The state of New York stands squarely in the shadow of America's biggest and most celebrated city. Say "New York" and you immediately think of the Statue of Liberty, skyscrapers, Central Park. But to overlook the rest of the state is to miss out on the Adirondacks' wild peaks, the vineyards of the Finger Lakes, and the rolling beauty of the Hudson Valley. It's called the Empire State for a reason: there's a whole kingdom waiting beyond the world's most famous city.

STATE MOTTO Ever Upward

STATE FLOWER Rose

STATE ANIMAL North American beaver

STATE BIRD Eastern bluebird

FUN FACT New York is unique in that it's the only state that borders both the vast Atlantic Ocean and the magnificent Great Lakes (specifically Lake Erie and Lake Ontario).

Discover the Adirondacks by kayak

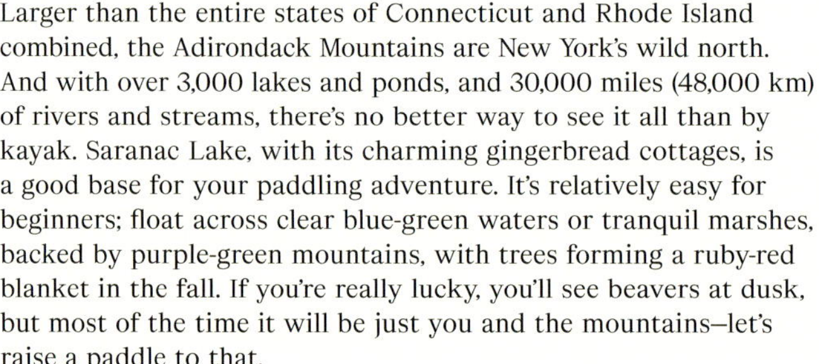

Larger than the entire states of Connecticut and Rhode Island combined, the Adirondack Mountains are New York's wild north. And with over 3,000 lakes and ponds, and 30,000 miles (48,000 km) of rivers and streams, there's no better way to see it all than by kayak. Saranac Lake, with its charming gingerbread cottages, is a good base for your paddling adventure. It's relatively easy for beginners; float across clear blue-green waters or tranquil marshes, backed by purple-green mountains, with trees forming a ruby-red blanket in the fall. If you're really lucky, you'll see beavers at dusk, but most of the time it will be just you and the mountains—let's raise a paddle to that.

◉ Check out the Adirondacks Welcome Center (visitadirondacks.com) or the Saranac Lake Area Visitor Center (saranaclake.com) for more details.

Hike through the Hudson Valley

Stretching some 315 miles (507 km), the mighty Hudson River slices through the Hudson Valley, a region of wooded hills, lakes, and historic towns. It's one of the most rewarding parts of the state to explore—something best done on a leisurely drive that follows the river north from New York City. Stop wherever the road tempts you: Washington Irving's Sunnyside for a touch of literary history, the lavish Vanderbilt Mansion to learn about the barons of the Gilded Age, or the homes of Franklin and Eleanor Roosevelt (both are buried at Springwood, in Hyde Park). All around are the lakes and tranquil peaks of the Hudson Highlands and the Catskills—park the car, pull on your hiking shoes, and get exploring.

◉ For an overview of the Hudson Valley highlights, check out travelhudsonvalley.com.

Dive into baseball in Cooperstown

There may be some disagreement as to whether it was really invented here, but one thing's for sure: baseball still finds its spiritual home in Upstate New York's Cooperstown. The gargantuan National Baseball Hall of Fame, which dominates the town's Main Street, is where the history of the beloved sport is chronicled in meticulous detail. Displays of rare memorabilia, from Babe Ruth's bat to Aaron Judge's 2017 home run jersey, bring key sporting moments to life. The Hall of Fame itself, expanded each year, is a shrine-like memorial to baseball's greatest players (over 350, so far). Disappointingly for fans, there's no evidence that writer James Fenimore Cooper, who lived here and whose father founded the town, ever played baseball.

◉ The National Baseball Hall of Fame is open 9am–5pm daily (9am–7pm late May–early Sep); see baseballhall.org.

When to visit

There's never a bad time to visit New York. Winters can be cold, sure, and summers hot, but the state shines year-round—picture blazing fall colors upstate, spring city blooms, and cozy escapes when the snow arrives.

Explore Fort Ticonderoga and Fort William Henry

For a glimpse into New York's wild frontier days, head north. Fort William Henry at the southern end of Lake George may be a replica, but it's a good one: here, you'll find timber-frame blockhouses and stockades, and uniformed reenactors firing muskets and cannons. Built in 1755, the original fort is best known for General Montcalm's siege in the French and Indian War two years later. Over at Fort Ticonderoga, at the south end of Lake Champlain, it's the Revolutionary War that's commemorated; it was captured from the British in 1775. Today, it's all incredibly peaceful—the only bang you'll hear will be the afternoon musket demonstration.

◉ Fort William Henry and Fort Ticonderoga are open May–Oct; see fwhmuseum.com and fortticonderoga.org for more.

NEW YORK CITY TOP 5

BROOKLYN BRIDGE
Cross the East River and enjoy stellar views of Manhattan.

THE STATUE OF LIBERTY
Take the ferry over to Lady Liberty, looming over New York Harbor since 1886.

CENTRAL PARK
Exploring this iconic green wedge by bike is the best way to take in its highlights.

THE MET
Stroll around one of the greatest collections of art in the world, spanning 5,000 years of history.

BAGELS WITH LOX
Enjoy the quintessential New York breakfast: a toasted bagel smeared with cream cheese and smoked salmon.

Take in the sights of New York City

The city so nice they named it twice, the Big Apple, or simply NYC. Almost everyone knows something about New York City, its icons appearing in countless movies and TV shows: the Empire State Building, Central Park, Brooklyn Bridge, the Statue of Liberty, and Grand Central, to name a few. But nothing beats seeing it all in person. Stroll the High Line, see the art of the Guggenheim, enjoy a world-class Broadway musical, and stop for cheesecake, hot dogs, and pastrami on rye in between. With so much to take in, you'll find there's little time for sleep–well, this is New York City, after all.

New York City's official tourism website is nyctourism.com, and there's a visitor center at 1 Times Square (onetimessquare.com).

Trace history at Seneca Falls

Elizabeth Cady Stanton spoke first. Women, she said, should "understand the height, the depth, the length, and the breadth of her own degradation." Thus opened the Seneca Falls Convention of 1848, the world's first to address women's rights. In the 1840s, American women had few rights. They couldn't inherit property, sign contracts, or vote. Suffrage wouldn't be granted for another 70 years, but the meeting got the ball rolling. Today the Women's Rights National Historical Park preserves the church where the convention took place and Stanton's home, while the nearby National Women's Hall of Fame honors hundreds of pioneering women.

◉ The Women's Rights National Historical Park Visitor Center is open 10am–4pm Mon–Thu & 9am–5pm Fri–Sun.

Tour the Finger Lakes

Covering much of central New York, the Finger Lakes comprise 11 narrow channels that range from 38-mile- (61-km-) long Seneca and Cayuga, to minnows like Canadice and Honeoye. The hilly scenery here is charmingly rustic, and much of the allure comes from surrounding attractions like the awe-inspiring Taughannock Falls (taller than Niagara), and Watkins Glen, a waterfall-studded gorge. Most enticing of all, though, are the wineries. Seneca Lake, Cayuga Lake, and Keuka Lake especially are lined with vineyards producing surprisingly good wines, with a fraction of the tasting costs—and crowds—of Napa.

◉ The Finger Lakes Welcome Center is in Geneva at 35 Lake Front Drive (9am–6pm Sun–Thu, 9am–8pm Fri, 8am–8pm Sat).

Discover history in Rochester

Long overshadowed by its bigger city rivals, Rochester's cultural offerings are nonetheless plentiful—especially when it comes to key figures in American history. This is the city where the Kodak film brand was born; today, you can see the oldest photography collection in the world at the George Eastman Museum, set up in the former home of the Kodak founder. The Susan B. Anthony Museum & House was the home of the pioneering suffragette; she's buried in the city's Mount Hope Cemetery. Also buried here is the celebrated abolitionist Frederick Douglass, honored with a monument and statue.

◉ The Rochester Visitor Information Center opens 9am–5pm Mon–Fri (visitrochester.com).

Learn about Indigenous history

New York state was once at the heart of the powerful Haudenosaunee (Iroquois) Confederacy, an alliance of six Indigenous peoples: the Mohawk, Oneida, Onondaga, Cayuga, Seneca, and Tuscarora. It fell after the arrival of European colonists and the Revolutionary War, when most of their land was ceded. The Ganondagan State Historic Site preserves the site of a 17th-century Seneca town, while on Onondaga Lake, the Skä•noñh Great Law of Peace Center tells the Haudenosaunee story, with a focus on the Onondaga Nation: here, you'll learn of their legends and customs—and that they still exist today, governing themselves as they always have done.

◉ For more on Ganondagan, see ganondagan.org; for the Skä•noñh Great Law of Peace Center, visit skanonhcenter.org.

Explore Letchworth State Park

With three huge waterfalls plunging through a gorge lined by forest and bald eagles soaring above, you'd be forgiven for thinking you're in the Rockies. But this is a sliver of upstate New York, on the western edge of the Finger Lakes. Some 80 miles (129 km) southeast from Niagara Falls, the far less busy Letchworth State Park is one of the natural wonders of the East. Here, the Genesee River flows through a steep canyon, cascading over Upper, Middle, and Lower Falls. The Middle Falls is especially fierce, but you'll get the best view of all three, lining up like steps, from the gorge bottom.

◉ Letchworth State Park is open year-round 6am–11pm daily (letchworthpark.com); the visitor centers are usually open 10am–5pm daily.

Get to know Buffalo

New York's second city is a long way from Manhattan. Some 385 miles (620 km) west on the shores of Lake Erie, Buffalo seems more like a Midwestern city than an East Coast one. You'll hear the difference as well as feel it: the local accent is more like in Chicago, and the winters are fierce, with snow blasting Buffalo each year. It has an intriguing roster of sights: the Theodore Roosevelt Inaugural National Historic Site commemorates the place where he took the oath of office in 1901, while the Buffalo AKG Art Museum is full of world-class art. And don't forget the food. It's true: "buffalo wings" aren't made of bison, and the spicy wings were really invented at Buffalo's Anchor Bar in 1964.

◉ For tourist information, head to 403 Main Street, Suite 630, or check out visitbuffaloniagara.com.

Gaze at Niagara Falls

Nothing beats your first view of Niagara Falls. Every second, huge amounts of water plummet over a jagged cliff edge in a mass of foam and mist. There are three distinct parts to Niagara Falls: the American and Bridal Veil falls on the American side, and the wider Horseshoe Falls on the Canadian side. On the American side you can view the action from an observation tower, but it's worth making time for a trip on the *Maid of the Mist*. This open double-decker boat floats right up to the falls, the water gushing like a tsunami about to swamp it, the crowd squealing with delight as the inevitable walls of spray soak the decks. Don't worry —a hooded rain poncho is included.

◉ Niagara Falls U.S.A. Official Visitor Center is at 10 Rainbow Boulevard (8:30am–5pm daily; niagarafallsusa.com). For the *Maid of the Mist*, see maidofthemist.com.

The Tar Heel State

North Carolina has it all. Stretching "from Manteo to Murphy"—a local way of referring to the whole state—it offers up beautiful beaches in the east; rugged mountains in the west; and rolling, forested Piedmont in between. There's a cosmopolitan vibe here, partly thanks to the state's big student population, with cool microbreweries, creative craft galleries, and boisterous college bars. Add to this coastal islands, colonial history, and high-octane adventures, and you'll want for nothing.

STATE MOTTO To Be, Rather Than To Seem

STATE FLOWER Flowering dogwood

STATE ANIMAL Eastern gray squirrel

STATE BIRD Cardinal

FUN FACT In 1799, a young boy, Conrad Reed, found a large golden nugget near his family's farm, which was then used as a doorstop in his home for many years. It was the first documented discovery of gold in the U.S.

Road trip on the Blue Ridge Parkway

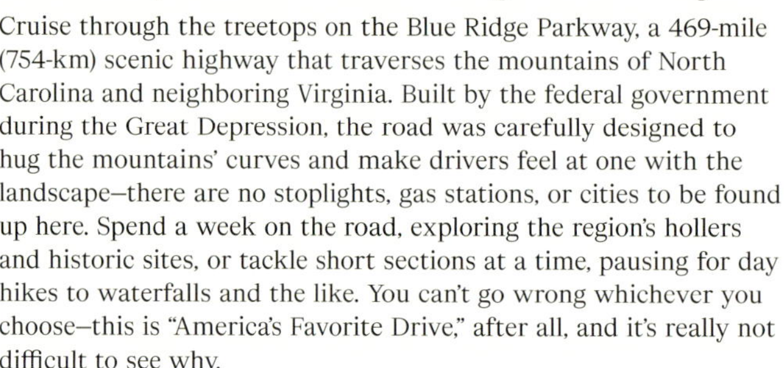

Cruise through the treetops on the Blue Ridge Parkway, a 469-mile (754-km) scenic highway that traverses the mountains of North Carolina and neighboring Virginia. Built by the federal government during the Great Depression, the road was carefully designed to hug the mountains' curves and make drivers feel at one with the landscape—there are no stoplights, gas stations, or cities to be found up here. Spend a week on the road, exploring the region's hollers and historic sites, or tackle short sections at a time, pausing for day hikes to waterfalls and the like. You can't go wrong whichever you choose—this is "America's Favorite Drive," after all, and it's really not difficult to see why.

◉ The Blue Ridge Parkway begins at Rockfish Gap, Virginia, and ends in Cherokee, North Carolina; there are 41 access points along the way.

Summit Mount Mitchell

At 6,684 ft (2,037 m), Mount Mitchell towers over the other peaks of the Appalachian Mountains, a central ridgeline that stretches from Alabama to Canada. There are two ways to reach the summit: on a windy, 4.5-mile (7-km) drive, or by taking the more strenuous out-and-back hike up the mountain's slopes. You'll gain 3,600 ft (1,097 m) of elevation on your trek through the dense evergreen forests—along with bragging rights for climbing the highest peak east of the Mississippi River. Whatever way you get there, at the top you're greeted with 360-degree views of the Blue Ridge Mountains, vibrant wildflower blooms, and a well-earned snack from the mountaintop café.

⦿ Drivers take N.C. Highway 128 from the Blue Ridge Parkway; hikers begin from the Black Mountain Campground in Burnsville.

Sip on a craft beer in Asheville

Asheville might be a small mountain town, but it's a true beer-lover's paradise, with more than 50 microbreweries to choose from. At Wicked Weed's Funkatorium, sample experimental sours in the East Coast's first sour-focused taproom. Next, enjoy a bluegrass jam at Green Man—known for English ales—before heading to Burial's Forestry Camp, which pours craft brews in an old Civilian Conservation Corps outfit. Asheville's breweries are infused with the town's artsy culture and Appalachian spirit, with many incorporating local and foraged ingredients, as well as spring water, into their recipes. Cheers to that, we say!

⦿ Plan a walking tour of the South Slope, a stretch of downtown with a high concentration of breweries.

Take in the regal setting of the Biltmore Estate

America may not have a royal family, but the business tycoons of the 1800s were the country's de facto nobility, with the estates to prove it. The Biltmore, built by the Vanderbilts (of shipping and railroad fame), is the United States' largest private home, rivaling many a royal estate. The more than 179,000-sq-ft (16,600-sq-m) mansion sits on 8,000 acres (3,237 ha) outside of Asheville, where you can admire the grand rooms, stately library, and indoor bowling alley on a tour. Don't miss the gardens, designed by renowned landscape architect Frederick Law Olmsted, and end your visit with a wine tasting fit for a king.

⦿ The Biltmore is especially popular at Christmas, when the halls are decked with more than 100 hand-decorated holiday trees; reserve tickets well in advance (biltmore.com).

HISTORIC OAKWOOD
Stroll through the oldest residential neighborhood in Raleigh, with 30 blocks of Victorian homes.

FRANKLIN STREET
Bar hop along Chapel Hill's iconic block of college bars.

AMERICAN TOBACCO CAMPUS
Explore this former tobacco factory in Durham, now packed with local shops, restaurants, and a baseball stadium.

UMSTEAD STATE PARK
Hike, bike, or horseback ride along 60 miles (96 km) of trails in this urban oasis.

CARRBORO
Stroll this creative haven, home to a natural foods co-op and popular music venue.

Explore The Research Triangle

Raleigh, Durham, and Chapel Hill—together known as The Research Triangle, or simply The Triangle—make up the state's main urban corridor. These once-small Southern cities grew into a hub of science and higher education, comprising three major universities and the country's largest research park. And each city in The Research Triangle has a distinct character. Raleigh, the state capital, is filled with oak-lined streets and a thriving business district, while hipsters flock to Durham's converted tobacco warehouses and booming food scene. Chapel Hill, a quaint college town, offers a slower pace. Visit all three, or stay a while in one.

The cities that make up The Triangle are no more than a 45-minute drive from one another, making this a great weekend destination.

Catch a college basketball game

The South may be known for college football, but in North Carolina, basketball reigns supreme. The mid-state is home to four rival universities—UNC, Duke, NC State, and Wake Forest—affectionately referred to as "Tobacco Road." The most heated rivalry exists between UNC and Duke, two championship schools that are only 8 miles (13 km) from each other, but a world apart in culture. If you're lucky enough to score tickets to a game, you'll never forget the atmosphere in the arena—the noise is deafening, emotions run high, and each match is a nailbiter as teams fight not just for the win, but for glory over their enemies.

◉ The UNC-Duke feud occurs twice a year, with games typically played in February and March. Get your tickets from the UNC website (goheels.com).

Discover Cherokee's history

The area of Cherokee is many things: the southern end of the Blue Ridge Parkway, gateway to Great Smoky Mountains National Park, and the capital of the Eastern Band of Cherokee Indians, a sovereign Indigenous nation. Above all, it honors Cherokee ancestral lands and traditions, and sites invite visitors to explore and learn about local culture. Come in summer to visit the Oconaluftee Indian Village, a living museum that showcases 18th-century Cherokee life through replica buildings, traditional dances, and artisan demonstrations; in the evening, book tickets to a performance of Unto These Hills, an outdoor drama about the Cherokees' struggle to remain on their land.

◉ Visiting outside of the summer season? Then head to the Museum of the Cherokee People, open year-round.

See lighthouses at the Outer Banks

The Outer Banks, a 120-mile (193-km) stretch of barrier islands off the mainland, lure vacationers with their white-sand beaches, seaside towns, and idyllic inns. But historically, this stretch was known as "the Graveyard of the Atlantic," with over 3,000 shipwrecks recorded. To make the coast safer, lighthouses were built, from the red-brick beacon at Currituck Beach to the black-and-white-striped Hatteras tower. Today, these icons of the region lure travelers, as do the islands' wild horses, stories of pirates' coves, and lost colony (where early English settlers mysteriously disappeared).

◉ The best way to see the islands is via the Outer Banks National Scenic Byway (nsbfoundation.com).

When to visit

None of North Carolina's four seasons are too harsh, making this the perfect year-round state for visitors. March is lively in The Research Triangle thanks to college basketball games, while foliage draws visitors to the mountains in late fall.

Take flight at Kitty Hawk

On the remote, sandy beaches of Kill Devil Hills near Kitty Hawk, brothers Wilbur and Orville Wright made history by conducting the first powered, controlled airplane flight. After experimenting with gliders for years, Orville gained liftoff on a December morning in 1903, piloting the *Wright Flyer* for 120 ft (36 m). Sure, he was only airborne for 12 seconds, but that was 12 seconds more than any plane had flown before, paving the way for air travel as we know it. Head to the Wright Brothers National Memorial to see replicas of the *Flyer* and walk the first flight's route. You'll soon see why it's a huge point of pride around here—so much so that "First in Flight" is the slogan on the state's license plates.

◉ The Wright Brothers National Memorial is open 9am–5pm daily (nps.gov/wrbr/index.htm).

The Peace Garden State

In the northern heart of the Great Plains, North Dakota is a land of vast skies, sweeping horizons, and a history rooted in the rhythms of the prairie. It was here that Theodore Roosevelt forged his conservation ideals, and where Indigenous nations continue to share their living cultures. Adventure runs through it all: bison thunder across the landscape, rodeo events bring the Old West back to life, and trails weave around the state's epic badlands. It really is a state worth protecting.

STATE MOTTO Liberty and Union, Now and Forever, One and Inseparable

STATE FLOWER Wild prairie rose

STATE ANIMAL Nokota horse

STATE BIRD Western meadowlark

FUN FACT North Dakota holds the world record for the most snow angels made in one place. In February 2007, 8,962 people gathered to flap their arms and legs simultaneously in the snow on State Capitol grounds.

Heed the call of the wild in Theodore Roosevelt National Park

Few parks capture wildness as viscerally as Theodore Roosevelt National Park. In these painted canyons, bison graze, and bands of wild horses move across the ridges. Scenic drives thread past prairie-dog towns, while trails dip into valleys striped with red and gold clay. It was here, in the 1880s, that Roosevelt found refuge after personal tragedy (the deaths of his wife and mother on the same day in 1884), crediting the Badlands with shaping his conservation ethos. Today, the park remains underrated, but stand on a bluff at dusk and you might feel as inspired as the 26th U.S. president was.

◉ Drive the park's scenic loops for epic Badlands views and the chance to spot wildlife from the safety of your car.

Get a taste of the Old West in Medora

Medora wears its cowboy heritage proudly. Wooden storefronts lean against the Badlands, saloons swing open to country tunes, and shops sell frontier gear fit for any would-be ranch hand. At the North Dakota Cowboy Hall of Fame, exhibits honor ranchers, rodeo legends, and Indigenous equine traditions. Come summer, the town really leans into its cowboy roots, with rodeo events and Western-themed dinners, like the Pitchfork Steak Fondue, where skewered steaks are flash-fried as the sun sets over the Badlands. Between horseback rides and wagon tours, you'll really feel like you've stepped into the Old West (spurs optional).

◉ Don't miss the nightly Medora Musical, an outdoor show blending Western music, comedy, and local history.

When to visit

Summer is the best time for hiking, biking, and road trips in North Dakota, with warm days and long, light-filled evenings across the plains. The fall months, meanwhile, bring golden foliage and harvest festivals.

Bike along the impressive Maah Daah Hey Trail

Stretching more than 140 miles (225 km) through the Badlands, the Maah Daah Hey Trail is a ribbon of dirt and dust that tests even the most seasoned bikers. Its name comes from the Mandan language, meaning "an area that has been or will be around for a long time"—a fitting nod to the landscape here, which has been carved over millions of years by wind and water. Out on the trail, riders climb buttes, skirt sandstone spires, and plunge into gullies where mule deer scatter. Overnight camps dot the route, too, so you can make an adventure of it—an adventure made all the better by views of North Dakota at its most wild.

◉ Arrive with a standard bike—this is a non-motorized trail. For more information on the trail, see mdhta.com.

Delve into the arts scene in Fargo

Fargo might just be one of America's most underrated art hubs. This is a city that has learned to thrive on the edges of the prairie, and its artistic expression reflects that frontier spirit. The result? A thriving, offbeat art scene where creativity runs wild. Stop by the Plains Art Museum to see regional and national works, from Indigenous textiles to bold contemporary pieces. Outside, enjoy bright murals splashed onto brick walls, transforming streets and alleyways into open-air galleries. Nearby, Brewhalla gathers artisans under one roof: bakers, potters, brewers, and makers all bring Fargo's craft culture to life.

◉ Organized by the Folkways cultural organization, the Night Bazaar festival in Sep is a great place to enjoy Fargo's arts scene (folkways.org/nightbazaar).

Discover Scandinavian heritage in Minot

Minot's Scandinavian Heritage Park celebrates the immigrants who helped shape the northern plains. In the late 19th and early 20th century, settlers from Norway, Sweden, Denmark, Finland, and Iceland arrived in waves, drawn by the promise of farmland and freedom. Their legacy lives on here, in monuments that honor each nation's culture and traditions: stroll past a full-scale replica of a Norwegian stave church, its dark timber walls etched with dragons, or a soaring Swedish Dala horse painted in bright colors. There's no better place to get into all things Scandinavia—well, in the U.S. anyway.

◉ The park's outdoor exhibits are open year-round, with tours available in the summer (scandinavianheritage.org).

Unpack North Dakota's story in Bismarck

Prepare to time-travel through millions of years at Bismarck's North Dakota Heritage Center and State Museum. One moment you're face-to-face with dinosaur skeletons and the fossilized remains of ancient sea creatures; the next, you're wandering through galleries focused on Indigenous culture, frontier life, and modern statehood. Artifacts on display range from chipped spear points to a moon rock, tracing our journey from the plains to deep space. It's a crash course in geology and history–and a reminder of just how far the people of North Dakota have come.

◉ The museum is open 8am–5pm daily (from 10am Sat & Sun); for more information, see statemuseum.nd.gov.

Visit Fort Berthold Reservation

North Dakota has a rich Indigenous heritage, and one of the best places to experience it is at the Fort Berthold Reservation. Located in the state's northern plains, it's home to the Mandan, Hidatsa, and Arikara Nation, together known as MHA Nation, or the Three Affiliated Tribes. The nations' history is complex, marked by alliances, epidemics, and displacement, yet their presence endures powerfully here. At the reservation, you'll find exhibits tracing agricultural and artistic traditions; outside, there are opportunities to enjoy the landscape, like the sweeping views across Lake Sakakawea seen from Crow Flies High Butte.

◉ Visit Great Plains Indian Trading on Main Street in New Town, part of the reservation. You can browse beadwork, pottery, and other handmade pieces by local artists.

Get behind the wheel on the Enchanted Highway

The Enchanted Highway, a 32-mile (50-km) ribbon of road between Gladstone and Regent, turns a drive through the prairie into a journey of pure imagination. Giant metal sculptures rise from the fields: geese with wings outstretched, a grasshopper taller than a house, and a family of tin figurines waving from the roadside. Local artist Gary Greff created these whimsical sculptures to breathe new life into his hometown of Regent–and you might say it worked. Today the drive feels almost surreal, as though the prairie has leapt straight from the pages of a storybook.

◉ For a map to guide you to each sculpture, see enchantedhighwaynd.com.

See Jamestown's giant buffalo

Welcome to Jamestown, aka Buffalo City. Why the nickname? That's due to the city's most famous resident: a 26-ft- (8-m-) tall concrete bison that's towered over the plains since 1959. This massive sculpture isn't just a roadside curiosity; it's a nod to the animal that once thundered across North America in the millions. To learn more, head to the North American Bison Discovery Center, where exhibits trace the species' near extinction and remarkable comeback–the center has two bison herds, too. After, wander the clapboard streets of the adjoining Frontier Village, which offers a glimpse into 19th-century life, bison and all.

◉ Time your visit for summer, when guided tours of the bison pastures bring the story to life (buffalomuseum.com).

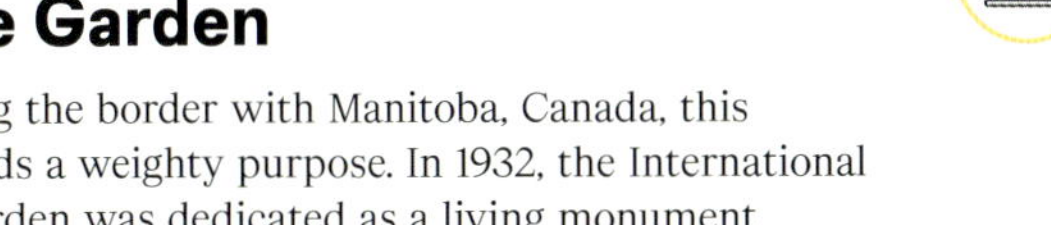

Stroll around the International Peace Garden

Straddling the border with Manitoba, Canada, this space holds a weighty purpose. In 1932, the International Peace Garden was dedicated as a living monument to friendship between Canada and the United States. Strolling among the lush floral displays–which change color with the seasons, from summer blooms to fall reds–it's the perfect place to contemplate its founding ethos. Along the way, you'll find a chapel for quiet reflection and a 9/11 memorial, made from steel beams from the World Trade Center. You can even cross onto the Canadian side–just don't forget your passport.

◉ If you can, time your visit for summer's peak blooms; for more details, visit peacegarden.com.

The Buckeye State

The Midwest buckle of the "rust belt," Ohio has been at the center of American history for much of its existence. It was the birthplace of seven U.S. presidents, where American businessman John D. Rockefeller established his empire, and the Wright Brothers gave life to the aviation industry. Today, its trio of "C" towns (Cleveland, Columbus, and Cincinnati) embody the modern state of Ohio—a place of industry, creativity, and reinvention. Think you know Ohio? Think again.

STATE MOTTO With God, All Things Are Possible

STATE FLOWER Red carnation

STATE ANIMAL White-tailed deer

STATE BIRD Cardinal

FUN FACT Designed by architect John Eisenmann in 1901, the state flag of Ohio, the Ohio Burgee, is the only state flag that isn't a rectangle. Instead, it's a triangular, swallowtail shape.

Explore Cuyahoga Valley National Park

A green oasis on the edge of suburban Cleveland, Ohio's only national park makes for a handy escape. At the heart of this preserve, the Cuyahoga River Valley now shelters enveloping forests and serene old millponds. It's hard to imagine this was once a busy, industrial waterway, given the profound peace of its rolling hills. Of the park's 125 miles (201 km) of hiking trails, the boardwalk through Beaver Marsh makes for a lovely stroll, surrounded by reeds, bright green water lilies, and the stumps of old poplars, cottonwoods, and willows. Alternatively, walk the tranquil 19.5-mile (31-km) Towpath Trail, which shadows a now abandoned stretch of the old Ohio and Erie Canal.

◉ The national park is open 24 hours every day, though some areas close at dusk. You'll need your own car to make the most of the park.

Ferry to the Lake Erie Islands

Here's a head-scratcher: Ohio is miles from the ocean and yet has 312 miles (502 km) of coastline. How? It's thanks to Lake Erie, one of the mighty Great Lakes. While the mainland shore keeps a low profile, the Lake Erie Islands are the ultimate summer escape. Think fishing, swimming, partying, and lazing in the sun. Want a taste? Hop on the ferry over to tranquil Kelleys Island and zip around on a bike or golf cart. It's peppered with 100-year-old buildings, a treasure trove of archeological sites (including ancient Indigenous pictographs), and even a sandy beach at the island state park. It may not be the Caribbean, but come July and August, the water is perfectly warm for a refreshing dip.

◉ You'll find ferry times at shoresandislands.com. It's worth visiting one of the welcome centers at 125 E. Water Street, Sandusky, and 770 S.E. Catawba Road, Port Clinton.

See ancient mounds at Hopewell

Picture this: a series of smooth rises in a meadow of neatly mown grass; on a summer morning, steam rises from the ground, enveloping the mounds in swaths of mist. There are no trails, and nothing else here. This is the Hopewell Culture National Historical Park, the site of six massive earthwork sites, created by people from an advanced Indigenous civilization some 2,000 years ago. Who built them, and why? No one knows for sure, but they were undoubtedly spiritual places: some of the mounds appear to be burial chambers, with remnants of necklaces, bone carvings, pottery, and even stone smoking pipes.

◉ The historical park is open daily, dawn–dusk, but the Mound City Group Visitor Center is open 9am–4pm (16062 SR-104, Chillicothe; nps.gov/hocu).

Rock around the city of Cleveland

Ohio's port city is most famous for the Rock & Roll Hall of Fame, an I. M. Pei–designed glass labyrinth that pays homage to America's greatest music legends, and takes a full day to explore. But it's not all that the Great Lakes city has to offer. Since the 1990s, the city has been revitalized, with spaces like the Public Square and the Great Lakes Science Center transforming the riverfront. Dive into culture at University Circle's superb art, natural history, and vintage car museums. Then, for some festive fun, visit the home from *A Christmas Story*, which has been restored to appear exactly as it did in the 1983 holiday flick.

◉ Cleveland's visitor center is at 334 Euclid Avenue (10am–6pm Tue–Sat; thisiscleveland.com). Download RTA's free CLE mobile app for info on city buses, or visit rideRTA.com.

Wander the streets of Columbus, the state capital

Ohio's capital often gets short shrift from visitors, though there's a lot to love about this city, including top-notch nightlife and a welcoming LGBTQ+ scene. Reminders of the city's 19th-century German roots thrive in the brick-paved lanes of German Village, where local icon Schmidt's has been knocking out sausages, schnitzel, and strudel since 1886. All roads lead to the Ohio Statehouse, one of the few state capitols not to have a dome. Completed in 1861, it's presided over by a giant statue of President William McKinley, who was assassinated by an anarchist from Ohio in 1901.

You'll find more about the city at its visitor centers, which can be found at 277 W. Nationwide Boulevard and 188 Easton Town Center (experiencecolumbus.com).

Journey through aviation history in Dayton

Dayton, the Birthplace of Aviation. Here, Wilbur and Orville Wright grew up, started their first business, and invented their first successful aircraft, the *Wright Flyer*. Today a string of sights charts their story: the cycle shop (now a museum), where their understanding of bicycles led to flying machines; Huffman Prairie, where they tested their aircraft; and Hawthorn Hill, Orville's elegant mansion, completed using the financial rewards of his invention (Wilbur died young). Finally, the National Museum of the Air Force, nearby, charts aviation's evolution. Just think: from horse-drawn carriages to the dawn of supersonic flight, Orville Wright saw it all.

◉ Most sites are free to enter, though an admission fee is required for Hawthorn Hill.

Learn about the trailblazing Buffalo Soldier, Charles Young

Charles Young was one of the most remarkable Americans of the 19th century. Born into slavery in 1864, Young moved to Ohio and went on to serve with the segregated Ninth Cavalry in Nebraska and Utah as one of the Buffalo Soldiers (Black soldiers serving on the frontier). He became the first African American colonel in 1916, though was forced to retire a year later. Today, visitors can learn about his life and legacy at the Charles Young Buffalo Soldiers National Monument in Wilberforce, Ohio, at the home he purchased in 1907 and where he lived until 1922.

◉ Charles Young Buffalo Soldiers National Monument is open 9am–4:30pm Wed–Sun; Nov–Feb it's open 9am–4pm Fri–Sun (nps.gov/chyo).

When to visit

June through September is the best time to enjoy the lakeshore and Erie Islands, but you'll avoid the crowds by seeing the rest of the state in shoulder seasons. Spring is great for maple syrup and tulip festivals, while fall erupts with color.

Visit Cincinnati

Cincinnati is Ohio's cultural center. It grew from a small village and fort built in 1788, strategically placed on the Ohio River. Once an industrial hub, it's largely shaken off this past to reinvent itself as a modern cosmopolitan center–one with a huge mix of highlights. In Cincy, you can enjoy everything from games played by the NFL's Cincinnati Bengals to drinks at the world's second-largest Oktoberfest. Over at the National Underground Railroad Freedom Center, the city's role in helping African Americans escape slavery is commemorated, while the Cincinnati Art Museum and Taft Museum showcase masterpieces by the likes of Rembrandt, Picasso, and Turner. With so much to see and do, Cincinnati will keep you on your toes.

◉ For Cincinnati tourist information, see visitcincy.com. To catch a Cincinnati Bengals game, check bengals.com.

The Sooner State

Swathed in windswept plains and grassy prairies, Oklahoma was forged by a pioneering spirit, by settlers who staked their land claims "sooner" than they should, and by cowboys driving cattle west. Long a crossroads for Indigenous nations, pioneers, and oil barons, it's a place where cowboy heritage mingles with rich Indigenous traditions, and where revitalized districts in Tulsa and Oklahoma City speak to Black heritage and musical legacies.

STATE MOTTO Work Conquers All

STATE FLOWER Oklahoma rose

STATE ANIMAL American bison

STATE BIRD Scissor-tailed flycatcher

FUN FACT Oklahoma has more artificial lakes than any other U.S. state. Over 200 have been built with various purposes, including water supply, flood control, and recreation.

Get active in Beavers Bend State Park

Tucked amid the pine-clad hills of southeastern Oklahoma, Beavers Bend State Park is a vast expanse of forest and water that lures lovers of adventure. Here, miles of trails weave between dense thickets, leading to waterfalls—such as the romantically named Moonshiner Falls—rocky overlooks, and picnic spots. Broken Bow Lake, with its gin-clear waters and craggy shores, is a haven for kayaking, boating, and stand-up paddleboarding, while the Mountain Fork River is perfect for canoeing and trout fishing. Whatever you do, be sure to look up: by day, bald eagles soar on the thermals; by night, the sky transforms into a star-spangled canvas.

◉ Hit the Friends Trail Loop; among the most popular routes in the park, it offers sweeping views of the Mountain Fork River on its short but relatively steep 1.5-mile (2.5-km) stretch.

Visit the Five Civilized Tribes Museum in Muskogee

Set in a 19th-century Indian Agency building overlooking Honor Heights Park, this museum today is dedicated to the heritage of the Cherokee, Chickasaw, Choctaw, Muscogee (Creek), and Seminole nations. Its exhibits trace their histories from ancestral homelands through forced removal and relocation to Indian Territory, highlighting their resilience, cultural survival, and achievements. Rotating exhibitions showcase traditional crafts and contemporary Indigenous art, while interpretive displays unpack the complex histories of treaties and sovereignty.

◉ Join a guided tour (fivetribes.org) to gain deeper insight into the stories behind the artifacts and the ongoing cultural contributions of these nations.

Learn about Cherokee culture in Tahlequah

In the leafy foothills of northeastern Oklahoma, Tahlequah is the capital of the Cherokee Nation and a center of its cultural life. The Cherokee National History Museum—housed in a historic 1860s building that was once the capitol building—traces the nation's story from pre-contact times through removal and revitalization, with poignant temporary exhibits showcasing ongoing fights for justice. Cherokee culture thrives in Tahlequah today, whether in its language immersion schools, the artisan studios keeping traditional crafts alive, or the identity-focused murals brightening downtown walls.

◉ Download a self-guided walking map from Visit Cherokee Nation (visitcherokeenation.com) to explore museums, murals, and heritage sites on foot.

Discover "Black Wall Street" in Tulsa

The Greenwood Rising Black Wall Street History Center tells the story of one of America's most prosperous Black communities—and the devastating 1921 Tulsa Race Massacre that sought to obliterate it. Through immersive exhibits, oral histories, and powerful art, the museum honors this once buzzing artery of Black enterprise, creativity, and pride, and celebrates the community that was rebuilt from the ashes. Today, the museum is surrounded by the revitalized Greenwood District, where murals, memorials, and locally owned businesses keep the modern spirit of "Black Wall Street" alive.

◉ Join a guided walking tour of the Greenwood District with the Greenwood Cultural Center (greenwoodculturalcenter.org) to see key landmarks, from the Black Wall Street Memorial to the John Hope Franklin Reconciliation Park.

Embrace cowboy culture in Oklahoma City

Many of the major cattle trails established in the late 1800s ran through Oklahoma, and working cowboys who drove vast herds along routes like the Chisholm Trail—which cut through modern-day Oklahoma City (OKC)—helped shape the cattle industry and the culture of the west. At OKC's National Cowboy and Western Heritage Museum, cowboy exhibits and re-created frontier streets trace this most American of stories, while Stockyards City Historic District adds a living layer to the tale: century-old cattle pens still host live auctions and shops are full of the likes of leather boots, saddles, and Stetsons.

⦿ Visit during the Oklahoma State Fair in Sep to experience rodeos, livestock shows, and live country music.

Drive Oklahoma's portion of Route 66

Few states can claim a connection to Route 66 quite like Oklahoma. It was Tulsa entrepreneur Cyrus Avery who first had the idea of stitching together America's roadways into one continuous highway, and the route is today officially known as the Will Rogers Memorial Highway, after the beloved Oklahoma cowboy. In the 400 miles (644 km) that run through Oklahoma—the longest drivable stretch of the "Mother Road" in any state—all the route's classic elements combine: neon signs, roadside diners, retro gas stations, and quirky Americana, like POPS 66 Soda Ranch and the gloriously kitschy Blue Whale of Catoosa.

⦿ POPS 66 Soda Ranch is found at 660 W. Highway 66, Arcadia (pops66.com).

Learn about Oklahoma's Indigenous history at the First Americans Museum

In the 19th century, Oklahoma was designated "Indian Territory," and many Indigenous peoples were forcibly removed from their homelands and relocated here, most infamously on the Trail of Tears, a series of brutal removals that claimed thousands of lives. Through storytelling galleries, art exhibitions, and hands-on workshops, the striking First American Museum in Oklahoma City explores how the state's communities endured, adapted, and continue to thrive here today.

⦿ Check the museum's busy events calendar for storytelling, music sessions, and artist residencies (famok.org).

Discover musical heritage in Tulsa

Tulsa's musical roots run deep, from folk hero Woody Guthrie, who grew up in nearby Okemah, to Bob Dylan, who chose the city for his vast archives. At the Bob Dylan Center, rare recordings and handwritten lyrics trace the evolution of the American icon, while the neighboring Woody Guthrie Center celebrates the Dust Bowl balladeer's life and legacy, and the ways he inspired a young Dylan. For more on the city's storied music scene, visit the Church Studio, founded by Leon Russell in 1972 and known as the birthplace of the "Tulsa Sound," a soulful fusion of rock, country, and blues.

⦿ Catch live performances in bars and venues in the Blue Dome district and throughout Tulsa's Arts District.

Explore Chickasaw Country

Stretching across south-central Oklahoma, Chickasaw Country is rich in Indigenous heritage and living culture. The immersive Chickasaw Cultural Center in Sulphur explores the eponymous nation's history and traditions through interactive exhibits, reconstructed villages, and storytelling—try to catch one of the Stomp Dance Demonstrations, brought alive by community members in traditional dress. Nearby, the Chickasaw National Capitol Museum shares the story of Chickasaw Nation governance in a striking building. Natural beauty weaves through this region, too, from the sparkling waters of the Lake of the Arbuckles to the trails of the Chickasaw National Recreation Area.

◉ Time your visit to coincide with Native American Heritage Day at the Chickasaw Cultural Center (chickasawcultural center.com), when the air fills with drumbeats and dance.

When to visit

It's worth braving the summer heat for events such as the Woody Guthrie Folk Festival in July, an homage to the folk icon in his hometown of Okemah, and the Red Earth Festival in June, a celebration of Indigenous culture in OKC.

Hike in the Wichita Mountains Wildlife Refuge

Sprawling across more than 59,000 acres (24,000 ha) of rugged granite peaks, sweeping prairie, and oak forest, this refuge protects some of Oklahoma's wildest landscapes. Trails wind through dramatic scenery, with the chance to spot grazing bison or colonies of prairie dogs standing sentry beside their burrows. Hike to the summit of Mount Scott—a steep but paved 3-mile (5-km) trail, or explore the peaceful shores of Lake Jed Johnson, named for a durable Oklahoma politician.

◉ To overnight, camp in Wichita Mountains Wildlife Refuge (you'll need to reserve ahead), or pitch up in the backcountry.

The Beaver State

Oregon has always been something of a beacon. In the 1800s, thousands followed in the footsteps of explorers Lewis and Clark, enduring the hazards of the Oregon Trail to carve out a new life on the edge of the American frontier. Trappers were drawn by the abundance of beavers, the trade in their furs fueling Oregon's early economy—and earning the state its nickname. Today, the call comes from thick forests ripe for hiking, a wildlife-rich coast, and quirky cities.

STATE MOTTO She Flies With Her Own Wings

STATE FLOWER Oregon grape

STATE ANIMAL American beaver

STATE BIRD Western meadowlark

FUN FACT Oregon is home to the world's only Bigfoot trap. Found in the Siskiyou National Forest, it consists of a large wooden box held together by metal bands. So far, it's still waiting for its first catch.

Explore the stunning Oregon Coast

Charming villages, historic landmarks, and natural beauty combine on the Oregon Coast to create a place that feels almost too good to be true. *Goonies* fans will relish a nostalgic self-guided tour of Astoria, where most of the movie was filmed. History buffs will enjoy visiting the skeletal remains of a century-old shipwreck at Fort Stevens. And everyone will wonder at the wildlife: barking sea lions greet visitors in Newport's historic bayfront, elk roam Ecola State Park, and boat tours from tiny Depoe Bay promise sightings of majestic gray whales.

◉ For more on the Oregon Coast, see visittheoregoncoast.com. Depoe Bay whale-watching tours are run by Tradewinds Charters (tradewindscharters.com) and Dockside Charters (docksidedepoebay.com).

Hit the historic Oregon Trail

Stretching west for over 2,000 miles (3,200 km), from Independence, Missouri, to Oregon's Willamette Valley, the Oregon Trail carried settlers, ranchers, and anyone else who was in search of a better life. Replica wagon trains and historic reenactments put flesh on the trail's bones at Baker City's National Historic Oregon Trail Interpretive Center; you can even see some of the 200-year-old trail ruts on a nearby hike. In Pendleton, meanwhile, the Tamástslikt Cultural Institute gives the Indigenous perspective, detailing the devastating effects this expansion had on the Cayuse, Umatilla, and Walla Walla peoples–and how, despite this, they have continued to keep their traditions alive.

◉ You can check opening hours and admission fees at blm.gov/learn/interpretive-centers and tamastslikt.org.

When to visit

If you're looking to delve into Oregon's great outdoors, plan your visit between April and September. Crater Lake is at its best from late July through September. Planning a ski trip instead? Expect deep, crisp snow in February.

Visit Crater Lake National Park

Crater Lake may be Oregon's sole national park, but it has a big claim to fame–here lies the deepest lake in the U.S., formed over 7,000 years ago by the eruption of mighty Mount Mazama. Subsequent eruptions created Wizard Island, which pokes its head above the lake's surface and is the destination for boat tours departing from the end of Cleetwood Cove Trail. Some of the finest views of the park can be had from up high, along the Rim Drive. Here, dozens of overlooks provide stop-offs to admire the lake and its fringing coniferous forest. Time your drive with sunset, when the waters glow a beautiful shade of purple and gold.

◉ Crater Lake National Park's west and south entrances are open year-round; the north entrance is typically closed from November through May/June. See nps.gov/crla for more.

POWELL'S CITY OF BOOKS
Browse the shelves of the largest independent bookstore in the country.

WASHINGTON PARK
Walk among fragrant roses and sip tea in a Japanese teahouse in this urban park.

FOOD CART PODS
Dip into Portland's delicious street-food culture at food carts throughout the city.

PORTLAND ART MUSEUM
Admire the works of a wide range of artists at the city's largest art museum.

PITTOCK MANSION
This mansion-turned-museum displays Portland's early history, and enjoys incredible views from its hilltop location.

Explore Portland

Portland exhibits the best of the Pacific Northwest. Within the city limits, you'll find a forest, a dormant volcano, and, come summer, an explosion of roses in its many parks. On Portland's outskirts lie rainforests laden with waterfalls, snowy mountain peaks, and the Pacific Ocean. Once a logging town, today's Portland is progressive, socially active, and has just the right dose of quirky—here, the niche is celebrated. Come to Portland for big-city amenities; stay for the slowed-down, casual pace of life, where local is preferred, biking is best, and the food and the beer are unbeatable.

◉ Portland (travelportland.com) is a fine city to cycle around. Rent bikes from Cycle Portland (portlandbicycletours.com) and Everybody's Bike Rentals and Tours (pdxbikerentals.com).

Go waterfall-spotting along the Columbia River Gorge

The largest Natural Scenic Area in the U.S., Columbia River Gorge runs for 80 miles (130 km) along the Columbia River between Washington and Oregon. On the eastern side, windsurfers flock to Hood River. On the western side, it's all about the dazzling waterfalls: Multnomah Falls, plunging 620 ft (190 m) between rock walls carved by Ice Age floods; Loutrell Falls; Horsetail Falls; and, deep in the forest, the mystical, moss-shrouded Hole-in-the-Wall Falls.

◉ Timed entry permits are required to visit Multnomah Falls late May–early Oct, and can be booked at recreation.gov.

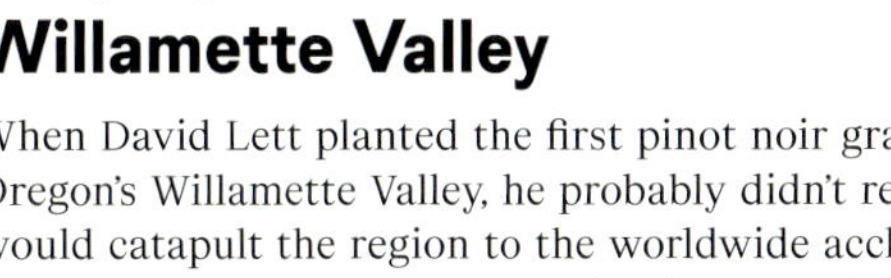

Stop by wineries in the Willamette Valley

When David Lett planted the first pinot noir grapes in Oregon's Willamette Valley, he probably didn't realize it would catapult the region to the worldwide acclaim it enjoys today. There are 700 wineries spread across the valley, primarily on the west side of the Willamette River, where the ideal temperatures, humidity, and mineral-rich soil make it perfect for pinot. The valley's location along the I-5 corridor means Willamette is an unusually accessible wine region; base yourself at McMinnville, starting point for a variety of wine tours.

◉ NW Wine Shuttle (nwwineshuttle.com) and A Great Oregon Wine Tour (agreatoregonwinetour.com) offer wine tours.

Visit Bend for ale and activities

In a state renowned for beer and outdoor recreation, it's a bold claim to say you have the best of both. But Bend just might. In spring, hike the Oregon Badlands Wilderness, when superblooms fill the high desert with color. In summer, get your adrenaline fix with some white-water rafting. Fall has perfect conditions for climbing Smith Rock, while winter offers excellent runs on quality powder at Mount Bachelor Ski Resort. Your reward for all this activity? A crisp craft beer. Enjoy a pint at Deschutes Brewery, the oldest brewery in Bend, before discovering more of the town's best brews along the Bend Ale Trail.

◉ Plot your beer-filled route through Bend using the Bend Ale Trail Map (bendaletrail.com/#map).

Admire the otherworldly landscape at John Day Fossil Beds National Monument

The fascinating John Day Fossil Beds National Monument tells the story of the region nearly 45 million years ago. You can view fossils here at the Thomas Condon Paleontology Center, in Sheep Rock, and directly on the trail at Clarno, while the colorfully striated hummocks at Painted Hills illustrate the state's changing climate over millions of years—and remain a picturesque dreamscape for photographers today.

◉ There's no cell service or internet access at the John Day Fossil Beds (nps.gov/joda), except for at the visitor center.

Spot wild horses in the remote Steens Mountain Wilderness

Tucked away in the high desert of southeast Oregon, Steens Mountain Wilderness is little known and seldom explored. Follow the Steens Mountain Loop Road to overlooks at glacier-carved Kiger Gorge and the East Rim, where you can peer down into the Alvord Desert. Bighorn sheep and coyotes roam these parts, but the most coveted sightings are of the wild Kiger mustangs—book a riding tour with Steens Mountain Guest Ranch for a guaranteed glimpse of these beautiful horses.

◉ The best time to visit Steens Mountain (blm.gov/visit/steens-mountain-wilderness) is spring or early fall. See steensmountainguestranch.com for details of riding tours.

Ski or board Mount Hood

Winter is magical in Mount Hood. Oregon's tallest mountain gets snow year-round, but it starts settling like a heavy blanket come fall. When the lifts open for the season, skiers and snowboarders flock to Mount Hood Meadows, with its variety of trails and Nordic skiing tracks, while most locals gravitate toward Mount Hood Ski Bowl, a haven for those craving solitude—and night skiing. Cinephiles, meanwhile, seek out the Timberline Lodge Ski Area, whose eponymous lodge (or its facade, at least) stood in for The Overlook Hotel in the classic horror movie *The Shining*. Curious visitors can stay here, too, and without the threat of a haunting.

◉ The ski season begins end of November or early December, depending on snowfall. See skihood.com, skibowl.com, and timberlinelodge.com for more on the ski areas.

The Keystone State

Just as a keystone is essential to a building's structure, Pennsylvania played a pivotal role in the founding of the United States. American history was made in the lofty halls of Philadelphia and the steel mills of Pittsburgh. But the state isn't stuck in the past. Its modern cities have a lively, creative energy, while small towns, dark skies, and hiking and biking trails provide plentiful opportunities to get outdoors and make the most of the present.

STATE MOTTO Virtue, Liberty, and Independence

STATE FLOWER Mountain laurel

STATE ANIMAL White-tailed deer

STATE BIRD Ruffed grouse

FUN FACT The "Pretzel Belt" is an area in Pennsylvania where a large concentration of pretzel and snack producers are located. This has led to the state's unofficial title as the "Snack Food Capital of the World."

Gawk at the night sky at Cherry Springs State Park

Surrounded by the vast tracts of Susquehannock State Forest, remote Cherry Springs State Park has some of the darkest nights in all of the Northeast. With clear skies, a lack of cloud cover, a decent pair of binoculars, and a dose of good luck, you might see Venus, the Milky Way, the Space Station, and various asteroids and meteor showers streaking across the sky. There are three areas designated for stargazing, with the Overnight Astronomy Observation Field the darkest of the three.

◉ The state website (pa.gov) has information on Cherry Springs State Park and its stargazing opportunities. Reservations are required, and fees are charged.

See Pittsburgh

With roots in the steelmaking industry, Pittsburgh has evolved into a vibrant city. Located in western Pennsylvania, at the confluence of three rivers (there's an impressive 446 bridges here), Pittsburgh is known for its outdoor spaces, including green parks, a vast network of trails, and mountain-biking areas within city limits. The city also has a wealth of cultural institutions, including the Carnegie Museums of Pittsburgh, Phipps Conservatory and Botanical Gardens, and the Andy Warhol Museum, dedicated to the pop artist who had the good fortune to grow up here.

◉ Visit Pittsburgh's website (visitpittsburgh.com) features a comprehensive visitor's guide. Many of the major attractions are in the East End neighborhood.

Explore Fallingwater

In 1936, when Frank Lloyd Wright designed a private residence for the Kaufmann family, owners of the namesake department store in nearby Pittsburgh, he sought to not only embrace nature but also to defy it. He succeeded on both accounts, and this incredible work of architecture, now known as Fallingwater, is arguably the most famous house in America. The finished product is marked by cantilevered outdoor terraces and locally quarried sandstone, and a roaring stream that runs right through the house—Wright wanted the Kaufmanns "not simply to look at the waterfalls, but to live with them." The house and grounds have been open to the public as a museum since the 1960s.

◉ Fallingwater (fallingwater.org) is located 70 miles (113 km) south of Pittsburgh in the town of Mill Run, Pennsylvania.

Venture out on the Great Allegheny Passage

Running from Pittsburgh to Cumberland, Maryland, the Great Allegheny Passage is one of the longest and best hiking and biking trails in the Northeast. The transformation of a former railroad route into a 150-mile (241-km) trail took more than 25 years, but the result, unveiled in 2013, was well worth the wait. Beginning in downtown Pittsburgh, the trail weaves through the Allegheny Mountains, diving into tunnels, crossing high-wire bridges, and serving up plenty of idyllic scenery and fascinating history along the way.

◉ If you only have a day, the trail's first stretch from Point State Park in Pittsburgh is easily accessible. The section around Ohiopyle State Park is considered the most scenic.

PHILADELPHIA

TOP 5

INDEPENDENCE NATIONAL HISTORICAL PARK
Visit Independence Hall, site of the signing of the Declaration of Independence in 1776.

MAGIC GARDENS
A once-vacant lot, Magic Gardens has been transformed by artist Isaiah Zagar.

PHILLY CHEESESTEAK SANDWICH
This iconic roll is stuffed with sliced beef and melted cheese.

BARNES FOUNDATION
See the largest collection of works by Pierre-Auguste Renoir and Paul Cézanne in the world.

ITALIAN MARKET
South 9th Street hosts the nation's oldest continuously operating outdoor market.

Dive into Philadelphia

Founded in 1682, Philadelphia, nicknamed the "City of Brotherly Love," is Pennsylvania's largest city and a true original. One of America's most historic cities, Philly served as the nation's first capital before Washington, D.C., and was home to such luminaries as Founding Father Benjamin Franklin and Betsy Ross, who made the original American flag. It's also known for its art, with more outdoor sculptures and murals than any other city in the country. From bustling Center City to Fairmount Park, there's a lot to explore here. You'll want to visit for at least a long weekend, but a full week is better.

Visit Philadelphia (visitphilly.com) has a wealth of information on the city and its attractions.

Visit the Kennett Underground Railroad Center

South of Philadelphia, Kennett Square was a hub of the abolitionist movement in the 1800s. It was also a major way station on the Underground Railroad, a network of safe houses used by escaped enslaved people–among them future abolitionist Harriet Tubman–on their way north. Covering a number of key sights within the region, the Kennett Underground Railroad Center runs regular bus tours of the town's documented safe houses and the historic homes of local abolitionists, offering an insightful lens into the town's proud history.

◉ Bus tours are offered monthly from spring to fall; purchase tickets in advance via the center's website (kennettundergroundrr.org).

When to visit

If you're here for the night sky, plan your trip around the moon cycles; ideally avoid a full moon, so the stars are that bit brighter. New Year's is spectacular in Philadelphia, when the Mummers Parade takes over the city on New Year's Day.

Hike to Bushkill Falls

Nicknamed "The Niagara Falls of Pennsylvania," this series of eight waterfalls cascades through the woodlands of Lehman Township in the Pocono Mountains. Fed by a creek that ultimately joins the Delaware River, the tallest waterfall here drops over 100 ft (30 m) into the foaming waters, stained brown by natural tannins from oak, hemlock, and white pine. A short walk leads to a viewing platform, or you can follow a longer, 2-mile (3.2-km) trail that provides lovely views of all eight falls. This is also a great spot for bird-watching: keep an eye out for woodpeckers, blue jays, and even bald eagles as you follow the falls.

◉ As Bushkill Falls is privately owned, an admission fee is required to hike the trails here. The park's website (visitbushkillfalls.com) has detailed visitor information.

See a movie at Shankweiler's, the oldest drive-in in the U.S.

When Shankweiler's Drive-In Theatre opened in Orefield in April 1934, the screen was described as "a bedsheet hung between two poles." Founder Wilson Shankweiler had drawn inspiration from the world's first drive-in theater in New Jersey, launching a budget version to draw customers to his restaurant and lodging. Nearly a century later, Shankweiler's has outlasted its lone predecessor, as well as thousands of other drive-ins. Catch a movie here when you can—of 4,000 drive-ins in the U.S. that were operating in the 1960s, only about 300 were still going as of 2025.

◉ Shankweiler's Drive-In Theatre (shankweilers.com) is open year-round. It also hosts events like food festivals and artisan markets.

Try a plate of scrapple

In Pennsylvania Dutch Country, in the state's southeast, scrapple is a breakfast delicacy made of pork, cornmeal, and spices that's simmered in a pan until it browns. The result is a bit polarizing: many Pennsylvanians consider scrapple a nostalgic treat and a morning mainstay alongside eggs and bacon, but others find the inclusion of a wide range of pork by-products ("everything but the oink," some say) to be unsettling. Regardless, scrapple is one of Pennsylvania's most iconic foods. It's available at restaurants all over the state, from Pennsylvania Dutch Country to Philadelphia and beyond.

◉ In Philadelphia, the Dutch Eating Place (dutcheatingplace.com) at Reading Terminal Market is known for its scrapple. Dienner's Country Restaurant (dienners.com) is a good bet in Pennsylvania Dutch Country.

Stop in at the Colonial Complex in York

Get into Pennsylvania's fascinating colonial history at the Colonial Complex in York. Landmark buildings await at every turn. In 1777–78, the Second Continental Congress met in the rebuilt Colonial Courthouse to debate, revise, and ultimately adopt the Articles of Confederation, which guided the U.S. government until it was superseded by the Constitution in 1789. Step back in time to 1741 at the Golden Plough Tavern, which showcases daily colonial life, and visit the General Horatio Gates House, where the namesake General stayed for a winter during the Revolutionary War.

◉ The Colonial Complex (yorkhistorycenter.org) is open Apr–Nov, Tue–Sat; all visitors must schedule their hour-long tours in advance.

Delve into Civil War history at Gettysburg

The Civil War's bloodiest battle unfolded at Gettysburg in July 1863, a three-day fight that marked the Confederate Army's most audacious foray into the North. Its 50,000 casualties were not only the highest of the Civil War, but the most of any military operation in U.S. history. The Union prevailed, and historians consider it a major milestone in the North's ultimate victory. Today, Gettysburg National Military Park memorializes the event with a museum detailing the battle, a cemetery where 6,000 soldiers were laid to rest, and the house where President Abraham Lincoln completed his renowned speech, the Gettysburg Address.

⦿ Gettysburg National Military Park (nps.gov/gett) is open daily year-round. The battlefield itself is open dawn–dusk; the museum and visitor center have more limited hours.

Tour the candy factory at Hershey's Chocolate World

Chocoholics, this one's for you! It's possible to build an entire vacation around the attractions in Hershey, home of the United States' most famous chocolate brand. Start with the free tour of the chocolate factory, a ride that takes visitors on the journey from cocoa beans to chocolate bars—with a free sample at the end. Then hop on a trolley tour of the town itself and learn the story of its namesake and the company's founder, Milton Hershey. Serious chocoholics will want to create their own bar, and browse the world's largest Hershey's store. A whole chocolate-filled world awaits.

⦿ Hershey's Chocolate World (chocolateworld.com) is open daily year-round except major holidays. Next door is Hersheypark (hersheypark.com), an amusement park.

The Ocean State

Rhode Island may be the smallest state in the Union, but its impact has been disproportionately large. It enacted the first law against slavery in North America in 1652; in 1793, the nation's first water-powered textile mill initiated America's Industrial Revolution; and in 1881, Newport hosted the nation's first tennis championship. This history provides much of its allure, but there's plenty more going on in Rhode Island, if you know where to look.

STATE MOTTO Hope

STATE FLOWER Blue violet

STATE FISH Striped bass

STATE BIRD Rhode Island red

FUN FACT Rhode Island once had the longest state name in the country: the State of Rhode Island and Providence Plantations. In 2020, however, Rhode Islanders voted to drop "and Providence Plantations."

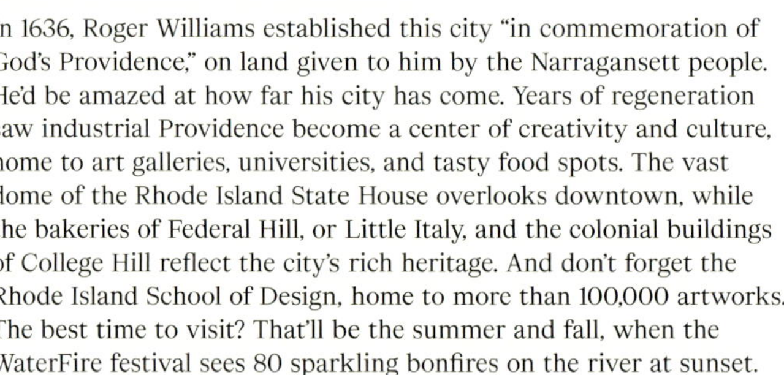

Discover Providence

In 1636, Roger Williams established this city "in commemoration of God's Providence," on land given to him by the Narragansett people. He'd be amazed at how far his city has come. Years of regeneration saw industrial Providence become a center of creativity and culture, home to art galleries, universities, and tasty food spots. The vast dome of the Rhode Island State House overlooks downtown, while the bakeries of Federal Hill, or Little Italy, and the colonial buildings of College Hill reflect the city's rich heritage. And don't forget the Rhode Island School of Design, home to more than 100,000 artworks. The best time to visit? That'll be the summer and fall, when the WaterFire festival sees 80 sparkling bonfires on the river at sunset.

◉ For visitor information, see goprovidence.com. The WaterFire festival bonfires take place on select weekends May–Nov (waterfire.org).

Visit oyster bars and clam shacks

There's something about South County's clam shacks. They just look, feel, and smell different. Here, the salty ocean air mixes with the rich fragrance of clams, lobster, and bubbling pots of chowder. Top-tier dishes are served up on humble paper plates and enjoyed by seafood fans on battered picnic tables—and the best places are family owned. The Ocean State's very first clam shack, Aunt Carrie's, was opened in 1920 by Carrie and Ulysses Cooper; it's still knocking out Carrie's invention, crispy clam cakes in corn batter, alongside other seafood "Shore Dinners." Wherever you go, battered and fried belly clams are an irresistible order, as is a bowl of Rhode Island chowder (with a clear broth), clam fritters, or maybe even a lobster roll or two.

◉ To learn more about Rhode Island's iconic seafood, check out visitrhodeisland.com/food-drink.

When to visit

Summer is busy in Rhode Island, drawing crowds to events like the WaterFire festival and Newport Jazz Festival. Consider visiting in fall or winter, when things cool off and the state's cozy inns and seaside towns reveal a quieter charm.

Tour one of Newport's Gilded Age mansions

Gold, porcelain, truckloads of Renaissance art, and enough marble to sink a battleship—nothing epitomizes the stratospheric wealth of the Gilded Age like the mansions of Newport. With its gorgeous seaside location, fleets of posh yachts, and pink sunsets, the likes of the Astors and Vanderbilts summered here in the late 19th century, building opulent "cottages" to escape their humid New York townhouses. Some of the best are open for public viewing, including the relentlessly over-the-top Breakers, built for Cornelius Vanderbilt and practically covered in gold plating.

◉ The Preservation Society of Newport County maintains the bulk of houses and gardens open for public viewing (newportmansions.org).

Explore the varied beaches of South County

When it comes to beaches, Rhode Island has a little bit of everything. And the best of these can be found in Washington County, better known locally as South County. For family fun, head out to South Kingstown Town Beach, which is backed by rolling dunes, or the huge swaths of sand along Scarborough State Beach; if you're looking to catch a wave, look no farther than East Matunuck State Beach, where there are swells big enough to surf; and if you like your beaches wild, head for East Beach in the Ninigret State Conservation Area, with sugar-fine sand and zero concessions.

◉ Most beaches in South County are officially open from Memorial Day (late May) to Labor Day (early Sep), 9am–6pm daily; for more details, see southcountyri.com.

Try local culinary specialties

Rhode Island has a sweet tooth. Just take a look at the official state drink: coffee milk, a riff on a chocolate milk made with coffee syrup instead (preferably crafted by local supplier Autocrat). The version served in White Electric in Providence is a classic. Rival for the state drink title is Del's Frozen Lemonade: a mix of crushed ice, lemon juice, and sugar originally created in the 1940s on a humble food cart and now sold statewide. Prefer savory? The "New York System wiener" is the Rhode Island version of a Coney Island hot dog, topped with celery salt, yellow mustard, chopped onions, and a spicy meat sauce. Olneyville NY System has been selling them in Providence since 1946–with a "special secret sauce" you'll just have to try in person.

◉ For more on Rhode Island's culinary offerings, check out visitrhodeisland.com/food-drink.

Learn about the American Industrial Revolution

The quiet towns of the Blackstone River Valley once hummed with industry. And it was all thanks to Samuel Slater. The Brit emigrated to the U.S. in the late 1790s, and using technology (illegally) imported from his native land, he built the first successful water-powered cotton-spinning mill in North America, initiating the American Industrial Revolution. Slater Mill Historic Site preserves the mill, while the Museum of Work & Culture nearby chronicles those who arrived to work the valley's factories. Folks back home considered him a traitor, but he never looked back: "I gave out the psalm and they have been singing to the tune ever since."

◉ The Blackstone River Valley Visitor Center is at 175 Main Street in Pawtucket (open 10am–4pm daily; tourblackstone.com); Old Slater Mill at 67 Roosevelt Avenue is open seasonally (nps.gov/blrv).

Visit Block Island and hike along the Mohegan Bluffs

Martha's Vineyard without the stars? Block Island, 12 miles (19 km) off Rhode Island's southern coast, may lack the ex-presidents and celebrities of its larger, better known Massachusetts neighbors, but it retains the same laid-back charm and arguably better beaches. It's home to a year-round population of under 1,500, swelling to 20 times that in summer. They come for endless ocean vistas, the quaint Victorian architecture, 28 miles (45 km) of hiking trails, and especially the beaches. To get to the beach on Block Island, the joke goes, simply walk in any direction—there are 17 miles (27 km) of sand all around it.

◉ The island visitor's center is located on Water Street opposite the ferry dock in Old Harbor (blockislandinfo.com).

The Palmetto State

Though it shares a name with its northern neighbor, South Carolina is a world all its own. Much of the South's culture took root here, blending African traditions brought by enslaved people with European customs. The Lowcountry's colonial cities, beaches, and cuisine draw many visitors, while Upstate offers another perspective from the foothills of the Blue Ridge Mountains. From Gullah dishes to palmetto groves, there's plenty that makes South Carolina unique.

STATE MOTTO While I Breathe, I Hope

STATE FLOWER Yellow jessamine

STATE ANIMAL White-tailed deer

STATE BIRD Carolina wren

FUN FACT A colony of approximately 3,500 free-ranging rhesus monkeys resides on South Carolina's Morgan Island, also fittingly known as Monkey Island. The only other U.S. rhesus monkey colony is in Florida.

Explore Canoe Congaree National Park

Some of the country's tallest and most majestic trees can be found, surprisingly, in the middle of a river—the Congaree River, to be exact. And bordering the river is Congaree National Park, an active floodplain that has helped keep this forest of towering trees alive for centuries. Stroll along the park's wooden boardwalks, which wind their way around the trees, some of which reach the lofty heights of a 17-story building. Or find solace in the swamp-like surroundings by paddling through the floodplain and up Cedar Creek in a canoe, with just the ancient cypress and looming pines for company.

◉ The park is open year-round, 24 hours a day. For a magical experience, visit in late spring, when fireflies illuminate the canopy in a natural light show (nps.gov/cong).

Shag dance in Myrtle Beach

Myrtle Beach is known as the "shag" capital of the world—a reference to shag dancing, a variation of swing that originated in the resort city's African American community and caught on along the beaches of the Carolinas. In the 1940s, local teens and spring-breakers flocked to seaside clubs to try the smooth shuffle, perfect for maneuvering through sand with a drink in hand. A laid-back version of R&B, aptly titled "beach music," was created in step. Today, shag dancers are a tight-knit community of young and old, who welcome newcomers wanting to embrace the dance's carefree vibes. Put on your boogie shoes and join them.

◉ Take part in the dancing fun over at Fat Harold's Beach Club, a popular spot for shag dancing (fatharolds.com).

Picnic at Falls Park in Greenville

In the middle of Greenville's Main Street—a leafy block lined with boutiques, breweries, and cafés—an urban oasis appears. Falls Park was built where the Reedy River flows through historic downtown, seamlessly integrating the Upstate's natural beauty into the heart of its largest city. The park's centerpiece is a 28-ft (8.5-m) waterfall, surrounded by a curved suspension bridge that winds you through the treetops above the river. Pack a picnic basket with charcuterie from nearby Curean or macarons from Old Europe Coffee, and stroll along wooded trails in search of wildlife. A trip to Falls Park always feels like an escape—even if it's just a lunch break.

◉ Falls Park is located at 601 S. Main Street. For more information on Curean, see cureangvl.com; for Old Europe Coffee, head to oldeuropedesserts.com.

Hike the hills of the Upstate area

A paradise for outdoor enthusiasts, South Carolina's Upstate area teems with peaks, picturesque lakes, and challenging hiking trails in the state parks, like Table Rock State Park. Its scenic trail of the same name is challenging but rewarding; it climbs 2,000 ft (600 m) to a crag with panoramic mountain views. On your way up, you'll trek through a dappled forest, balance across wooden footbridges, and pause at overlooks with sneak peeks of what awaits. After drinking in the view, consider linking to the Foothills Trail, a 76-mile (122-km) through-hike that resembles a mini Appalachian Trail. Either way, the descent will feel like a welcome respite—your heart full and breath steadying, you'll savor every step down the mountain.

◉ The challenging 7-mile (11-km) round-trip Table Rock Trail starts at the Nature Center in the middle of the park.

Stroll through Middleton Place

When colonizers arrived in South Carolina, they took full advantage of the state's balmy summers to create expansive crop plantations, with the wealthiest growing gardens for pleasure. Take picturesque Middleton Place, the oldest landscaped garden in America and an homage to the grand palace gardens of Europe. Wander along its grassy terraces to the banks of the Ashley River, and admire the native dogwood and magnolia trees, which provide a lush backdrop for imported plants, including some of the very first camellias to be introduced to the Americas. Want to grow a piece of Middleton magic in your own backyard? The garden shop sells seedlings from its centuries-old nurseries, plus gorgeous pots made by the resident potter.

◉ The Middleton Place gardens are open 9am–5pm daily, with guided tours taking place every hour.

When to visit

Spring in South Carolina brings gardens in bloom, parties in Myrtle Beach, and Charleston's Spoleto Festival. Fall is beautiful in the Upstate area, as leaves change color and locals head out for Fall for Greenville, a multiday food and music festival.

Nosh on a Lowcountry boil

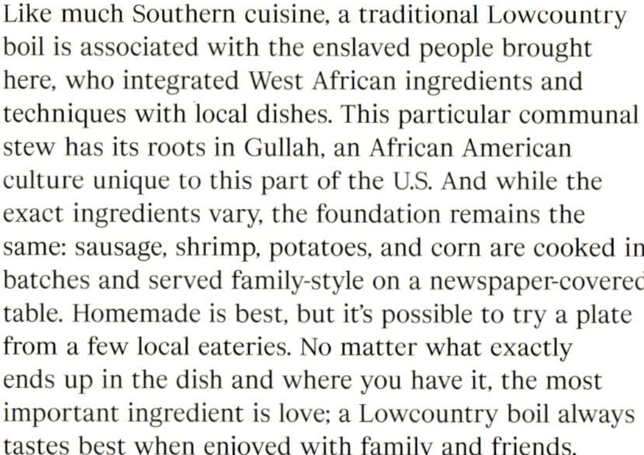

Like much Southern cuisine, a traditional Lowcountry boil is associated with the enslaved people brought here, who integrated West African ingredients and techniques with local dishes. This particular communal stew has its roots in Gullah, an African American culture unique to this part of the U.S. And while the exact ingredients vary, the foundation remains the same: sausage, shrimp, potatoes, and corn are cooked in batches and served family-style on a newspaper-covered table. Homemade is best, but it's possible to try a plate from a few local eateries. No matter what exactly ends up in the dish and where you have it, the most important ingredient is love; a Lowcountry boil always tastes best when enjoyed with family and friends.

◉ Try a ready-to-eat or ready-to-cook "boil bucket" from Lowcountry Boil Company (lowcountryboilcompany.com).

Tee off on Hilton Head Island

South Carolina is one of the best golf destinations in the world, thanks to its beautiful scenery, four seasons of mild weather, and enduring popularity among PGA pros. With more than 350 courses to choose from, the real challenge is deciding where to play, especially on Hilton Head Island, which is home to a whopping 28 of them. For a scenic course, head to Sea Pines Resort, where not one but three beautifully designed, championship-level courses are framed by ocean views, blue lagoons, and the greenest greens around. After the final putt, cart yourself to a nearby beach for a well-earned rest, sweet tea vodka in hand.

◉ Watch the world's top golfers take on the Harbour Town Golf Links course during the RBC Heritage tournament, held each April at Sea Pines (seapines.com/golf/rbc-heritage).

Charleston Top 5

FORT SUMTER
Ferry to the island citadel where Confederate shots were first fired.

CHARLESTON CITY MARKET
Shop traditional handmade goods in an open-air market that's nearly 200 years old.

RAINBOW ROW
Stroll along this picture-perfect block of colorful 18th-century houses.

KING STREET
Check out the high-end boutiques here, housed in buildings from the 1700s.

FOLLY BEACH
Head out for a day of catching waves and sun at one of Charleston's beaches.

Travel back in time in Charleston

Old-world charm and an appreciation for life's finer things await in genteel Charleston. Founded in 1670, the city has seen a lot: a siege during the American Revolution, the first shots of the Civil War, and the harrowing realities of the slave trade. Though downtown might look unchanged from the outside, behind the doors of former carriage houses and old Victorians, you'll find some of the best shopping and dining in the South (think fresh-caught seafood and heirloom vegetables). Add Southern style and storybook aesthetics—colorful homes, cobblestone streets, and romantic waterfronts—and there really is nowhere else like it.

For more information, visit the Charleston Visitor Center at 375 Meeting Street (open 8:30am–5pm daily; charlestoncvb.com).

Mount Rushmore State

Some call South Dakota the land of Great Faces and Great Places, so here are a few of each: the giant sculpted visages of Mount Rushmore and Crazy Horse, looming large in the Black Hills; the bison-dotted Badlands National Park and town of Deadwood, wild and storied. You'll want to visit them all (and much, much more) to experience the best of this truly epic state, celebrated for its pioneer spirit, Indigenous heritage, and rich natural wonders.

STATE MOTTO Under God, the People Rule

STATE FLOWER American pasqueflower

STATE ANIMAL Coyote

STATE BIRD Ring-necked pheasant

FUN FACT The world's fastest recorded drop in temperature took place in Spearfish, South Dakota, in 1943. The temperature fell from 54°F (12°C) to -4°F (-20°C) in just 27 minutes.

Marvel at Badlands National Park

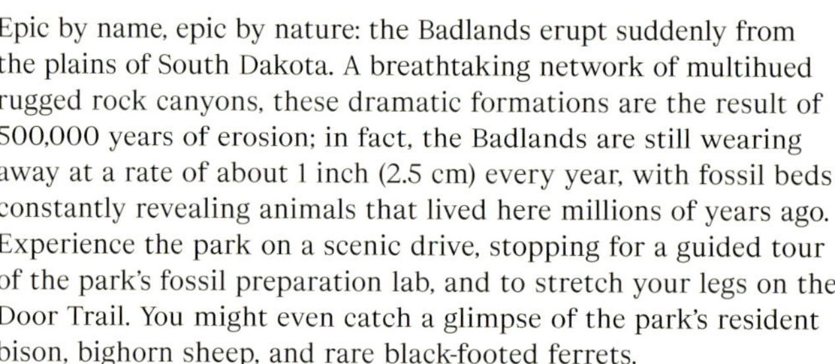

Epic by name, epic by nature: the Badlands erupt suddenly from the plains of South Dakota. A breathtaking network of multihued rugged rock canyons, these dramatic formations are the result of 500,000 years of erosion; in fact, the Badlands are still wearing away at a rate of about 1 inch (2.5 cm) every year, with fossil beds constantly revealing animals that lived here millions of years ago. Experience the park on a scenic drive, stopping for a guided tour of the park's fossil preparation lab, and to stretch your legs on the Door Trail. You might even catch a glimpse of the park's resident bison, bighorn sheep, and rare black-footed ferrets.

◉ Badlands National Park (nps.gov/badl) has two distinct areas: the North Unit is accessible via I-90, and the entrance to the less-developed South Unit is about 50 miles (80 km) south.

Gawk at the Corn Palace

With rolling farmland and strong agricultural roots, it follows that South Dakota would have a palace celebrating the humble corn kernel. Built in 1921, today's structure, in Mitchell, was predated by two smaller palaces, all celebrating the state's rich harvest of wheat, soybeans, and, of course, corn. Each year, the palace is decorated with crop art—murals made from corn and other grains—which are then removed after the annual Corn Festival, in August, to make way for the next works of corn art. Inside, the venue houses displays on its history and the decorating process, and hosts events. Looking for a corny souvenir? Check out the gift shop across the street.

◉ The Corn Palace is open daily, with extended hours in the summer, and is free to visit (cornpalace.com).

Cruise along the Native American Scenic Byway

Journey across the sovereign lands of four Lakota Sioux peoples on the Native American Scenic Byway. Framed by wide rivers, rugged badlands, and huge plains, the 350-mile (563-km) byway is a history book of Indigenous culture. Stop to honor the legacies of political and spiritual Lakota leader Sitting Bull, and Sacagawea, the guide for the Lewis and Clark Expedition. You can also trace a path along the Lewis and Clark Legacy Trail near Lake Oahe. The drive culminates in the 50-ft (15-m) *Dignity of Earth and Sky* statue; a symbol of Lakota resilience, it's something of a must-see.

◉ The byway runs from Chamberlain to the North Dakota border, where it continues to the town of Cannon Ball.

Visit the Minuteman Missile National Historic Site

For most of the 1960s, until the early 1990s, 150 underground silos were ready to launch nuclear missiles from the western plains of South Dakota. Two of these facilities have been preserved for posterity as the Minuteman Missile National Historic Site, a reminder of the Cold War's tense and seemingly silent story. Start at the visitor center before taking a guided tour of the launch control facility, to see the cramped consoles where operators were ready to push the button on command. Afterward, you'll want to peer into the silo itself to see an unarmed Minuteman Missile from ground level through a thick, protective viewing window.

◉ Minuteman Missile National Historic Site (nps.gov/mimi) encompasses three sites spread across 15 miles (24 km), near I-90. Tours require advance reservations.

Gaze up at Mount Rushmore National Memorial

Always wanted to meet a president? You'll come face-to-face with four at Mount Rushmore, one of the country's most awe-inspiring landmarks. Carved into a granite mountainside in the Black Hills, the 60-ft (18-m) faces of George Washington, Thomas Jefferson, Theodore Roosevelt, and Abraham Lincoln gaze out protectively over the valley below. Sculptor Gutzon Borglum carved these colossal effigies from 1927 until his death in 1941, with his son finishing the project a year later. Visit the Sculptor's Studio to learn about the daring carving process and understand the vision that transformed the mountain into an icon.

◉ Mount Rushmore National Memorial (nps.gov/moru) is open daily year-round, and it's free to visit. The faces are illuminated at night, and a film is screened in the memorial's outdoor amphitheater during the summer months.

Spot bison at Custer State Park

Undoubtedly, the stars of the show at Custer State Park are the 1,300 bison, who roam freely across the open range, stopping to graze or for a much needed lie down. Take in the scene by driving the park's loop road or, better yet, come for the annual Buffalo Roundup and Arts Festival in late September. Pick a spot to set up a folding chair, and watch as cowboys and cowgirls drive the animals into corrals for branding and testing. This practice ensures the health of the herd (culled bison are later sold at auction). Beyond this tradition, the park's mountains and lakes offer a stunning backdrop for year-round hiking, fishing, and camping.

◉ Custer State Park (gfp.sd.gov) is located in the Black Hills region east of the town of Custer. A resort in the park boundaries (custerresorts.com) offers overnight lodging.

See the Crazy Horse Memorial

Sure, the presidential faces of Mount Rushmore are big, but the nearby Crazy Horse Memorial is much, much bigger. The 87-ft (27-m) head of Lakota Sioux warrior Crazy Horse, and his 263-ft (80-m) outstretched arm, have been under construction in the Black Hills since 1948. Intended to rival Mount Rushmore, and be the world's largest mountain sculpture, the monument may depict Crazy Horse, but it's intended to honor all Indigenous peoples. The work was the vision of the late sculptor Korczak Ziolkowski, who was employed by Lakota chiefs after seeing his work on Mount Rushmore. Ziolkowski's children and grandchildren continue to chip away at the sculpture; carving will likely continue for decades.

◉ The Crazy Horse Memorial (crazyhorsememorial.org) is open daily year-round. There is a fee to view the memorial.

When to visit

Summers are the best time to visit South Dakota, with events like country music festival Rock the Country in July and the Sturgis Motorcycle Rally in early August. Spring and fall are mild, but the weather can be unpredictable.

Shoot the breeze in Deadwood

Want a taste of the Wild West? Look no further than Deadwood. After a gold strike in 1874, the town quickly became one of the most infamous towns in the West, attracting a who's who of prospectors, gunfighters, and cattle rustlers. By 1877, at least 12,000 people had settled in the boomtown, making the most of its bars and saloons. Lawlessness and murders were not uncommon here. Thankfully, things are much more civilized these days; the town is a National Historic District, with daily reenactments of the shooting of famed frontiersman Wild Bill Hickok at Saloon No. 10. You can even visit the grave of sharpshooter Calamity Jane. Base yourself in the historic town and make the most of its proximity to other Black Hills sights.

◉ The website for the Deadwood Chamber of Commerce (deadwood.com) lists information on the town's attractions.

The Volunteer State

Tennessee is known for many things: natural beauty, delicious food, and really nice people (it's called the "Volunteer State," after all). But more than anything, it's famous for its music. Its humble towns launched some of the world's biggest artists, from Dolly Parton to B.B. King, and four genres, including country and Memphis blues, have their origins here. Today, cities like Nashville and Memphis keep the spirit alive, all with a helping of Southern hospitality, of course.

STATE MOTTO Agriculture and Commerce

STATE FLOWER Iris

STATE ANIMAL Tennessee walking horse

STATE BIRD Northern mockingbird

FUN FACT Women's right to vote in the U.S. is thanks to the state of Tennessee. It was the 36th state to ratify the 19th Amendment, in 1920, making women's suffrage legal in the U.S.

Raft the Ocoee River

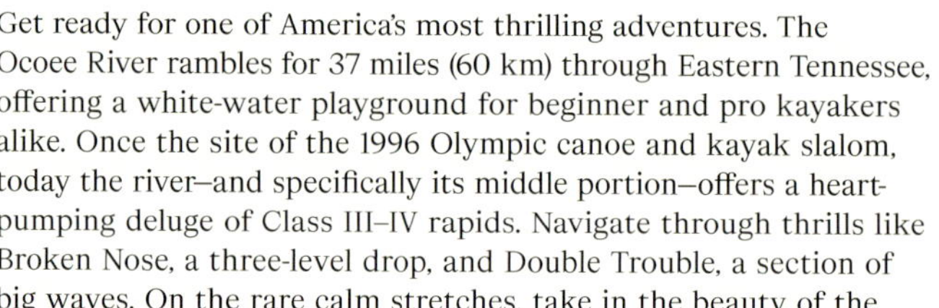

Get ready for one of America's most thrilling adventures. The Ocoee River rambles for 37 miles (60 km) through Eastern Tennessee, offering a white-water playground for beginner and pro kayakers alike. Once the site of the 1996 Olympic canoe and kayak slalom, today the river—and specifically its middle portion—offers a heart-pumping deluge of Class III–IV rapids. Navigate through thrills like Broken Nose, a three-level drop, and Double Trouble, a section of big waves. On the rare calm stretches, take in the beauty of the Cherokee National Forest, scanning the shore for a black bear or bobcat before being plunged into your next adventure.

◉ Unless you're an experienced paddler, it's best to go on a guided trip, which are organized on both the Upper and Middle Ocoee. Find a list of outfitters at theocoeeriver.com.

See Rock City for yourself

Drive through the southeast of the state and you'll spot dozens of barn roofs painted with the phrase "See Rock City." In the 1930s, some 900 barns bore this advertisement for the fairyland-inspired rock garden atop Chattanooga's Lookout Mountain. Built by Tennessee entrepreneur Garnet Carter and his wife Frieda, Rock City opened to the public in 1932 and became an instant hit. Step onto the winding paths and you'll immediately see why. Search for hidden garden gnomes, wind your way through the ancient rock formations, and stand at the edge of Lover's Leap, where legend says you can gaze out and see seven states spread out beneath you.

◉ Only 50 or so "See Rock City" barns remain, mostly in Tennessee. You can see Rock City year-round; hours vary by season (seerockcity.com).

When to visit

Music lovers flock to Tennessee in June for CMA Fest and Bonnaroo. When fall arrives, though, trade festivals for hiking trails and explore the beauty of the Smokies, which are ablaze with bright folliage.

Sip Tennessee whiskey

Some things just go together: bacon and eggs, peanut butter and jelly, and Tennessee and whiskey. So what is the alchemy behind the state's famous whiskey? It's filtered through maple charcoal and aged in oak barrels; this isn't just tradition, there's actually a state law that legally determines what can be labeled "Tennessee whiskey." Speaking of legality, whiskey and the law have had a rocky relationship over the years, with multiple bouts of prohibition threatening to kill the industry's buzz. Fortunately, the distilling laws were eased in 2009, and today there are more than 30 distilleries across the state. The most famous is Jack Daniel's in Lynchburg, where they've been crafting world-famous whiskey with local limestone spring water since 1866.

◉ Tours and tastings take place at the Jack Daniel's Distillery daily (jackdaniels.com).

STAX RECORDS
Visit the movie theater turned studio, where crooners like Otis Redding got their start.

EXPERIENCE GRACELAND
See the famous "Jungle Room" and over 100 jumpsuits at the King's mansion.

THE LORRAINE MOTEL
Now a Civil Rights museum, this hotel is where Martin Luther King Jr. was shot in 1968.

SPEND TIME IN THE MEMPHIS ROCK 'N' SOUL MUSEUM
Journey through Memphis's musical history at this one-of-a-kind museum.

THE RENDEZVOUS
A historic restaurant where the original Memphis ribs rub was developed in the 1950s.

Jam to the blues in Memphis

Nashville might be known as Music City, but Memphis takes the cake. Elvis Presley called it home, and soul and rock 'n' roll got their start here. But before all that, there was the blues. After the Civil War, musicians traveled from the Mississippi Delta to pluck strings on Beale Street, a hub of African American culture. Perhaps the most famous was W.C. Handy, the first to commercialize the blues for a mass audience; the tradition continues today, with clubs like B.B. King's and Alfred's serving up foot-stomping jams. It's tough to find a city with more soul–no wonder it's mentioned in more songs than any other city in the world.

◉ Memphis Visitor Center is found at 3205 Elvis Presley Boulevard, and is open 9am–3pm Wed–Sat (memphistravel.com).

See the waterfalls of the Cumberland Plateau

Tennessee might be landlocked, but with an abundance of lakes and waterfalls you'll never hear the locals complain. Day-trippers and backpackers head to the Cumberland Plateau for their weekend water fix, this sprawling natural playground offering family-friendly strolls, world-class hikes, and plenty of places to cool off after. Go for a swim in Cummins Falls, or kayak to the base of Burgess Falls, a stunning 136-ft (41-m) cascade. Feeling adventurous? Trek the Fiery Gizzard Trail, which traverses a rocky river gorge with countless waterfalls pouring into turquoise-blue pools. With this much wild water, who needs the beach?

◉ Visit tnstateparks.com for a rundown of some of the most stunning and accessible waterfalls in the state.

Drive the Natchez Trace Parkway

Stretching from Mississippi *(p120)* into Tennessee, the scenic Natchez Trace Parkway winds drivers through rolling hills and millennia of history. You could easily spend a week exploring its notable sites, but it's just as perfect for a spontaneous day trip. Start with Southern essentials: fill up on biscuits and jam before hitting the road. As you drive, you'll discover wooded trails, peaceful picnic spots, and breathtaking overlooks, as well as glide beneath the dramatic arches of the Birdsong Hollow Bridge. With something new around every bend–be it a historic burial mound or a quiet waterfall–this is a journey designed for discovery. Turn off your GPS and watch the South unfold.

◉ Visit nps.gov/natr for a list of entrances and exits, historic sites, and need-to-know travel information.

Make memories at Dollywood

When Tennesseans need a break from working 9 to 5, they head to Pigeon Forge for a refreshing dose of mountain air and a day at Dollywood. Set against the breathtaking backdrop of the Great Smoky Mountains, this is much more than a theme park—it's an homage to its namesake, Dolly Parton. Expect all the classic amusement park fare—roller-coasters, waterslides, and live shows—but with a side of Appalachian heritage. Enjoy bluegrass concerts, a replica of the cabin Dolly grew up in, and a variety of crafts classes. Beyond the thrills, Dollywood is an investment in the community. Its success funds the Imagination Library, Dolly's literacy organization, and other local nonprofits. Just one more reason why we will always love the Queen of Country.

◉ Tickets for the amusement park and a water park can be purchased separately or in combination (dollywood.com).

Step into Franklin's Civil War past

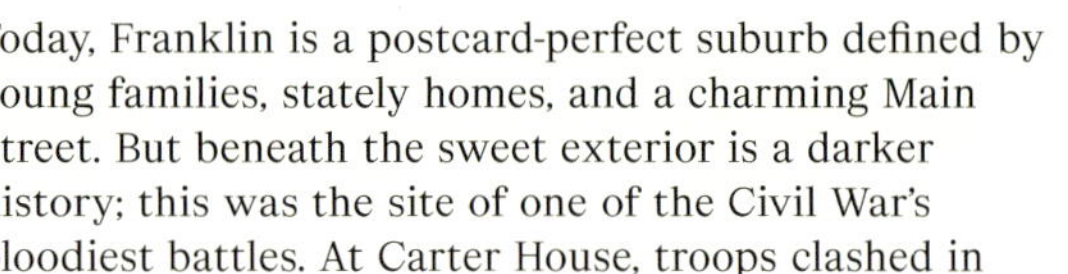

Today, Franklin is a postcard-perfect suburb defined by young families, stately homes, and a charming Main Street. But beneath the sweet exterior is a darker history; this was the site of one of the Civil War's bloodiest battles. At Carter House, troops clashed in a brutal five-hour conflict that left 9,500 soldiers dead or wounded. A makeshift hospital and Confederate graveyard were set up a mile away, on the Carnton Plantation. You can still see bloodstains permanently etched into the mansion's floors, and some say they've heard soldiers' ghosts wandering the halls. Franklin stands as a reminder that the war isn't merely an event in the history books; it forever changed the course of real people's lives and still haunts the South today.

◉ Tours of both Carter House and Carnton Plantation are provided through The Battle of Franklin Trust (boft.org).

Explore Great Smoky Mountains National Park

Anchoring East Tennessee, the Great Smoky Mountains are one of the world's oldest mountain ranges, defining the landscape with ancient, old-growth forests, spring-fed swimming holes, and the iconic hazy summits that give the park its name. The biodiversity here is unmatched: an astounding 19,000-plus species, from massive black bears to rare native salamanders, call these hills home. See it for yourself by hiking to LeConte Lodge, or discover early mountain life at Cades Cove, a grassy valley of log cabins. Sure, this national park is one of the country's most popular, but wilderness is always just a few steps away.

◉ Great Smoky Mountains National Park has four visitor centers, and covers two states (Tennessee and North Carolina). One way to access it is from Gatlinburg, at the Sugarlands entrance (nps.gov/grsm).

NASHVILLE
TOP
5

THE COUNTRY MUSIC HALL OF FAME
Pay your respects at this rhinestone-studded tribute to country music's biggest stars.

HONKY-TONKS ON BROADWAY
Don your cowboy boots and line dance to country covers on the ultimate party street.

THE RYMAN AUDITORIUM
Soak in the impeccable acoustics at the "Mother Church of Country Music."

EAT NASHVILLE HOT CHICKEN
A spicy take on fried chicken, this fiery dish is served at spots like Prince's and Hattie B's.

CHECK OUT THE PARTHENON
Visit the copy of the Greek temple in Centennial Park.

Go boot-scootin' in Nashville

They don't call Nashville "Music City" for nothing. It's the world's country music capital, where giants like the Grand Ole Opry and the legendary hit-makers of Music Row set the stage. And the sound of music is everywhere. Walk down neon-lit Broadway and you'll find it pouring out of honky-tonks, where bachelorette parties sing karaoke and tourists try line dancing. And second to the city's music scene is its food scene, with locals noshing on home cooking and James Beard–winning fare. Sound like fun? Pack your dancing boots, bring a healthy appetite, and get ready to move to Nashville's tune.

◉ Nashville Visitor Center is open 9am–5pm at 501 Broadway (visitmusiccity.com).

The Lone Star State

Everything feels larger than life in Texas, so much so that it can feel more like a country than a state. Sweeping scenery, big flavors, and epic histories all run deep here. And though the Lone Star State earned its nickname from the single star on its state flag—a symbol of its time as an independent republic—you'll never find yourself feeling alone or lonely in Texas. Not with culture-packed cities, welcoming dude ranches, tempting wineries, and truly stunning national parks on your doorstep.

STATE MOTTO Friendship

STATE FLOWER Bluebonnet

STATE ANIMAL Texas longhorn

STATE BIRD Northern mockingbird

FUN FACT "Texas" comes from the Caddo word "taysha," meaning "friend." When the Spanish arrived, they met the Indigenous Caddo people and adopted and adapted the word, referring to the people and region as "Tejas."

Explore Big Bend National Park

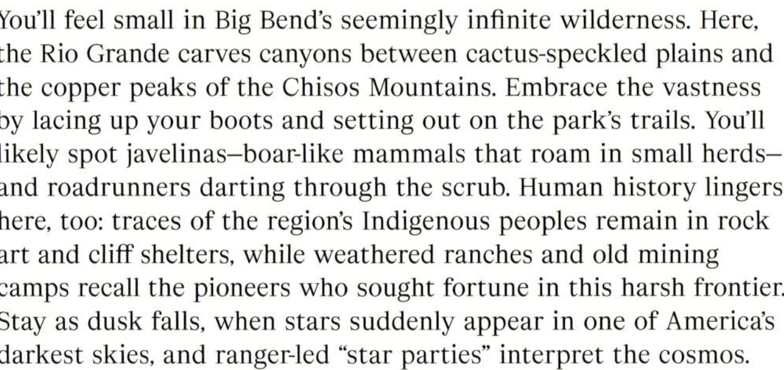

You'll feel small in Big Bend's seemingly infinite wilderness. Here, the Rio Grande carves canyons between cactus-speckled plains and the copper peaks of the Chisos Mountains. Embrace the vastness by lacing up your boots and setting out on the park's trails. You'll likely spot javelinas—boar-like mammals that roam in small herds—and roadrunners darting through the scrub. Human history lingers here, too: traces of the region's Indigenous peoples remain in rock art and cliff shelters, while weathered ranches and old mining camps recall the pioneers who sought fortune in this harsh frontier. Stay as dusk falls, when stars suddenly appear in one of America's darkest skies, and ranger-led "star parties" interpret the cosmos.

◉ The Ross Maxwell Scenic Route is a 30-mile (48-km) road through Big Bend's heart, past the Sam Nail Ranch ruins and the Sotol Vista overlook.

See otherworldly exhibits at Space Center Houston

Prepare for launch at Space Center Houston. The visitor hub for NASA's Johnson Space Center tells America's spaceflight story and the defining role that Houston played. Exhibits showcase everything from moon rocks, astronaut suits, and, of course, space craft. See early Mercury capsules—tiny one-person craft that first carried astronauts into orbit—and a towering 363-ft (111-m) Saturn V rocket that launched Apollo crews to the moon in the center's Rocket Park. Be sure to join a tram tour to see behind the scenes of Mission Control and where astronauts train underwater for spacewalks.

◉ Pre-book the Level 9 Tour for behind-the-scenes NASA access, from astronaut training facilities to working labs.

Learn all about JFK in Dallas

One of America's most famous moments took place in Dealey Plaza, Downtown Dallas, on November 22, 1963. From the sixth-floor corner window of the former Texas School Book Depository, assassin Lee Harvey Oswald fired shots at then President John F. Kennedy as he passed through the city in a motorcade. Today, the Sixth Floor Museum chronicles Kennedy's life, legacy, and assassination through historic film footage, artifacts, and eyewitness accounts. Outside, visitors pause at the stark white and cenotaph-like Kennedy Memorial. Beyond this somber square, modern Dallas sprawls outward—a metropolitan center that thrives while acknowledging its past.

◉ Consider a walking tour to learn more. Dallas City Tour's JFK Assassination and Museum Tour traces key sites including Dealey Plaza and Oswald's former boarding house.

When to visit

Mild weather is promised March through May, and September through November. Spring is great for bluebonnet drives and wine trails, while fall brings outdoor festivals like Austin City Limits (October) and the State Fair (September/October).

Indulge in cowboy culture in Fort Worth

The Wild West is alive and kicking in Fort Worth, or "Cowtown" as it was known in the 19th century, when the town had a booming cattle market and served as the last major stop on the Chisholm Trail (which drove cattle north to Kansas). Sure, Fort Worth has museums like the Cowgirl Hall of Fame and Texas Cowboy Hall of Fame, but the real frontier spirit lingers at the Stockyards, where you can witness the drama of longhorn drives twice daily, plus the Stockyards Championship Rodeo, every Friday and Saturday night. Afterward, two-step over to Billy Bob's Texas—the world's largest honky-tonk—for live music and dancing.

◉ Grab an alfresco dinner in the modern downtown, centered around Sundance Square.

Take in the drama of Palo Duro Canyon

While the Grand Canyon takes top billing, Palo Duro Canyon, in the Texas Panhandle, steals the show. Why? For starters, the country's second-biggest canyon remains gloriously uncrowded, making it feel like it's all yours. Stretching out for 120 miles (193 km), its canyon walls plunge down for 800 ft (244 m), in sweeping bands of red, gold, and rust. Looking for adventure? Set out on a hike or a guided horseback ride, then pitch your tent amid the canyon's striking hoodoos. On summer nights, the epic *TEXAS Outdoor Musical*—a long-running open-air show celebrating Panhandle pioneer days—plays to a backdrop of stars.

◉ Drive the 16-mile (26-km) scenic loop through Palo Duro, descending into the canyon's depths, and pause at scenic overlooks. Trails from the road lead to Capitol Peak, Lighthouse Rock, and dramatic canyon views.

Discover Spanish and Mexican heritage in San Antonio

Centuries of culture await in the city of San Antonio, home to five Spanish Colonial Missions that comprise a UNESCO World Heritage Site. The most legendary is the Alamo, a limestone fortress that saw the 1836 battle for Texan independence. In the city center, Mexican mariachi music, *papel picado* bunting, and bustling *mercados* speak to San Antonio's enduring cross-border heritage. This really comes to the fore each October, when the city hosts the country's largest Día de los Muertos (Day of the Dead) celebrations. The festival celebrates and remembers loved ones passed, transforming the streets with candlelit altars and parades honoring ancestors.

◉ Cycle the 8-mile (13-km) Mission Trail, linking the Alamo with five other missions along a scenic riverside route.

Unwind on the Texas Coast

When it comes to planning a summer vacation, many travelers overlook Texas's 350 miles (563 km) of coastline, but they're missing out. Take Galveston, with its charming Victorian mansions that recall the wealth of the Golden Age. Today, the port city's water-front and Strand district teem with cafés, antique shops, and galleries that will have you parting with your pay-check in a heartbeat. Along the shore, charter boats bob on the water at Port Aransas marina, guiding anglers and dolphin watchers, while kayakers drift through the quiet wetlands of Mustang Island State Park. Sound good? Texas's coastline is ready when you are.

◉ Don't miss the Tall Ship *Elissa* in Galveston, a restored 19th-century barque that honors the island's seafaring past.

Snoop around ghost towns

Ruined saloons stand stalwart. Weathered signage creaks. Tumbleweed rolls past. Texas's ghost towns might be abandoned, but they still tell the raw stories of the boom-and-bust cycles driven by mining, ranching, and the expansion of the railroads. Mainly scattered across the vast landscape of the west of the state, standouts include Terlingua, with its crumbling adobe houses and shells of its old-school saloons, and Glenrio, once a bustling pit stop on Route 66, now a silent spot on the Texas–New Mexico border, its empty motels and gas stations frozen in time.

◉ Make your base at Terlingua Ranch Lodge, with its cabins and campground space. Here, the low-key Bad Rabbit Café hosts regular live music events and excursions.

Get outdoors in Guadalupe Mountains National Park

Near the New Mexico border, the Guadalupe Mountains rise abruptly from the desert plains, their tall cliffs preserving a 250-million-year-old fossil reef that was once submerged beneath the sea. Trails climb through agave and juniper trees to the pine-clad heights and Guadalupe Peak, the highest point in the state. Here, mule deer graze along shaded canyon floors while golden eagles drift overhead. In fall, McKittrick Canyon ignites with scarlet maples and cottonwoods. It's one of the last true wildernesses in Texas.

◉ Focus your visit on the Pine Springs area, which has a campsite and a visitor center for information.

Find the arty side of Marfa

Sitting on the high-desert plain of West Texas, Marfa was once a modest ranching town where troops were based during both World Wars. Then, in the 1970s, minimalist artist Donald Judd arrived, reshaping the city into a shimmering creative beacon. How? By taking the empty barracks and reimagining them as art installations. His Chinati Foundation transformed the whole outpost into a pilgrimage site for art lovers. Today, contemporary galleries draw visitors from around the world, along with the famous Prada Marfa, a much-loved art installation near the town that's styled as a designer boutique on an empty stretch of desert highway.

◉ Watch for the mysterious Marfa Lights from the roadside viewing area east of town. Are they car headlights, or UFOs?

Dig into Tex-Mex

When it comes to comfort food, Tex-Mex is tough to beat—think sizzling fajitas, cheese-smothered enchiladas, and breakfast tacos sprinkled with spice. Bringing together Mexican roots and local Texas flavor, the cuisine originated in border ranch kitchens and has evolved into a foundational part of the state's identity. So, where to sample it? San Antonio's culinary clout has earned the city a designation as a UNESCO City of Gastronomy. Head for Casa Rio, on the River Walk, and colorful Rosario's Mexican Café y Cantina. Meanwhile, El Paso stays true to its roots with red-and-green chile-smothered enchiladas and downhome spots such as the L&J Café, a local landmark since 1927.

◉ Learn how to make tamales and South Texas–style soups at Sylvia's Enchiladas in Houston.

Rope your way onto a dude ranch

Ranching runs deep in Texas. The first great ranches grew from Spanish land grants and open-range cattle drives, laying the foundations for the state's cattle industry and enduring cowboy traditions. Across the state, places like the King Ranch near Kingsville and the J.A. Ranch in the Panhandle shaped cowboy culture, pioneering large-scale cattle operations and horsemanship that became central to Texas identity. For a true, hands-on dude ranch experience, head north to Bandera, the self-proclaimed "Cowboy Capital of the World." Standouts like Dixie Dude Ranch or Mayan Dude Ranch invite you to saddle up for sunrise rides, learn to rope, and share barbecue suppers.

◉ Time your trip for the Bandera Rodeo Memorial Weekend Stampede, a three-day event of competitions and live music.

TOUR THE TEXAS CAPITOL
This striking pink-granite landmark was built in 1888 and is set in tree-lined grounds.

BARTON SPRINGS POOL
Take a refreshing dip in Zilker Park's spring-fed natural swimming hole.

MOODY THEATER
Catch the legendary Austin City Limits Live music series at the city's ultimate venue.

WATCH BATS OVER THE CONGRESS AVENUE BRIDGE
Witness a million Mexican free-tailed bats take flight as the sun sets.

KAYAK ON LADY BIRD LAKE
Drift beneath tree-shaded trails and city bridges.

Feast on the delights of Austin

Austin's streets are alive with the sound of music—and the scent of smoked brisket. The self-styled "Live Music Capital of the World" has more live music venues per capita than anywhere else in the country, and meandering around its streets you're guaranteed to hear guitar riffs spilling out from open doors. After all, this is the city that shaped legends like Willie Nelson, and continues to launch new stars at SXSW and Austin City Limits festivals. Between sets, grab a quick bite from taco trucks or join locals lining up for plates piled high with barbecue at institutions like Franklin or La Barbecue.

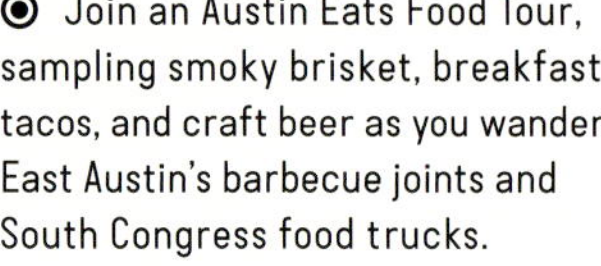
⦿ Join an Austin Eats Food Tour, sampling smoky brisket, breakfast tacos, and craft beer as you wander East Austin's barbecue joints and South Congress food trucks.

Uncover German heritage in Fredericksburg

Founded in 1846 by immigrants from the Rhineland, the city of Fredericksburg wears its German heritage proudly. Take Main Street, which looks like it's been plucked from the pages of a German storybook with turreted buildings and flower-filled *biergartens*. Visit the Pioneer Museum and the octagonal Vereins Kirche to trace the city's pioneer story; the museum's 19th-century log cabins, smokehouse, and schoolhouse reveal how settlers built new lives on the frontier. Swing by the reconstructed church in Marktplatz, which recalls the city's first communal hall. Then round off the day with schnitzel and a pint of German-style lager–*prost!*

◉ In fall, join locals for Oktoberfest, when German music, bratwurst, and frothy steins fill Marktplatz.

Drink wine in Texas Hill Country

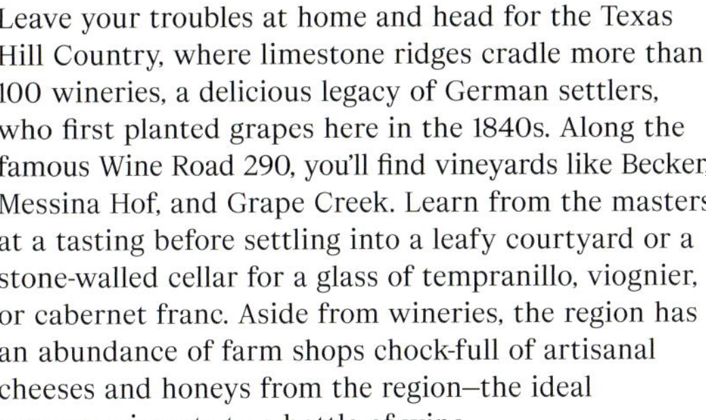

Leave your troubles at home and head for the Texas Hill Country, where limestone ridges cradle more than 100 wineries, a delicious legacy of German settlers, who first planted grapes here in the 1840s. Along the famous Wine Road 290, you'll find vineyards like Becker, Messina Hof, and Grape Creek. Learn from the masters at a tasting before settling into a leafy courtyard or a stone-walled cellar for a glass of tempranillo, viognier, or cabernet franc. Aside from wineries, the region has an abundance of farm shops chock-full of artisanal cheeses and honeys from the region–the ideal accompaniments to a bottle of wine.

◉ Wine Road 290 stretches for roughly 30 miles (48 km) between Johnson City and Fredericksburg. Make the most of the 290 Wine Shuttle, which runs continuously between wineries, allowing visitors to hop on and off every 15 minutes.

Sample classic Texas barbecue

Barbecue isn't just a means to a meal, it's a Texas ritual. Since the 1800s, pitmasters have slow-smoked meat over oak coals until tender and aromatic. Rooted in the meat markets and smokehouses opened by German and Czech settlers, barbecuing became a community affair–a way to gather, feed neighbors, and celebrate. Today, it's a Lone Star State staple and many spots have a cult following. At Franklin Barbecue in Austin and Snow's in Lexington, early-morning lines form for melt-in-your-mouth brisket, ribs, and sausage, served simply on butcher paper. Wash yours down with a classic sweet tea or a local craft beer.

◉ Follow the Central Texas Barbecue Trail, a 75-mile (121-km) loop through Lockhart, Luling, Elgin, and Taylor, and sample the breadth of Texas's barbecue.

The Beehive State

If there's one word to describe Utah, it's otherworldly—red-rock cliffs, gravity-defying arches, salt lakes, and snow-covered peaks make for some of the most jaw-dropping landscapes in the U.S. Settled by the Mormons, who saw it as a promised land, Utah feels both older than time and still undiscovered. You can hunt for dinosaur bones, explore prehistoric Indigenous dwellings, and find radioactive rocks at a former uranium mine—and be back in town in time for dinner.

STATE MOTTO Industry

STATE FLOWER Sego lily

STATE ANIMAL Rocky Mountain elk

STATE BIRD California gull

FUN FACT Utah is home to one of the world's largest organisms. Pando, also known as the Trembling Giant, is a one-tree aspen forest, made up of over 47,000 trunks, all of which share a root system.

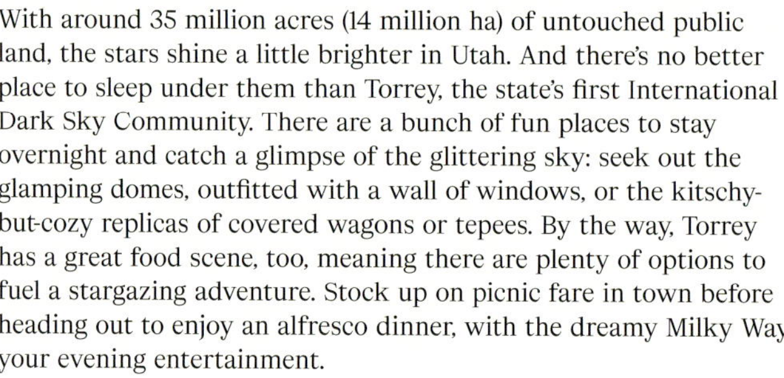

Sleep under the stars in Torrey

With around 35 million acres (14 million ha) of untouched public land, the stars shine a little brighter in Utah. And there's no better place to sleep under them than Torrey, the state's first International Dark Sky Community. There are a bunch of fun places to stay overnight and catch a glimpse of the glittering sky: seek out the glamping domes, outfitted with a wall of windows, or the kitschy-but-cozy replicas of covered wagons or tepees. By the way, Torrey has a great food scene, too, meaning there are plenty of options to fuel a stargazing adventure. Stock up on picnic fare in town before heading out to enjoy an alfresco dinner, with the dreamy Milky Way your evening entertainment.

◉ Torrey is located right outside of Capitol Reef National Park, making it the perfect base for stargazing (torreyutah.gov/visit-torrey).

Squeeze through a slot canyon

Slot canyons are deep, narrow gorges carved by water rushing through Utah's sandstone cliffs. They're generally deeper than they are wide–some of the narrowest are only 10 inches (25 cm) across–making them a playground for canyoners and a nightmare for the claustrophobic. South-central Utah's Escalante area is popular among slot canyon newbies, home to many cheekily named gullies like "Spooky" and "Peek-a-Boo." Ready to tackle one for yourself? Climb inside and enter a world of winding passages, formidable boulders, and tight corridors, before heading out the other side, feeling adventurous... and in need of some personal space.

◉ The staff at the Escalante Interagency Visitor Center can offer advice and safety information before you head out (blm.gov/visit/escalante-interagency-visitor-center). Canyons are dangerous in flash floods; never hike if storms are forecast.

When to visit

If you're headed to southern Utah's national parks, plan to go April through May or September through October, when the heat isn't as brutal. Park City has hosted the Sundance Film Festival in the winter, which is also an ideal time for skiing.

Go mountain biking in Moab

The buzzing city of Moab, in eastern Utah, is a favorite for outdoor adventure of all kinds. The most popular activity of all? That's got to be mountain biking. Bucket-list-worthy rides skirt the bases of buttes, scale grippy "slickrock" dunes, and fly down the sides of mesas, attracting riders from all over the world. Take your shot at a trail like "Captain Ahab" or "the Whole Enchilada," where you'll find unbeatable views, leg-burning climbs, and death-defying drops that you'll recount time and time again back home. Finish off a day on the trails with a drink at the Moab Brewery, where retired two-wheelers hang from the rafters.

◉ Don't want to travel with your steed? Shops specialize in bike rentals and shuttles to and from the trailhead. Trail maps and ratings can be found at discovermoab.com.

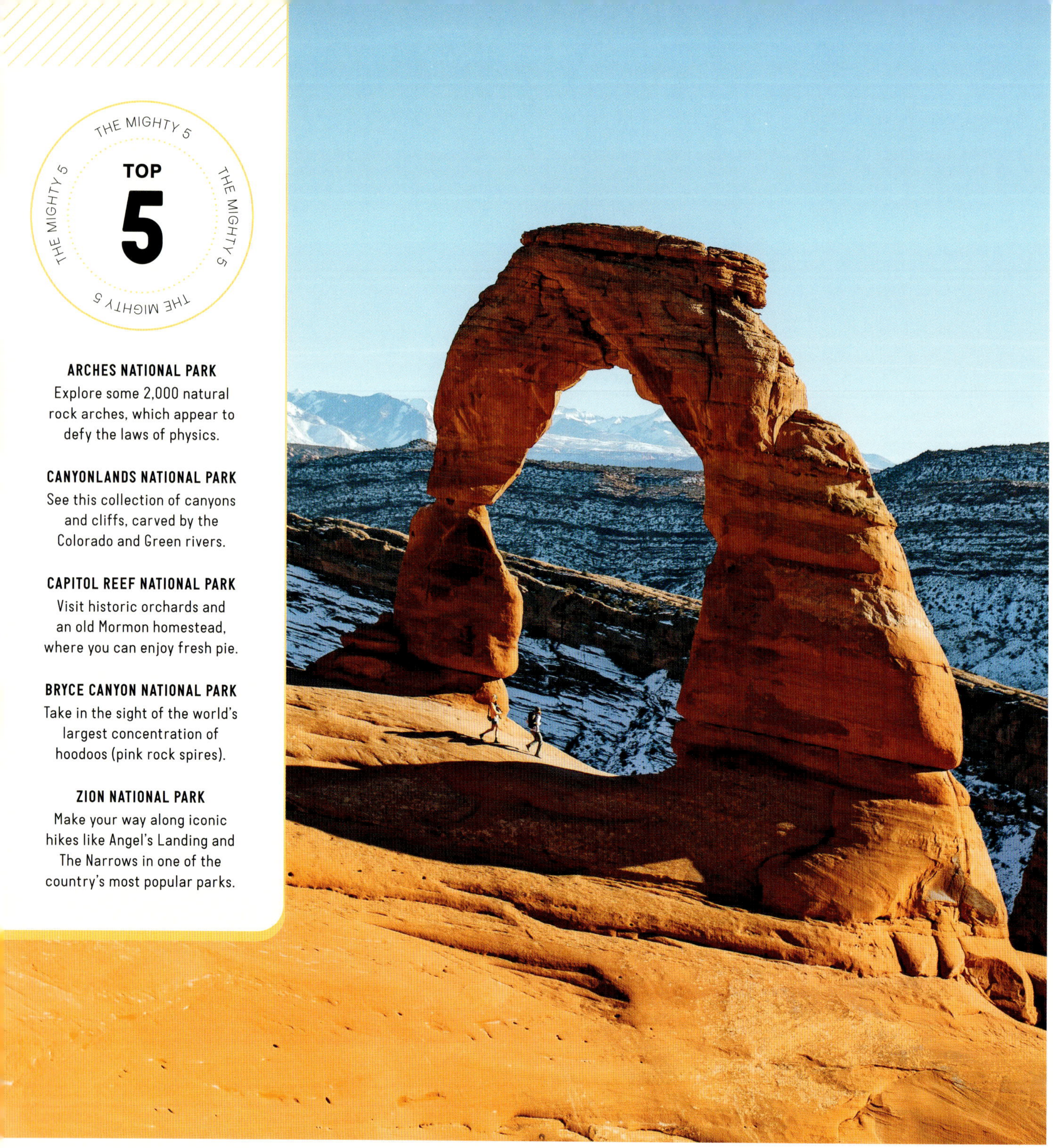

ARCHES NATIONAL PARK
Explore some 2,000 natural rock arches, which appear to defy the laws of physics.

CANYONLANDS NATIONAL PARK
See this collection of canyons and cliffs, carved by the Colorado and Green rivers.

CAPITOL REEF NATIONAL PARK
Visit historic orchards and an old Mormon homestead, where you can enjoy fresh pie.

BRYCE CANYON NATIONAL PARK
Take in the sight of the world's largest concentration of hoodoos (pink rock spires).

ZION NATIONAL PARK
Make your way along iconic hikes like Angel's Landing and The Narrows in one of the country's most popular parks.

See The Mighty 5

Southern Utah's canyon country—a high desert of towering buttes and rugged mesas—is so remarkable that it claims five national parks, affectionately known as The Mighty 5. They're all packed with stunning canyons, funky rock formations, and amazing history. But each has a unique claim to fame, from arches clinging to the sides of cliffs to a hike upriver through a narrow gorge. Got time on your hands? The best way to see The Mighty 5 is on an epic, 900-mile (1,448-km) drive between the parks. Vintage diners, frontier towns, desert highways, and endless adventure? It's the stuff road-trip dreams are made of.

◉ Start in Springdale and loop through the parks. They are just a few hours from each other, but give yourself a week to explore—there's much to see along the way.

Hit the slopes in Park City

A silver-mining town until the 1950s, today Park City is a top destination for skiers, mountain bikers, and wellness junkies seeking a little rest and relaxation. The 2002 Winter Olympics and annual Sundance Film Festival put this resort town on the map, and its menu of unforgettable experiences keeps it there. Beyond hitting the slopes, you can enjoy paddleboard yoga in a geothermal crater; sip whiskey at a distillery in an old saloon; or feel the rhythm, feel the rhyme, and roll down the Olympic bobsled track in the summertime. And, of course, there's no better way to see off a day on the slopes than at one of the many après-ski spots, no matter what activity kept you busy in the day.

◉ The visitor center is located inside the Park City Museum at 528 Main Street (parkcityutah.com).

Race on the Bonneville Salt Flats

Picture a flat plain, covered in white dust, stretching out as far as the eye can see. This isn't snow on the tundra. It's salt, 147 million tons of it. The Bonneville Salt Flats formed after Lake Bonneville evaporated nearly 13,000 years ago, leaving behind mineral deposits, most of which are common table salt. The most popular activity here, besides taking lots of social media–worthy photos, is motor racing. The flats are famously used for record-breaking speed tests, but you can also take the family car for a spin. Don't expect to break any records, though—that's reserved for the expert racers who tackle this terrain during the annual Speed Week event.

◉ The flats are driest in the summer, and Speed Week typically takes place in August.

Hunt for dinosaur bones

Seeing dinosaur bones at the science museum is cool, but nothing beats spotting them in the wild. Skeletons can be found all over Utah, along the side of the road, in rock faces, and in dried-up riverbeds, offering a snapshot not just of dinosaur anatomy, but also of how these creatures lived. The state has one of the most complete fossil records on the planet, including marine life, mammoths, and petrified wood (turns out all that sandstone is great for preserving things). Step back in time to the Mesozoic era and head to Dinosaur National Monument, where you can see and touch 1,500 bones exactly as they were found, frozen in a moment in prehistory.

◉ Dinosaur National Monument is located on the border between Utah and Colorado. It's open daily, but hours vary depending on the season. Dig for details before you go at nps.gov/dino.

Go boating on Lake Powell

Something you don't expect to see in the desert? A 250-sq-mile (647-sq-km) lake where sandstone cliffs reflect off the water's surface and rock formations loom like orange-painted icebergs. In 1963, the Colorado River was dammed, flooding Glen Canyon and creating Lake Powell, providing access to ravines and overlooks that were previously inaccessible. Follow a side canyon to a landmark like Rainbow Bridge, one of the largest natural bridges in the world, or sunbathe on a secret beach. The best way to experience the lake is via houseboat, where you can hike, fish, and swim in the sun, then doze off in a cove at night, waves rocking you to sleep.

◉ Set off from Bullfrog Marina on the north end of the lake or Wahweap Marina in the south (lakepowell.com).

See the bison at Antelope Island

The Great Salt Lake is one of Utah's most impressive features: an inland dead sea 75 miles (120 km) long and saltier than the ocean. In the middle of the lake sits Antelope Island, fed by freshwater springs and home to—you guessed it—antelope and American bison. The bison were introduced in 1893 and remain one of the largest free-range herds in the U.S. Pick your favorite mode of transportation—hiking, mountain biking, or horseback riding—and explore its grassy hills in the hope of a wildlife sighting (the area is also famous for bird-watching). End your visit with a refreshing float in the lake, weightless and full of wonder.

◉ You can make a day trip to Antelope Island State Park or camp overnight (stateparks.utah.gov/parks/antelope-island).

Wander through ghostly Grafton

Visiting Grafton feels like stepping onto a movie set—and in many ways, you are. One of the most photographed ghost towns in the U.S., it's appeared in Westerns like *Butch Cassidy and the Sundance Kid* and *Ramrod*. Founded in 1859 by Mormon settlers and abandoned 85 years later, Grafton's preserved buildings are free to wander as you see fit. Stroll past the adobe brick chapel, crawl into earthen cellars, sit on stately porches, and read gravestones, piecing together family trees. As cattle graze beneath the cinematic cliffs, you can't help but wonder if John Wayne might just ride around the corner, searching for a saloon and a showdown.

◉ Grafton sits on the Virgin River; most vehicles can handle the dirt road into town, but drive carefully so your car doesn't become another abandoned relic here.

Explore the world of the Ancestral Puebloans

There's much we don't know about the Ancestral Puebloans, who inhabited the Southwest before the recognized Indigenous peoples of today, but signs of their lives are everywhere. Kivas, homes, and granaries can be spotted in the cliffs above hiking trails. Highways are lined with rock carvings depicting bighorn sheep and alien-like creatures. Even old corn cobs have been found, slow to decompose in the desert air. At Hovenweep National Monument, tour the castle-like ruins of six Puebloan villages that date back to around 1200 C.E. With detailed stonework, these ancient sites are as impressive as they are mysterious.

◉ For more information on how to access the park, head to the visitor center at Montezuma Creek (nps.gov/hove).

Visit Temple Square in Salt Lake City

When Brigham Young, leader of a persecuted religious sect, arrived in the Salt Lake Valley in 1847, he dedicated a spot in the uncharted desert as sacred land for the group's temple. Today, that spot is Temple Square in Salt Lake City, a five-block complex home to the Church of Jesus Christ of Latter-day Saints. The center point of the square—and the city—is a striking 210-ft (64-m) granite temple, where one of the most famous choirs in the world, the Tabernacle Choir, performs. You can't separate Utah's history from the Mormon story; visit the Church History Museum on the square to learn about the state's visionary origins.

◉ Only members of the church can attend services at the temple, but the square's grounds and museums are open to all.

The Green Mountain State

Churches, mountains, clapboard houses, maple syrup: Vermont is the quintessential New England state, and one that (predictably) is at its best in fall, when its forests put on a spectacular show. It's full of historical significance, too: its constitution was among the first in the world to ban slavery and grant universal (male) suffrage. Come for the history or come for the New England ideal; there's plenty to love about this picture-perfect state.

STATE MOTTO Freedom and Unity

STATE FLOWER Red clover

STATE ANIMAL Morgan horse

STATE BIRD Hermit thrush

FUN FACT Before Vermont became the 14th state of the U.S., it existed as an independent nation for 14 years (between 1777 and 1791) and was known as the Vermont Republic.

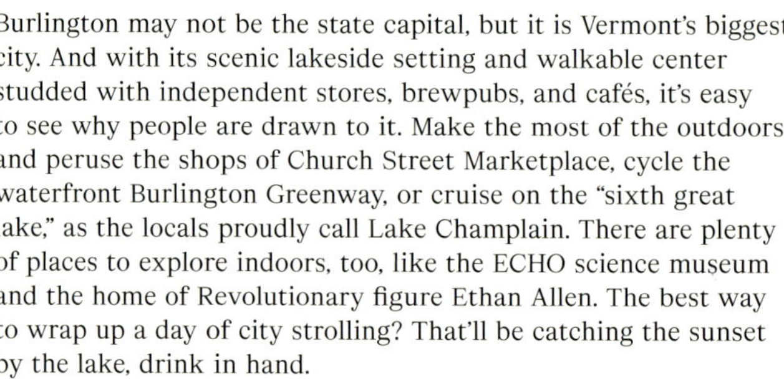

Stroll around Burlington

Burlington may not be the state capital, but it is Vermont's biggest city. And with its scenic lakeside setting and walkable center studded with independent stores, brewpubs, and cafés, it's easy to see why people are drawn to it. Make the most of the outdoors and peruse the shops of Church Street Marketplace, cycle the waterfront Burlington Greenway, or cruise on the "sixth great lake," as the locals proudly call Lake Champlain. There are plenty of places to explore indoors, too, like the ECHO science museum and the home of Revolutionary figure Ethan Allen. The best way to wrap up a day of city strolling? That'll be catching the sunset by the lake, drink in hand.

◉ For more information on Burlington, visit helloburlingtonvt.com. You can rent bikes at Local Motion on the waterfront (localmotion.org).

Hop on board the Champlain Valley Dinner Train

Vermont is known for its scenery, and there's no better way to see it all than by train. Relive the golden era of train travel on the Champlain Valley Dinner Train, where you'll be served a three-course meal in restored 1930s dining cars while the landscape rolls by. The two-and-a-half-hour round-trip starts in Burlington, trundling south along the shore of Lake Champlain. On the far side of the lake loom the Adirondack Mountains of New York; farther south, you'll pass farmland and pastures, with patches of forest. The journey stops at the small town of Vergennes before heading back to Burlington the same way, so you can enjoy it all over again.

◉ Trains run on weekends late Jun–Oct; for the full schedule, visit rails-vt.com/champlain-valley-dinner-train.

Hike the Long Trail

Vermont is crisscrossed with scenic hiking paths, but there's one that comes out on top. The Long Trail runs the length of the Green Mountains, some 272 miles (438 km) from the Massachusetts border to Québec. The oldest long-distance trail in the U.S., it was built between 1910 and 1930, becoming the inspiration for the much longer Appalachian Trail. It's a multi-week challenge to hike the whole thing, but you can also tackle it in sections; the northern half is wilder and more arduous, crossing some of Vermont's highest peaks like Mount Mansfield and the Jay Peak Range. Finish the whole thing and you'll officially be a rare "End-to-Ender" (just over 3,000 brave hikers have earned this title).

◉ For more on the Long Trail, visit greenmountainclub.org/the-long-trail; those planning on hiking the entire trail should count on spending 25–30 days on the route.

Ascend Mount Mansfield

Climbing Mount Mansfield, the highest point in Vermont at 4,395 ft (1,340 m), is a strenuous proposition. But get to the summit and you'll be rewarded with views of forest-smothered peaks all the way to Lake Champlain, the Adirondacks, and Canada. Want an easier way up? Drive up the winding Toll Road, following the old carriage path some 4.5 miles (7 km) to the summit from Stowe. The road ends at a tiny visitors' center, from which it's a short scramble to the ridge along the mountaintop and on to the peak, known as "the Chin." Spectacular scenery awaits, however you get there.

◉ The Mount Mansfield Toll Road is usually open late May–Oct, 9:30am–4:30pm daily. No motorcycles, bicycles, or RVs are allowed (stowe.com).

Tackle some of Vermont's best slopes

Vermont may not have the Rockies, but with around 20 diverse ski areas and resorts, it's still the top ski destination in the East. One of the most popular spots is Killington, known as the "Beast in the East" since 1958 thanks to it having the highest vertical drop in New England; it's also home to 155 trails that sprawl over seven mountains. To tackle the slopes of Vermont's highest peak, head to one of over a hundred trails in the Stowe Mountain Resort. There are plenty of stunning places to stay, too, where you can kick back in front of a wood fire, legs tired but great memories made.

◉ For Stowe Mountain Resort visit stowe.com; for Killington check out killington.com; and for general information on skiing in Vermont, see skivermont.com.

Sample Vermont's maple syrup

You can't come to Vermont without trying maple syrup. Sugaring season usually starts around mid-February or early March: the rise in temperature after winter makes the maple sap flow. The trees are "tapped," with the sap collected in metal buckets before it's slowly boiled down to make thicker syrup. Locals add it to almost everything: look out for a "creemee," a version of soft-serve made with real maple syrup, and the unique "sugar on snow," hot maple syrup drizzled over packed snow, resulting in a chewy, caramel-like treat (usually eaten as a popsicle or on a fork).

◉ Try the full range of Vermont maple treats over at Sugarbush Farm in Woodstock (sugarbushfarm.com) or at Morse Farm Maple Sugarworks in Montpelier (morsefarm.com).

Visit the Shelburne Museum

Electra Havemeyer Webb was an avid art collector in the 20th century, with a particular taste. She turned away from fashionable French Impressionism and instead mainly filled her Vermont summer cottage with Americana: folk art, quilts, tiger maple furniture, and hooked rugs. With nowhere to store her growing collection, she opened Shelburne Museum, south of Burlington, in 1947. Today, this huge museum houses over 150,000 works across 39 buildings. Among them are a lighthouse, carousel figures, and even a sidewheel steamboat. It would take weeks to see everything here, but even an afternoon is a good place to start.

◉ The Shelburne Museum is open mid-May–late Oct, 10am–5pm daily (shelburnemuseum.org).

When to visit

Vermont in fall is legendary; you'll no doubt enjoy this time, but you won't be alone. The winter months (November through February) are the best time to hit the state's stunning slopes.

Try some Vermont cheese

Wisconsin may be famous for its cheese production, but Vermont claims the highest number of cheese makers per capita in the U.S.–around 50 at the last count. Sheep's milk, feta, Camembert, goat's milk, and a bewildering range of Cheddars are all produced here, and there's even a Cheese Trail. In short? Cheese is a serious business. Many producers remain small batch, or attached to a local dairy farm, and some open their doors to the public. Take Cabot Creamery, known for its Cheddar: visit its store in Waterbury to try samples, or the Yellow Barn store in Hardwick for an even bigger selection, including a rich 10-year aged Cheddar.

◉ To eat your way along the Cheese Trail, check out the Vermont Cheese Council (vtcheese.com).

Tour the Ben & Jerry's Factory

Whether it's a movie night snack or a spoonful of comfort, Ben & Jerry's is the go-to ice cream for many. What started as a small stall in a Burlington gas station in 1978 has today grown into a global empire. Learn all about it on a tour of the brand's headquarters in Waterbury, where you can see how it's made and try different combos for yourself. Found a new favorite flavor? You can buy more at the gift shop and ice-cream counter on site. Real aficionados can pay their respects to beloved, long-lost (read: discontinued) flavors at the "Flavor Graveyard" on the way out. It really is all "Peace, Love, and Ice Cream" here.

◉ The Ben & Jerry's Factory is open 10am–8pm daily; advanced reservation recommended (benjerry.com).

Drive the scenic Route 100 Byway

Winding along the central spine of Vermont, the Route 100 Byway provides the perfect introduction to the state's rustic charms. Heading north from Wilmington, the road climbs into the Green Mountains, where you'll spy ski lodges and ski runs on the slopes. Stop off at tiny Jamaica, a scenic village of brightly painted clapboard homes. Farther north, you'll pass through Plymouth Notch and the Calvin Coolidge Historic Site, where weathered barns and timber homesteads make up the childhood home of former president Calvin Coolidge. After an obligatory stop for Ben & Jerry's in Waterbury, you'll reach Stowe, gateway to the state's premier ski resort. The route is especially photogenic in the fall, when the beech, birch, and maple woods erupt in color, but you won't be disappointed during the rest of the year. In fact, the alpine landscapes are so scenic, they attracted the real Von Trapp family in the 1940s (of *Sound of Music* fame); you can still visit (and stay at) the Trapp Family Lodge today.

◉ For more on the Route 100 Byway, see vermontvacation.com. For the Calvin Coolidge Historic Site, visit coolidgefoundation.org.

The Old Dominion State

Virginia is steeped in the stories that shaped a nation. It's where English colonists first settled in the early 1600s and where the Revolution and Civil War were later fought on fields still scarred by history. The state's stunning nature sets the scene for its storied past: from its tidewater shores to its Blue Ridge peaks, the past and present are always entwined here. It really is a place where America began and where its story keeps unfolding.

STATE MOTTO Thus Always to Tyrants

STATE FLOWER American dogwood

STATE ANIMAL Virginia big-eared bat

STATE BIRD Northern cardinal

FUN FACT Virginia is nicknamed the "Mother of Presidents" because it's the birthplace of eight American presidents (more than any other state), including four out of the first five.

Delve below the surface in the wonderland of Luray Caverns

Hidden beneath Virginia's Shenandoah Valley, Luray Caverns—a vast underground world of extraordinary natural beauty—was stumbled upon by chance in 1878. What greeted its no-doubt bedazzled discoverers back then still sends shivers down the spines of visitors today: towering stalagmites rise from the cavern floor, delicate stalactites drip from the ceiling, and mirrored pools double the spectacle. The cavern's cathedral-like chambers are home to the "Great Stalacpipe Organ," a one-of-a-kind instrument that uses the stalactites themselves to create haunting music.

◉ Join a 45-minute guided tour to hear how the caverns were discovered; for more information, head to luraycaverns.com.

Wander around the streets of Fredericksburg

Fredericksburg reveals its layered past at every turn. Its cobbled streets and Georgian townhouses speak to its colonial roots, while traces of Civil War battles can be seen in its surrounding fields. At Fredericksburg and Spotsylvania National Military Park, walk through preserved battlefields, see earthen trenches and fortifications still etched into the landscape, and learn how the war changed the city forever. It's not all about the past, though. Today, Fredericksburg blends its history with modern living, with boutiques, galleries, cafés, and craft breweries occupying its historic 18th- and 19th-century buildings.

◉ Set off on a self-guided tour of the battlefields to learn about the major clashes fought here (nps.gov/frsp/index.htm).

Step back in time on the streets of Colonial Williamsburg

The past really does spring to life in Colonial Williamsburg. This living-history museum captures colonial America more vividly than anywhere else. Costumed interpreters go about daily tasks in restored homes, workshops, and taverns, while fife-and-drum parades echo down cobbled streets. You can watch blacksmiths hammer glowing metal, listen to debates about independence, and even dine in historic taverns that once hosted the likes of Thomas Jefferson. It's immersive, atmospheric, and endlessly detailed—a journey back to the tumult and optimism of the Revolutionary era. Don a tricorne and join in the fun.

◉ Join a tour with Williamsburg Walking Tours to trace over 300 years of history (williamsburgwalkingtours.com).

Explore Virginia's Eastern Shore

Virginia's Eastern Shore is a world apart from the state's cities—a quiet, unspoiled region of barrier islands, salt marshes, and long, empty beaches. A high, narrow peninsula stretching between Chesapeake Bay and the Atlantic, the shore is ripe for exploration. Set out along the wildlife-rich trails of Chincoteague and Assateague national wildlife refuges to spot wild ponies roaming the dunes, or navigate the creeks and channels of the Virginia Seaside Water Trail, a 100-mile (160-km) coastal paddling route that invites you to slow down and take it all in. After all that adventuring, quaint towns like Cape Charles and Onancock offer respite by way of seafood restaurants, galleries, and waterfront inns.

◉ For more information on how to plan your time on Virginia's Eastern Shore, including information on trails through the region, check out visitesva.com.

Visit Jamestown and Yorktown

Yes, there are a number of sights in Virginia that hark back to the colonial era, but the "Historic Triangle," encompassing Jamestown, Yorktown, and Williamsburg, might just be the cream of the crop. At the historic Jamestown Settlement, see re-created ships and costumed interpreters from this period, as well as a Powhatan village showing how Indigenous peoples lived here. A short drive from here along the Colonial Parkway leads to Yorktown, where Revolutionary War history takes center stage. It was here that British General Cornwallis surrendered to George Washington in 1781, securing American independence. You'll come away from the "Historic Triangle" with a better understanding of the nation's early chapters.

◉ The tree-fringed, 23-mile- (37-km-) long Colonial Parkway connects the sites (nps.gov/colo/parkway.htm).

Feast in northern Virginia

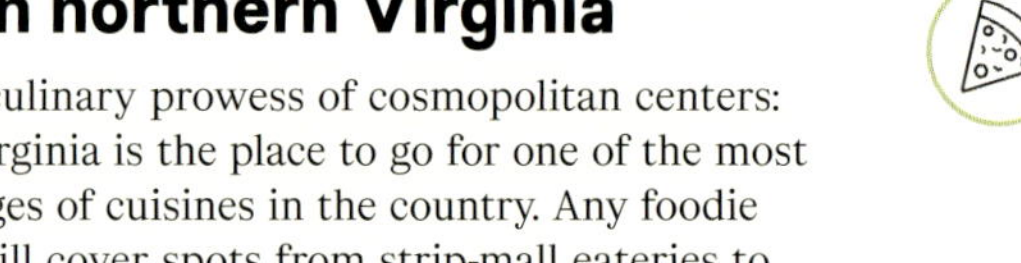

Forget the culinary prowess of cosmopolitan centers: northern Virginia is the place to go for one of the most diverse ranges of cuisines in the country. Any foodie tour here will cover spots from strip-mall eateries to sleek restaurants, united in their delicious offerings. Dive into steaming bowls of pho in Falls Church, Ethiopian injera in Alexandria, Korean barbecue in Annandale, or Bolivian *salteñas* in Arlington. Inspired to try your hand at a new dish? Stop by one of the state's many farmers' markets, which brim with produce from nearby Shenandoah farms. You may still be in northern Virginia, but eating here will take you on a journey far beyond the state's borders.

◉ Don't just follow your nose—join a guided food tour with companies such as DC Metro Food Tours (dcmetrofoodtours.com) or Blue Fern Travel (bluefernttravel.com).

Ascend to the top of the world on the Skyline Drive

Few drives in America rival the Skyline Drive. This 105-mile (168-km) route winds the length of Shenandoah National Park, hugging the crest of the Blue Ridge Mountains. Along the way, drivers are rewarded with sweeping views over forested valleys that blaze red and gold in fall and bloom with wildflowers in spring. Pullouts and overlooks invite you to stop and enjoy the scenes; you might even spot black bears, deer, and wild turkeys beyond the road. Over 500 miles (800 km) of hiking trails branch off from the drive, too—including parts of the Appalachian Trail—giving you ample opportunity to stretch your legs.

◉ More information on the Skyline Drive, part of Shenandoah National Park, can be found on the park website (nps.gov/shen).

Discover the past at the American Civil War Museum

The American Civil War was fought on Virginian soil, from the first major battle at Bull Run to the surrender at Appomattox Court House. The state was the epicenter of the history-changing conflict, and its legacies still run deep. So it's only appropriate that it's now home to a museum exploring how this war shaped the nation and its identity. The American Civil War Museum in Richmond tells this complex story from Union, Confederate, and African American perspectives, with displays that weave together letters, photographs, artifacts, and voices from the time. The dynamic exhibitions bring this defining conflict to life in an interesting way for the whole family.

◉ Join a guided tour, museum talk, or living-history event for deeper insight into the war (acwm.org).

When to visit

Spring and fall are ideal for exploring nature spots, when Shenandoah's flowers are in bloom and the leaves of the Blue Ridge Mountains turn. Summer brings hot, humid days, perfect for beach escapes on the Eastern Shore and Chesapeake Bay.

Stop by Thomas Jefferson's home near Charlottesville

No trip to Virginia is complete without a visit to Monticello, the former hilltop home and plantation of Thomas Jefferson. A UNESCO World Heritage Site, the house offers insight into the life and contradictions of America's third president: his Enlightenment ideals and architectural brilliance, but also the realities of the slavery on which his world depended. Guided tours of the house and grounds reveal Jefferson's innovations and ideas, while exhibitions explore the lives of the enslaved people who lived and labored here. The result is a complex, nuanced portrait of a pivotal figure in U.S. history.

◉ Monticello is open daily, year-round; see monticello.org for details on hours and occasional closures.

Go out in Richmond's Fan District

Richmond's Fan District—named for its fan-shaped street layout—is one of the city's most characterful neighborhoods. Developed between the 1890s and 1930s as the city expanded westward, it became a showcase for fashionable residential architecture, from Queen Anne homes to Colonial Revival townhouses. Today, though, the Fan's leafy avenues are alive with more than just a refined charm. It's the prime spot to head for a night on the town, where endless busy food spots, live-music venues, and vibrant bars line the colorful historic streets. Whether you end up in a laid-back craft brewery or a raucous speakeasy, one thing is for sure: in the Fan District, the best of Richmond's vibrant nightlife really comes to the fore.

◉ Not sure where to start? Start at Monument Avenue, the area's main boulevard, and see where the night takes you.

The Evergreen State

In Washington, it rains for almost half the year (around 150 days, to be precise), so it's no wonder that it's known as the Evergreen State. Fueled by the rain, this is a land of lush terrain, where wet forests, ancient waterfalls, and active volcanoes are the stars. Naturally, all this makes for invigorating excursions in the great outdoors. So, don your waterproof, lace up your boots, and get exploring—Washington state is ready when you are.

STATE MOTTO By and By

STATE FLOWER Pacific rhododendron

STATE ANIMAL Olympic marmot

STATE BIRD American goldfinch

FUN FACT Washington is the leading state for the production of apples in the U.S. and one of the top exporters in the world, with an incredible 10–12 billion apples harvested every fall.

Hike through Olympic National Park

Mossy rainforests and flourishing ferns, sky-high Sitka spruces and soft lichens: Olympic National Park must surely be the reason behind Washington's nickname, the Evergreen State. Dominating the northwestern end of the state, the park's landscape is varied to the extreme. On the western fringe, a string of untamed beaches and foggy coast; inland, a mountainous and glaciated expanse, crowned by the great Mount Olympus; and to the south, some of the only temperate rainforests in the country. Enchantment really does seem to lie in every corner of Olympic National Park—so much so, in fact, that the ape-like Sasquatch is said to roam among the trees.

◉ The park is open year-round, but those looking to avoid the really wet weather should go from June through September; see nps.gov/olym.

Catch a glimpse of an orca off the San Juan Islands

The Pacific Northwest coastline teems with whales, especially the distinctive black-and-white orca (there's a reason they based the movie *Free Willy* in these parts). For the chance of seeing one of these great creatures of the deep yourself, head out on a whale-watching tour from the remote San Juan Islands, an archipelago in northern Washington's Salish Sea. Guides will bring you close enough to see, but not disturb, the wildlife in the waters. Can't make it onto a tour? Then stake out a spot at Lime Kiln State Park, part of the San Juan Islands and an area where orcas are often seen from land.

◉ Board the ferry to the San Juan Islands from the city of Anacortes' ferry terminal, found on Washington's north coast.

When to visit

Summer in western Washington is unmatched: long daylight hours and warmer temperatures make for epic days soaking up the great outdoors. Across eastern Washington, sun-drenched deserts and gorges shine brightest in spring.

Head out on an adventure in the North Cascades National Park

In a state full of epic natural beauty, it's hard for any area to rank above another. But the North Cascades National Park makes a compelling push for the top. This national park is defined by its glaciated mountain peaks, less-trodden trails, and some of Washington's wildest nature. Experienced adventurers make for the alpine landscapes in particular, where some of the best trails require strenuous climbs and navigating snowy fields. The reward is unmatched: remote tranquility among mountain lakes and the park's 300 glaciers, the highest concentration in the lower 48 states.

◉ Mid-Jun–late Sep is generally the best time to visit, because much of the park is closed the rest of the year due to snow (nps.gov/noca).

Uncover the Alpine Lakes Wilderness Area

Thanks, in part, to its hard-to-reach locations, the Alpine Lakes Wilderness Area is home to some of Washington's most spectacular nature. Part of the Central Cascades mountain range, the area has 615 miles (989 km) of trails that wind past snowcapped peaks and pristine mountain lakes. The section known as the Enchantments is, as the name suggests, full of magical views, though day hikes here are strictly for experts. Waptus Lake nearby is much more accessible, and, while it may not compare to the Enchantments' grand views, there's little chance you'll be disappointed when looking out over tranquil waters.

◉ For more information on visiting the Alpine Lakes Wilderness Area, see fs.usda.gov/r06/okanogan-wenatchee.

Seek out waterfalls in Mount Rainier National Park

When it rains, it pours, and in Mount Rainier National Park that means waterfalls. The park is named after its gargantuan volcano, known by some Indigenous peoples as Tahoma, or "Mother of Waters." It's an apt name: cascading glacial waterfalls line the road to Paradise, the park's most popular area. Often snapped when it's covered in purple meadows, Paradise sees an average 645 in (1,640 cm) of snow yearly, feeding glaciers and waterfalls. Awestruck travelers can catch a glimpse of these falls from viewpoints throughout the park; arrive at sunrise to admire the view in solitude, long before the crowds descend.

◉ There are four entrances to Mount Rainier National Park. For more detail on opening times of these, see nps.gov/mora.

Visit Washington's wine country

Head east of the Cascades mountain range, and you'll find rolling hills, bountiful orchards, and, surprisingly, plenty of sunshine. This is Washington's premier wine region, home to the vineyards of Yakima Valley, Red Mountain, and Walla Walla Valley. Family-run wineries welcome visitors to sip on prized varieties, like full-bodied Merlots, fresh Syrahs, and earthy Cabernet Sauvignons. With so much sunshine, it's no surprise that agricultural industry also thrives here. The cherry on top? That'll be the literal Rainier cherry, which is produced in these parts alongside crisp apples and prized Walla Walla sweet onions.

⦿ Check Bacchus and Barley (bacchusandbarleyww.com) or Washington Wine Experience (wawinex.com) for wine tours.

Explore Whidbey Island

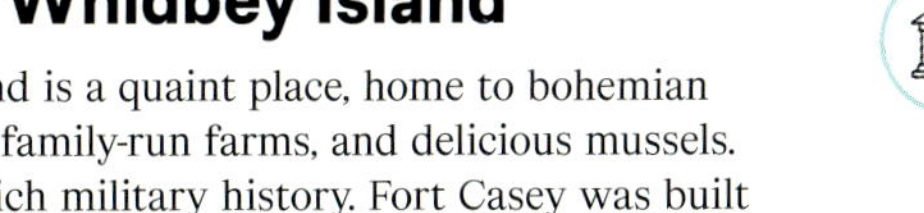

Whidbey Island is a quaint place, home to bohemian communities, family-run farms, and delicious mussels. It also has a rich military history. Fort Casey was built here in 1897, part of the state's trifecta of military bases known as the Triangle of Fire; Fort Ebey followed in the 1940s, hastily built during World War II. Both were decommissioned and turned into state parks in the years after the war. Visitors can discover Whidbey's past and present, freely exploring the abandoned bunkers and barracks, and renting out old officer houses. And while the horizon was once scanned for enemy warships, it's now the place to see a breathtaking sunset.

⦿ Fort Casey Historical State Park and Fort Ebey are both open 8am–dusk year-round (parks.wa.gov).

Harvest shellfish at Hood Canal

Western Washington is synonymous with excellent seafood. Wild salmon, Dungeness crab, and shellfish reign supreme, and the Hood Canal lays a strong claim to having the best of the latter. The 68-mile- (109-km-) long waterway is an ideal spot for gathering oysters, mussels, and clams, including the coveted geoduck. Apply for a shellfish license, don a pair of tall rubber boots, and grab a bucket. Dozens of beaches in state parks like Dosewallips and Potlatch are open for public harvesting. Prefer to focus on the slurping? Enjoy the canal's bounty with an overnight stay at an oyster farm or by dining at spots like Hama Hama Oyster Saloon.

⦿ Apply for a shellfish license at wdfw.wa.gov; regulations and guidance on safe harvesting can also be found here.

Shoot hoops in Spokane

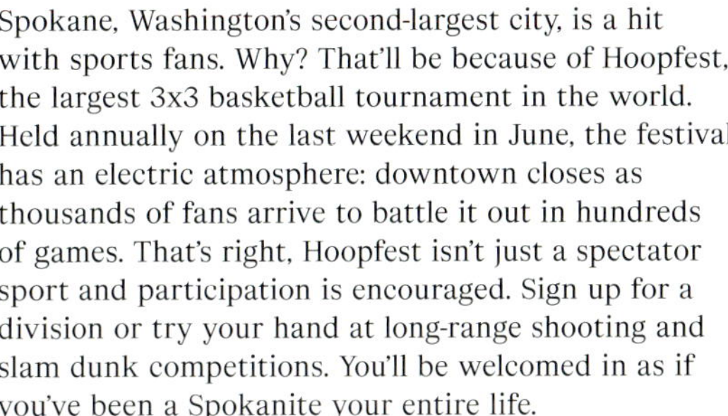

Spokane, Washington's second-largest city, is a hit with sports fans. Why? That'll be because of Hoopfest, the largest 3x3 basketball tournament in the world. Held annually on the last weekend in June, the festival has an electric atmosphere: downtown closes as thousands of fans arrive to battle it out in hundreds of games. That's right, Hoopfest isn't just a spectator sport and participation is encouraged. Sign up for a division or try your hand at long-range shooting and slam dunk competitions. You'll be welcomed in as if you've been a Spokanite your entire life.

⦿ For more information on Hoopfest, see spokanehoopfest.net. The Spokane Visitor Center is located at 620 W. Spokane Falls Boulevard (visitspokane.com).

Learn about Indigenous history

You can't fully understand Washington's history without knowing the stories of its Indigenous people. Today, there are 29 federally recognized tribes in the state. Dozens of museums and historic sites shed light on the histories and cultural traditions of these groups, which stretch back thousands of years. Of these, the Hibulb Cultural Center is a highlight, where you can hear stories narrated by Tulalip people and try your hand at basket-weaving. Another is the Suquamish Museum, where you can see the gravesite of Chief Seattle, a key 19th-century figure after whom the well-known city is named.

⦿ For the Hibulb Cultural Center, see hibulbculturalcenter.org; for the Suquamish Museum, see suquamishmuseum.org.

Hike around Mount St. Helens

Mount St. Helens made history and headlines around the world when it erupted in 1980, cloaking the whole landscape in ash, reducing the peak to a crater, and claiming the lives of 57 people. It's still one of the most active volcanoes in the U.S., but that doesn't stop the droves of visitors from arriving. In nearly 50 years, the land has transformed from barren devastation into an inviting medley of wildflower meadows and glassy lakes. Gorgeous treks can be taken along the west side of the mountain, where hikers can witness nature's tenacity and see first-hand how the environment has rebuilt itself, little by little.

⦿ For visitor information, check out fs.usda.gov/visit/national-monuments/mount-st-helens.

Traverse landscapes shaped by the Ice Age

Much of eastern Washington's landscape is epic, thanks to Ice Age Missoula floods–and the best way to take it all in is on a road trip. From Ellensburg, drive 40 miles (64 km) to the Frenchman Coulee area to see basalt pillars eroded by floods. Veer north to Soap Lake to squeeze in a soak in its mineral-rich waters, before a stop at Sun Lakes-Dry Falls State Park, where you can imagine the waterfall that flowed here years ago: at one time it was four times larger than Niagara Falls. From the viewpoint at the visitor center, it's easy to see just how forcefully the floods carved out the gorge, forever leaving their mark on this side of the state.

◉ Eastern Washington can get extremely hot in the summer and very cold in the winter, so the best time for a road trip is Apr–Jun.

Be inspired by Snoqualmie Falls

Over the years, the 268-ft- (81-m-) tall Snoqualmie Falls has inspired many. To the Indigenous Snoqualmie people, it has long been of spiritual importance, the surrounding area a traditional burial ground. Later, the 19th-century engineer Charles Baker saw the falls as the perfect spot for hydroelectric power, building the still-working power plant nearby. But most visitors will likely recognize the gushing waters from the eerie opening shot of the surreal 1990s series *Twin Peaks*. Filmmaker David Lynch shot much of this show here, including at the nearby Salish Lodge and North Bend's Twede's Cafe. The area is a huge part of the show–it's as if Agent Dale Cooper might drive past at any moment.

◉ Stop by the Snoqualmie Falls Gift Shop and Visitor Center (snoqualmiefalls.com), book a stay at the Salish Lodge (salishlodge.com), or see Twede's Cafe (twedescafe.com).

SEATTLE

TOP 5

PIKE PLACE MARKET
Take a food tour in the city's hundred-year-old market.

SEATTLE CENTER
Ride to the top of the Space Needle at the city's top arts and entertainment center.

DISCOVERY PARK
Explore Seattle's largest city park, full of birds, tidepools, and mountain views.

SEATTLE WATERFRONT
Watch ferries cross the Sound while dining on seafood.

BALLARD (HIRAM M. CHITTENDEN) LOCKS
Visit one of Seattle's engineering marvels.

Discover Seattle, the Emerald City

Welcome to the Emerald City. No, not of the Oz variety; this is Seattle, Washington's most populous city, named for its dense evergreen trees and abundant parks. Truth be told, it carries as much inspiration and wonder as its fictional namesake. This is the city at the heart of America's boutique coffee movement; the place where the grunge music scene shook the music industry in the 1990s; and where budding tech companies went on to change the world. Grab a coffee to go and set off for a walk along its streets and leafy parks, taking in this most dynamic of cities.

For tourist information, stop by Visit Seattle at 701 Pike Street, open 8:30am–5:30pm Mon-Fri (visitseattle.org).

The Mountain State

At the heart of Appalachia sits West Virginia, a truly enchanting state carved by rushing rivers and blanketed by mountains older than Saturn's rings. Ancient and dramatic, this landscape makes for a truly wild and utterly scenic outdoor playground for skiers, rock climbers, and whitewater rafters. But beyond its natural beauty is a layered history (mining was once big business here) and proud Appalachian culture, which give the state its cultural richness.

STATE MOTTO Mountaineers Are Always Free

STATE FLOWER Rhododendron

STATE ANIMAL Black bear

STATE BIRD Northern cardinal

FUN FACT The first modern Mother's Day celebration in the U.S. happened in West Virginia in 1908, when Anna Jarvis arranged a Mother's Day service of worship for her late mother.

Explore New River Gorge and beyond

New River Gorge, the United States' newest national park, has some of the best hiking in the country. Lace up your boots and trek one of the park's more than 40 trails, encountering abandoned coal mines, old-growth forest, and sweeping views of mountain ridges along the way. Afterward, recuperate with a stay at the Greenbrier Resort. Founded in 1778, the resort has a hallowed place in the annals of American hospitality. Soothe sore muscles in water from hot springs at its spa, relax with afternoon tea, or take a tour of the resort's secret Cold War–era bunker, where Congress could hide out in the event of a nuclear strike.

◉ Entry to New River Gorge National Park is free and the park is open daily, year-round (nps.gov/neri/index.htm). The Greenbrier is located in White Sulphur Springs (greenbrier.com).

Watch a Mountain Stage show

Music is at the heart of Appalachian culture, and trips through the region are soundtracked by a rich mix of country, bluegrass, and Americana galore. Among the country's best live music series is Mountain Stage, held each Sunday at Charleston's Culture Center Theater. Each show features several artists, from regional acts to nationally recognized names like Tyler Childers and the War and Treaty. At some performances, the sunny plinking of a banjo or the bright tones of an Appalachian dulcimer might immerse you in the traditional sounds of the mountains; at others, indie rock or world music show off the best of the region's contemporary soundscape.

◉ Can't make it to Charleston? Watch livestreams of Mountain Stage shows at mountainstage.org or past performances at livesessions.npr.org.

Drive the Hatfield-McCoy Trails

The Hatfield-McCoy Trails are among some of the most extensive ATV trail systems in the world, encompassing more than 1,000 miles (1,609 km) of track through the mountains and hollows of southwestern West Virginia. Rev your engine and ride through thick forests, along ridges, and up to mountaintops that put you above the clouds. Besides being an exciting way to experience the state's rugged terrain, the trails also provide the chance to experience small-town Appalachian life and to learn about the infamous family feud they're named after. Playing out in this region in the late 19th century, the Hatfield-McCoy rivalry was a sordid tale of arson, murder, star-crossed lovers, and a stolen hog.

◉ A trail permit is required to ride the Hatfield-McCoy Trails; see trailsheaven.com for more details.

Dig into West Virginia's coal-mining history

West Virginia's economy and identity were built, in large part, on coal mining. The industry boomed in the late 1800s, when nearly 50 mining towns popped up along the New River, and though many closed by the 1950s, it remains closely associated with the state. Take in this legacy at Beckley's Exhibition Coal Mine, where visitors can tour a former mine with a veteran miner. Back in the sunlight, set off on a road trip down the Coal Heritage Trail, which winds through mountains and valleys, passing historic sites, an old mining company store, and the town of Bramwell, once home to as many as 19 coal-mining millionaires.

◉ The Exhibition Coal Mine is open early Apr–early Nov (beckley.org/coal-mine). The Coal Heritage Trail follows SR 16/US 52 from Beckley to Bluefield.

Uncover John Brown's Fort

Harpers Ferry sits nestled at the confluence of the Shenandoah and Potomac rivers. However, the town's scenic setting belies its past: it was the site of one of the most consequential events in American history. On October 16, 1859, the abolitionist John Brown led a band of 21 men in a raid on the U.S. armory here. By seizing it, they hoped to incite revolts across the South that would end slavery. That didn't happen—and many members of the party, including Brown, were killed or executed—but the raid set the country on the path to the Civil War and, eventually, emancipation. Today, visiting the surprisingly diminutive armory, now known as John Brown's Fort, offers a singular opportunity to learn about this history.

◉ The fort is in Harpers Ferry National Historical Park (nps.gov/hafe/learn/historyculture/john-brown-fort.htm).

When to visit

Warm summers offer ample chances for hiking, kayaking, and riding ATVs, before ski resorts and sled hills open in the mountains in winter. Don't miss Bridge Day in October, when New River Gorge Bridge is turned over to pedestrians.

Go off grid in the National Radio Quiet Zone

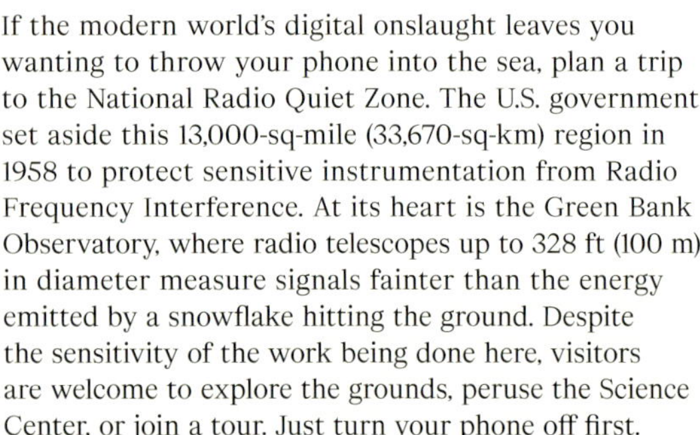

If the modern world's digital onslaught leaves you wanting to throw your phone into the sea, plan a trip to the National Radio Quiet Zone. The U.S. government set aside this 13,000-sq-mile (33,670-sq-km) region in 1958 to protect sensitive instrumentation from Radio Frequency Interference. At its heart is the Green Bank Observatory, where radio telescopes up to 328 ft (100 m) in diameter measure signals fainter than the energy emitted by a snowflake hitting the ground. Despite the sensitivity of the work being done here, visitors are welcome to explore the grounds, peruse the Science Center, or join a tour. Just turn your phone off first.

◉ Guided tours include the SETI Tour, focused on the site's role in the search for extraterrestrial intelligence.

Experience white-water rafting on the New River

Sometimes the natural world conspires to turn itself into a thrill ride. That's the case with West Virginia's New River, which offers some of the top white-water rafting in the country. Seasoned pro? Blitz the lower river, where challenging rapids serve up nasty crosscurrents and narrow chutes between menacing boulders, providing for a heart-pounding ride. New to the churn? Head for the upper river, where serene stretches let you take in the mountain scenery, and easier rapids provide just enough excitement to get your adrenaline pumping without making you wish you'd prepared a will before leaving home.

◉ Rafting season typically runs Apr–Oct. Reputable outfitters that run guided trips are listed on the New River Gorge National Park website (nps.gov/neri).

The Badger State

Ask someone what they know about Wisconsin, and they'll inevitably mention beer and cheese. Surely it says something about the state that its two most famous products are also two of life's great pleasures. Truth is, there's a lot to be pleased with here: Great Lakes and glacial landscapes, renowned buildings, close-knit communities. Being Midwesterners, you'll rarely hear Wisconsinites brag, but tell them you're headed to their state, and they'll raise a toast to the good life.

STATE MOTTO Forward

STATE FLOWER Common blue violet

STATE ANIMAL American badger

STATE BIRD American robin

FUN FACT The state's nickname comes from the name given to 19th-century miners, who dug holes in the state's hillsides to find lead and would then sleep in their caves, just like badgers sleep in dens.

See Apostle Islands National Lakeshore

Crumbling into Lake Superior from the Bayfield Peninsula are 21 islands that, together with a narrow strip on the mainland, make up the Apostle Islands National Lakeshore (a 22nd, Madeline Island, is not part of the preserve). The isolated gems are home to sandy beaches and northern hardwood forests that shelter martens, beavers, and black bears. Pilot a sea kayak along the coast and between islands to explore sea caves that waves have carved out of the red sandstone and the National Park System's largest collection of lighthouses, the oldest of which dates to 1856. Most of the islands have campsites, letting you turn the archipelago into a multiday adventure.

◉ There are guided kayaking trips as well as sightseeing cruises available on Lake Superior. Find info on both at nps.gov/apis.

Travel the Frank Lloyd Wright Trail

The most distinguished architect in American history designed such structures as New York's Guggenheim Museum and Tokyo's Imperial Hotel, yet the gravitational center of his life and work always remained his home state of Wisconsin. A drive down the 200-mile (320-km) Frank Lloyd Wright Trail offers an in-depth exploration of the man and his uniquely American Prairie Style, which sought harmony with the landscape and refused to distinguish between indoor and outdoor spaces. The trail's nine buildings range from Wright's own private residence to a school, reflecting his belief that everyone was entitled to beautiful design.

◉ The trail runs from Richland Center, Wright's birthplace, to Racine, primarily along U.S. Highway 14 and I-94.

When to visit

Wisconsin can seem to go into hibernation during its long winters, though snowshoers, snowmobilers, and cross-country skiers will find lots of fun. Summer brings beer gardens, outdoor adventure, and crowds to Lake Michigan beaches.

Peruse the Dane County Farmers' Market

This is America's Dairyland, but Wisconsin's milk, cheese, and butter are just a part of the agricultural bounty the state's farmers produce. To see everything else, head to Madison's Capitol Square on a summer Saturday. Surrounding the majestic State Capitol, the Dane County Farmers' Market is the largest producer-only farmers' market in the country. That means everything for sale—from sweet corn to bison steaks—was grown or raised by the Wisconsin farmer you meet at the stall. Grab some cheese curds or stuffed cookies to snack on as you pick out products to take from the state's farms to your table.

◉ The full Dane County Farmers' Market runs mid-Apr–Nov 6:15am–1:45pm Sat.

Have your mind blown at the House on the Rock

What do a giant circus wagon with an automated 40-piece band; a re-creation of a 19th-century street; one of the world's largest collections of dollhouses; an enormous carousel with 269 animals, 20,000 lights, and 182 chandeliers; a Japanese garden; and an "Infinity Room" with 3,264 windows that extends unsupported 140 ft (43 m) out over a valley all have in common? They're all part of the House on the Rock, the psychedelic architectural marvel/offbeat museum/quixotic fever dream created by mid-century eccentric and visionary Alex Jordan. You've never seen anything like it.

◉ Still not quirky enough for you? Visit in October, when the house is given a Halloween makeover some nights; see thehouseontherock.com for more information.

Watch a football game at Lambeau Field

The Green Bay Packers play at 81,441-seat Lambeau Field. The entire population of Green Bay is just 107,395; it is, by far, the smallest U.S. city with a professional sports team. Uniquely among pro teams, the Packers aren't owned by a multimillionaire but by the public, with 538,967 people holding stock in the team. This all means that attending a game at Lambeau isn't just a chance to have a fun day at the stadium, but to experience the sort of organic bond between town and team that's largely disappeared from contemporary, commercialized sports. Throw on some green and gold, don a cheesehead, and join the family.

◉ Purchase tickets at packers.com. Forget about season tickets, though—they have a renewal rate over 99 percent.

Trek the Ice Age Trail

Wisconsin looked a lot different 12,000 years ago. Near the end of the Ice Age, much of the state was buried beneath a giant glacier, and when it retreated it reshaped the landscape in ways that remain visible today. On Wisconsin's 1,200-mile (1,931-km) Ice Age Trail, which roughly follows the glacier's edge as it snakes through the state, you'll encounter ancient glacial signatures like kettles, moraines, and erratics. If geology isn't your thing, you'll still be treated to dense forests, wetlands, small-town Main Streets, and much more on this National Scenic Trail, one of just 11 in the country. The trail is just as good in winter, too, when visitors trade hiking boots for snowshoes.

◉ Good sections of the trail include the Southern Unit of the Kettle Moraine State Forest and Devil's Lake State Park; find detailed trail info at iceagetrail.org.

Escape to Door County

Rarely is life as good as it is in Door County. This slender peninsula jutting out into Lake Michigan is where Wisconsin—and much of the Midwest—goes to vacation. Join the regular vacationers here to gallery-hop in charming small towns, pick your own cherries on a family farm, spot 19th-century shipwrecks on a boat tour, or stroll through idyllic fields of lavender on Washington Island. In the evening, take in an alfresco performance at an outdoor theater, or catch some culinary drama at one of the county's iconic fish boils, a local tradition with Scandinavian roots that's usually finished off with a giant fireball.

◉ Door County is a 2.5-hour drive from Milwaukee and 1 hour from Green Bay, site of the nearest airport. For more travel information, visit doorcounty.com.

Take a brewery tour in Brew City

Wisconsin is famous for its beer, and that's especially true of Milwaukee, a city that was built on its barrels. Milwaukee's first brewery was founded before the city was even officially established, and the settlement's earliest years saw more than 30 breweries open, spurred on by its many German immigrants. The taps have never run dry, and Brew City remains a hotspot for beer lovers, who can learn about its history, see what's currently brewing, and sample the product on the many tours run by city breweries. Top options include the huge and historic Miller Brewery and local craft favorite Lakefront Brewery.

◉ Stay in part of what used to be the Pabst Brewery at the Brewhouse Inn & Suites, where you can still see the brewery's giant copper kettles.

The Equality State

Wyoming is the ultimate wide-open frontier. Explored for centuries, it's where towering mountain ranges meet endless stretches of rolling plains, and cowboy culture lives on. Home to Yellowstone—perhaps the nation's greatest national park—and Grand Teton's peaks, it's a playground for outdoors lovers and wildlife watchers alike. In Wyoming, the sky feels bigger, the air fresher, and the pace is slow enough that you can actually soak it all in.

STATE MOTTO Equal Rights

STATE FLOWER Wyoming Indian paintbrush

STATE ANIMAL American bison

STATE BIRD Western meadowlark

FUN FACT Although it's the country's tenth-largest state by area, Wyoming has the lowest population in the U.S., with only approximately 587,600 people living in its borders.

Experience Yellowstone National Park

You could spend a lifetime exploring Yellowstone National Park. The world's first national park has more geysers, hot springs, and other thermal features than anyplace else on earth. Water continues to shape the park in the form of world-class fly-fishing rivers and streams, and mighty falls flowing into the Grand Canyon of the Yellowstone and the vast Yellowstone Lake. Throughout are some of the best wildlife-watching spots in the U.S., with grizzly bears, gray wolves, and bison roaming the landscape. The best way to experience it all is not from your car, but in a pair of boots: there are more than 1,000 miles (1,609 km) of hiking trails in Yellowstone for all skill levels.

◉ Yellowstone National Park is open daily year-round, but most roads close Nov–late Apr (nps.gov/yell).

Hike through the Wind River Range

Quiet isolation, natural beauty, rugged wilderness: Wind River Range offers the best of the West's backcountry destinations. Home to most of the state's highest mountains (19 to be exact), the range's crowning glory is also Wyoming's highest summit, Gannett Peak, which looms 13,802 ft (4,207 m) above sea level. With so much terrain to explore, it's popular for multiday backpacking trips. Looking for just a taste of the backcountry? Then set out on a day hike, like the short Silas Lakes Trail near the town of Lander. There's really no better way to take it all in.

◉ Much of the range is located on the Wind River Indian Reservation (windriver.org). A permit is needed for hiking, camping, and fishing on these lands.

See the fossils at Fossil Butte National Monument

Fossil Butte National Monument is one of the most fertile fossil beds on the planet. About 50 million years ago, a large lake covered what is now the high desert of southwestern Wyoming. As it dried, it left behind a plethora of immaculately preserved fossils of fish, turtles, frogs, and other wildlife. Today, the visitor center's museum has one of the preeminent collections of fossils in the West, with more than 2,000 specimens from the Green River Formation. After visiting the museum and resident fossil lab, hike the 2.5-mile (4-km) Historic Quarry Trail to see the superlative source of the fossils.

◉ The site is open dawn–dusk year-round; for the museum's opening hours, check nps.gov/fobu.

Get into all things Western at the Buffalo Bill Center of the West

William "Buffalo Bill" Cody was America's first superstar. The scout-turned-showman toured the world at the turn of the 20th century with his Wild West shows, with feats of horseback riding, shooting, wild animals, and scripted sketches. He also founded the town of Cody, where the Buffalo Bill Center of the West tells his rich life story, with exhibits featuring his personal belongings and Wild West show memorabilia. But the center isn't focused solely on Cody: it's a world-class facility with five separate museums devoted to Western art, firearms, Indigenous history, and Yellowstone's ecosystem, as well as the one dedicated to Buffalo Bill himself.

◉ The Buffalo Bill Center of the West is open daily year-round, except major holidays (centerofthewest.org).

Visit the National Historic Trails Interpretive Center

The city of Casper was a major crossroads in the 1800s. The Oregon, California, and Mormon trails all intersected here, and a combined 500,000 westbound emigrants traveled on them in the mid-1800s. The completion of the transcontinental railroad in the 1870s made for a much easier trip, but the National Historic Trails Interpretive Center memorializes those early pioneers who took to the trails. You can learn about the fascinating history of these routes by way of a short film based on authentic journal entries and a variety of multimedia exhibits, each designed to show how arduous the journey really was.

◉ The National Historic Trails Interpretive Center is open 9:30am–5pm Tue–Sat (nhtcf.org). Admission is free.

Uncover the past at the Museum of the Mountain Man

In the first half of the 1800s, people began hunting and trapping beavers, deer, wolves, and other wildlife in the Rocky Mountains exclusively for their hides, prized in the U.S. and Europe. Many of these so-called mountain men came from Europe and were also some of the first white people to explore Wyoming and interact with Indigenous peoples here. In Pinedale, you can learn all about the Rocky Mountain fur trade at the Museum of the Mountain Man. The impressive collection features personal belongings of notable figures and explores the grueling lifestyle of a trapper in the Old West.

◉ The Museum of the Mountain Man is open May–Oct: daily (museumofthemountainman.com).

Soak your cares away in Hot Springs State Park

Looking to unwind? Few places offer as great a choice of thermal springs as Hot Springs State Park in the town of Thermopolis. The healing waters here have been in use for millennia, among them the aptly named Big Spring—the world's largest mineral hot spring. In 1896 the area's Indigenous peoples sold the springs to the U.S., on the condition that some of them would be reserved for public use. It's an agreement that's still honored today, with the State Bath House—home to three soaking pools kept at a constant temperature of 104°F (40°C)—completely free to use. Take a dip for yourself in these restorative mineral waters and leave feeling utterly relaxed.

◉ The State Bath House at Hot Springs State Park is open daily year-round, except holidays (wyoparks.wyo.gov). For the town, see the visitor's bureau website (thermopolis.com).

When to visit

For many, summer offers the best weather for hiking in Yellowstone and Grand Teton national parks, but you're more likely to spot elk, moose, and bears in fall. Winter is all about hitting the slopes in resorts like Jackson Hole.

See Grand Teton National Park

The iconic Teton Range in Grand Teton National Park has graced countless postcards, and with its blue-and-white mountains and verdant valleys it's really no wonder. While it may be tempting to spend an entire trip gawking at these stunning peaks, there's plenty more to do in the park. Spend time by the water, boating and fishing in Jenny Lake and Jackson Lake, hit the trails with a hike into Cascade Canyon for an up-close view of the Tetons, or discover pioneer history at Menors Ferry and Mormon Row. Like its mountains, the park's lodging and dining is superlative: Jenny Lake Lodge is one of the most luxurious places to overnight in any national park.

◉ Grand Teton National Park is open daily year-round, but the visitor centers and lodgings are closed early fall–mid-spring (nps.gov/grte).

INDEX

Page numbers in **bold** refer to main entries.

G

H

I

J

K

L

M

R

S

T

U

V

W

Y

Z

ACKNOWLEDGMENTS

DK would like to thank the following people for their contributions to this book:

EDITORIAL:

Jacqui Agate is a travel journalist, U.S. specialist, and the North America Editor at Wanderlust Magazine.

Chelsea Booker is a Seattle-based travel writer specializing in local travel in the Pacific Northwest.

Adam Karlin resides in New Orleans, where he teaches, and writes travel pieces and children's books.

Stephen Keeling is a New York-based travel writer and has worked on numerous books and travel guides.

Eric Peterson lives in Denver and writes about travel, business, beer, and neurology.

Kristen Shoates is a Nashville-based travel writer whose work appears in *The Infatuation* and various books.

Charles Usher lives in Milwaukee and writes about travel, food, and culture, specializing in the American Midwest.

DESIGN:

Marta Bescos is a Madrid-based photo editor who has contributed to countless DK travel books. www.martabescos.com

David Sierra Martínez is an illustrator from Galicia, Spain. His love for typography, detail, and color defines his unique style. www.dsierra.es

References for quotations:

p32 column 2, lines 1–2: Muir, John (1868).

p76 column 2, line 1: Vonnegut, Kurt. (1986).

p80 column 2, lines 1–2: Bryson, Bill. (1989) The Lost Continent. 1st edition. London: Secker and Warburg.

p85 column 2, line 1: Dorothy in The Wizard of Oz (1939).

p124 column 1, lines 9–10: Vandiver, William Duncan (1899).

p127 column 2, lines 2–3: Laura Ingalls in Little House on the Prairie (1974).

p159 column 2, line 1: Fox Mulder in The X Files (1993).

p163 column 1, lines 2–3: Stanton, Elizabeth Cady (1848).

p187 column 1, lines 18–19: Wright, Frank Lloyd (c. 1935).

p194 column 1, line 21: Slater, Samuel (1833).

The publisher would like to thank the following for their kind permission to reproduce their photographs:

(Key: a-above; b-below/bottom; c-centre; f-far; l-left; r-right; t-top)

123RF.com: gembuls 7fcr, iconisa 7bc, lalavida 7cr

4Corners: Guido Cozzi 106, Susanne Kremer 55t, Richard Taylor 50

Adobe Stock: Art Meripol 12, Matteo Colombo 10-11, Danita Delimont 129t, Derrick 28, Karina Eremina 159bl, f11photo 199, Zack Frank 31b, 81, fukez84 164-165, Jacob 120, Janine 60, Wangkun Jia 194, Chansak Joe A. 18t, Greg Meland 156, Stephen 186, TRAVEL EASY 198cr, Jason Valentine 64-65, Craig Zerbe 110

Alamy Stock Photo: aaron peterson.net 115cr, 116, Action Plus Sports Images / Scott Winters 177bl, All Canada Photos / Ryan Creary 171cr, BHammond 122t, Jon Bilous 100, Martina Birnbaum 203tr, Pat & Chuck Blackley 102, 174, 238, BLM Photo 183tl, Paul Brady 127, Courtesy of Philadelphia's Magic Gardens / Michael Brooks 188, Ron Buskirk 29bl, 176, 205cr, B. David Cathell 26cl, Cavan Images 23t, 98tl, 144-145, 217br, 244br, Felix Choo 72, CNMages 89t, 205bl, Jonathan Cohen 67, 189tr, Thornton Cohen 195, Richard Cummins 147cr, 147bl, Ian Dagnall 25b, 122, 130b, 201, Phil Degginger 158, Danita Delimont 137t, 139tl, 170, 171bl, Amel Dizdarevic 75b, Randy Duchaine 45, Worlds Largest Rocking Chair, Casey, Illinois – courtesy of Big Things in a Small Town. / Lori Epstein 71, EQRoy 29cr, EThamPhoto 22, Zachary Frank 77cr, 240br, Bildagentur Geduldig 236t, Nick Hanna 101t, Hisayuki Hayashi 142br, Heebphoto 132, Hemis / FRILET Patrick 206, Image Source Limited / Ron Dahlquist 62b, Jeffrey Isaac Greenberg 10+ 15bl, Jeffrey Isaac Greenberg 18+ 59, 231tl, 231cr, Andriy Kravchenko 76, John Lazenby 223, Lila Lee 61bl, Dan Leeth 39cr, Chon Kit Leong 181tr, Jon Lovette 49tl, Dennis MacDonald 79b, mauritius images GmbH 240tl, mauritius images GmbH / ClickAlps 17tl, mauritius images GmbH / Hanna Wagner 49cr, Mira 107cr, Rosemarie Mosteller 82, Michael Patrick O'Neill 55b, George Ostertag 151b, Sean Pavone 137b, Chris Pereira 146, Doug Perrine 63, PhotoSpirit 172b, Enchanted Highway Pheasants on the Prairie Sculpture in summer day courtesy of the Enchanted Highway, Gary Greff artist. / PhotoSpirit 173, 244t, Robert Quinlan 153bl, Edwin Remsberg 99br, James Schwabel 78, 135b, 200, scott sady / tahoelight.com 33cr, 142t, Alexey Stiop 90cr, Stock Connection Blue / Mardis Coers 77tl, Dawid Swierczek 83bl, Stephen Taylor 73bl, 183cr, Stan Tess 43, 43cr, 43bl, 193tl, Marek Uliasz 134, Michael Ventura 103tl, 225, Matthew Wakem 105tr, Jim West 86t, 239, Gary Whitton 77bl, Jennifer Wright 159tr, Zoonar GmbH / Galyna Andrushko 2, ZUMA Press, Inc. 62t, 101bl, ZUMA Wire / Brian Cahn 117bl

Arkansas Museum of Fine Arts: Iwan Baan 31tl

AWL Images: Jon Arnold 108, Walter Bibikow 47, 152, Cavan Images 14, Kav Dadfar 210, Danita Delimont Stock 171tl, Jeremy Flint 148, 187, 228, 233bl, Christian Heeb 92, Hemis 93bl, Hemis / Patrick Frilet 123bl, J.Banks 34, JRNY Magazine 57cr, 212br, Susanne Kremer 54, John Warburton-Lee 17bl

Cedar and Stone: 118cr, 118bl

Courtesy of Museum of the Mountain Man: 248

Depositphotos Inc: fireandstone 161cr, jewhyte 61tl, jimbrownphotography 115bl, miroslav_1 40b, sunsinger 155

Dreamstime.com: AevanStock 90tl, Cheri Alguire 69bl, Jon Bilous 230, Sandra Burm 204, Bonita Cheshier 136, Alexander Cimbal 202br, Gerald T. Coli 52, Sandra Foyt 180cl, 249tr, Georgesheldon 190, Krupal Ghori 7br, Alex Grichenko 138, Hannator92 36t, Joe Herlong 198tl, Icons Home 7clb, Gregory Johnston 69tr, James Kirkikis 211bl, Lequint 193bl, Lunamarina 107bl, Jacqueline Nix 205tl, Sean Pavone 197, 221, Kenneth A Sponsler 189bl, Alexey Stiop 90bl, Kelly Vandellen 196, Claire White 94br, Wirestock 24, 73cr, Lei Xu 193cr, Yobro10 219bl, Zoom1282 6-7, Zrfphoto 181bl

Eventide Oyster Co./NavadiseMedia: 99tl

Christian Fiedler: 153tr

Frank Lloyd Wright Visitor Center: Wingspread interior. Courtesy of The Johnson Foundation at Wingspread 243tl

Teri Genovese: 111b

Getty Images: 500px / Neil Miles 88, 500px / Sandra Lee Randle 207t, Cavan / Aurora Photos / Suzanne Stroeer 217tl, Cavan Images / Brent Doscher 149, Corbis Historical / Mark Reinstein 86b, De Agostini / DEA / L. ROMANO 26br, Denver Post / RJ Sangosti 41, Design Pics / Kevin Smith 19, Design Pics / Lucas Payne 16, Patrick Donovan 97, Francesco Vaninetti Photo 182, Ramesh Iyanswamy 128, L. Toshio Kishiyama 96, Chris McKay 58, NNehring 66, Photographer's Choice RF / Stuart Westmorland 20–21, Stringer / Dave Kotinsky 151t, The Image Bank / Jupiterimages 93cr

Getty Images / iStock: Adventure_Photo 216, Patricia Anderson 105b, Art Wager 61cr, BackyardProduction 141, benedek 25t, Bezvershenko 7bl, bluejayphoto 23b, Dee 207bl, DenisTangneyJr 46, 48, 49bl, 107tl, 229, George Dodd 13tl, DStarky 7crb, Erin Egnatz 191t, f11photo 124, fotoguy22 89b, franckreporter 232, gelyngfjell 208, jimfeng 131, 226–227, kavram 220, Khosrork 178, krblokhin 219cr, Jon Lauriat 79t, 234br, 249bl, LIKE HE 135tr, Dee Liu 80, Mariakray 53b, Timothy Mattimore 242, peeterv 203bl, Alex Potemkin 192, Purdue9394 70, Rakdee 7fbr, roclwyr 233tl, rodclementphotography 56, roman_slavik 237, Ron and Patty Thomas 42, RoschetzkyIstockPhoto 214, RudyBalasko 177cr, Angela Scapini 17cr, SeanXu 38, swisshippo 68b, tobiasjo 36b, Stefan Tomic 32, Vector designer 7cb, williamhc 247bl, Wiltser 111t, Wirestock 222, YayaErnst 33tl, Tammy Yeokum 87

Greenwood Rising, Inc.: Greenwood Rising History Center mural by artist D.Ross Scribe / JW Photography 179

Lakefront Brewery: 245

Lone Mountain Ranch: 129cr, Heidi A Long / Longviews Studios 129bl

Anna Petrow: 125bl, 126

Pilsen Photo Co-Op: 125cr

Plains Art Museum: Artwork by Anne Labovitz. Plains Art Museum interior. / Eric Muller 172t

Rock & Roll Hall of Fame: aerial agents 175

Shutterstock.com: Galyna Andrushko 247t, Bilanol 166, Martina Birnbaum 212tl, Bloodberry 94tl, Marty Castrogiovanni 243cr, Cat Dang Photography 133t, Yeilyn Channell 103bl, Ana S. Chao 75t, colcatkan 112–113, Caroline Elliott 167, EWY Media 73tl, f11photo 95, FashionStock.com 224, Matt Fowler KC 85tl, Stephen B. Goodwin 169, HN Works 7fcrb, DM Hurt 103cr, Asif Islam 233cr, Malachi Jacobs 241, LanaG 39bl, Kit Leong 85cr, 180tr, 211cr, lexfe 130t, lisafarov 114, Ranimiro Lotufo Neto 215, Lucky-photographer 140, magraphy 123tr, Denise McLane 85bl, melissamn 139bl, Debra Millet 161bl, Suriaya mollik 84, Natalie Jean Photography 33bl, Nicola Patterson 83tr, Sean Pavone 157, Angela N Perryman 53t, Bob Pool 68, Kent Raney 74, Jaden Roberson 243bl, schusterbauer.com 15tr, Rebecca Schwartz 117t, William Silver 154, Carmen K. Sisson 13br, Ventu Photo 143, Vineyard Perspective 139cr, Dak Vision 98br, Erin Westgate 51, Wileydoc 168, Nathan Yeagle 191bl, Jakub Zajic 184

Tippet Rise Art Center: Tippet Rise Art Center. The Geode, 2024. Designed by Arup. / James Florio 133b

Turpentine Creek Wildlife Refuge: 29tl

Unsplash: Tim Alex 150, Bell Chan 234t, Harry Gillen 162, Dennis Guten 202t, Drew Hays 209, Nils Huenerfuerst 57t, Vasilis Karkalas 183bl, Mick Kirchman 160, Alec Krum 40t, Matthew LeJune 37, Andrew Ling 119, José Matute 104, Lisha Riabinina 218, Rob Shields 236bl, Corey Simoneau 18tl, LaiLa Skalsky 246, Dennis Yu 27

Walter Anderson Museum of Art: 121

Senior Editor Lucy Richards
Senior Designer Michael Curia
Project Editor Tijana Todorinović
Editors Catrina Conway, Keith Drew, Rachel Laidler
Designers Louise Brigenshaw, Katie Thomas
Executive Editor, Americanization Lori Hand
Proofreader Kathryn Glendenning
Indexer Helen Peters
Picture Researcher Marta Bescos
Senior Cartographic Editors Suresh Kumar, James Macdonald
Jacket & Sales Material Coordinator Serena Sclocco
Illustrator David Sierra Martínez
Jacket Designer Michael Curia
Image Retoucher Michelle Briers
Production Editor Gillian Reid
Senior Production Controller Kariss Ainsworth
Managing Art Editors Gemma Doyle, Michael Duffy
Editorial Director Hollie Teague
Art Director Maxine Pedliham
Publishing Director Georgina Dee

First American Edition, 2026
Published in the United States by DK Publishing, a division of Penguin Random House LLC
1745 Broadway, 20th Floor, New York, NY 10019

First published in Great Britain in 2026 by
Dorling Kindersley Limited
20 Vauxhall Bridge Road,
London SW1V 2SA

The authorized representative in the EEA is Dorling Kindersley Verlag GmbH. Arnulfstr. 124, 80636 Munich, Germany

26 27 28 29 30 10 9 8 7 6 5 4 3 2 1
001–356870–Apr/2026

A CIP catalog record for this book is available from the British Library

ISBN: 979-8-2171-3796-1

DK books are available at special discounts when purchased in bulk for sales promotions, premiums, fund-raising, or educational use.
For details, contact:
DK Publishing Special Markets,
1745 Broadway, 20th Floor,
New York, NY 10019
SpecialSales@dk.com

Printed and bound in China
www.dk.com

This book was made with Forest Stewardship Council™ certified paper – one small step in DK's commitment to a sustainable future. Learn more at **www.dk.com/uk/information/sustainability**

Also available
Capture memories with the *50 States Travel Journal* (includes 50 state stickers).

A note from the publisher
Every effort has been made to ensure this book is accurate and up-to-date, but things can change in an instant. Opening hours change, attractions close their doors, and the natural world is influenced by so many variables; always check ahead when planning your next vacation. The publisher cannot accept responsibility for any consequences arising from the use of this book. If you notice we've got something wrong, we want to hear from you. Please get in touch at travelguides@dk.co.uk